THE CHIP ON
GRANDMA'S SHOULDER

ROBERT KEITH LEAVITT

J. B. LIPPINCOTT COMPANY

PHILADELPHIA AND NEW YORK

CONTENTS

WHY THESE MEMOIRS ARE UTTERLY UNTRUSTWORTHY

Anyone expecting to find this tome God's own truth in every detail had better fish the wrapper out of the wastebasket right now and trot the whole works back to the bookstore. For memoirs of this kind are invariably unreliable. The reminiscing gaffer may intend well, but once past the half-century mark he is betrayed by one or all of a variety of failings: senile decay of the faculties, vanity, the bemusement of nostalgia, the giddy lust to point a moral, or downright galloping depravity. His allegations of fact are fantastically untrustworthy, however true in essence his tale may be.

Some time in the early 1800's a group of bright young historians conceived the idea of collecting from such veterans of Lexington and Concord as had survived their sins and could be persuaded to talk, a symposium or anthology of personal recollections of that astounding day.

It was then only as long after the event as today is after World War I. So the enterprisers figured it would be easy to find among the survivors a few still in possession of their faculties, to buy them a drink or two apiece and — the Truth being proverbially in Wine — to draw from each a faithful picture of his part in the proceedings. These, when pieced together, would form an accurate mosaic for History through all time to come.

The first part was a cinch; there was, in fact, a surfeit of paunchy, graying one-time heroes about, and all so eager to talk that they even bought the drinks. Their recollections, pouring out faster than flying pens could take them down, were ample, minute, circumstantial, in every case buttressed with a wealth of detail and not infrequently attested with the most bloodcurdling oaths.

But when the historical scholars sat down to fit these parts together, they were confounded in their precise, literal minds, and shocked to the very cores of their scholarly souls. For the accounts were most deplorably inaccurate. They disagreed not only with one another, but within themselves and with the plainly ascertainable facts of the case: with the almanac, the weather records, the road maps and the conformation of God's green earth in Middlesex County itself. The simplest calculations showed that if all the colonists had marched as far and fast and shot as often and straight as each narrator said *he* did, ten million British would have bit the dust, no one of them less in grade than a Major, each and every one drilled through the head at four hundred yards — a range far in excess of the demonstrable capabilities of the Revolutionary musket.

So the historians tore the whole business into small pieces and sold the shreds to a box-board mill which shortly converted them into cartons for packaging McDono's Itch Salve for Man and Beast.

That was a pity, for almost certainly the gaffers' accounts, though erroneous or even mendacious in every detail, would have combined to give a far better picture of the night that was murmurous with hurrying footsteps and the day when the walls spat fire, than any painstaking reconciliation of times, distances and documentary evidence.

To get the nourishing truth out of any graybeard pantaloon, you have to harden your palate to tolerate a certain seasoning of misremembrances and borrowings and self-glorification and sheer mendacity. God knows I have eaten so much of these in my time — beating my gums with others in a similar stage of ripeness — that I have acquired a taste for them and maybe, like a cook who enjoys garlic, a habit of heaving the merest shovelful of them into my own concoctions.

My sources of information are equally unreliable. In the early stages of this composition I went back to the town I call Bradford, and there talked for most of a day to its present Chief of Police and Fire Chief. (Two substantial citizen-officials of great impressiveness, who were in my day reprehensible little contemporary hellions with me.) On a number of points having to do with their own departments they very grandly corrected my version of things as they had been in 1900-1908. But when — these changes having been duly recorded — they hauled out a bale of yellowing photographs, the camera's eye showed we were *all* wrong; my memory had been warped and colored by fond recollection *in absentia;* theirs had been twisted along the more prosaic but no less changing lines of the growth of the town. So I gave over trying to verify details. The hell with documentation. If I remembered a thing such-and-such a way, that was the way it was going to be.

On the other hand, it is one thing to call a horse a mare when you should have said gelding. But it is something else again to speak of an old lady as a Methodist, the way you remember her, when in reality she was a Holy Roller. By this time the horse is long since transfigured into glue, mattresses and baseballs, and unlikely to resent being called out of his or her sex. But the old lady may still be prowling around, and if you miscall her religion, however innocently, she will come after you with a buggy-whip.

So I not only altered the names of the town and of its streets and people, but I shuffled and redealt their attributes. In several cases I combined two or more people into one, so as to get them all into the story. I brought in people from other towns in the Old Colony, in three of which I customarily visited for long periods. This I did extensively, sometimes dispossessing eminent Bradfordians from their jobs or homes, to make room for Old Colonists from other towns. In fact, any characters not altogether praiseworthy whom I have put in the Bradford of this book are guaranteed to have been imported. Similarly, I have transported to Bradford certain happenings I had a part in or witnessed in other towns — but only those which might just as well, or even better, have happened in Bradford.

So let no one come after me with a shotgun, howling that his grandfather ate snuff, not chewing tobacco. No characters in this book, save those set down in love and admiration, are exactly portrayed. Except for the names of my own relatives and of public characters, no names — so far as I am aware — are those of actual persons, living or dead. And if, in using for flavor the family names and favorite given names common to that region,

I have inadvertently hit on a combination borne by any real person, I beg his (or her) pardon in advance, and offer to outfit him with a certificate attesting that he is not the John Doe who on page such-and-such of my book throttled his stepmother and made off with her store teeth.

1.

THE CHIP
ON GRANDMA'S SHOULDER

My grandmother, a frail and silver-seeming little old lady, carried an invisible chip on her shoulder.

This was easier to get away with in the opening years of the present century, and in the town of Bradford in the Old Colony of Massachusetts. For those were the last, sunlit hours of an unsuspecting era, and that was a green-and-golden backwater of intelligent, unhurried life. Time and place combined to make gentlemen gentle. They rarely yielded to the natural impulse to clip a combative old lady on the point of her outthrust jaw.

On the other hand, my grandmother was considerably limited in the indulgence of a natural taste for pugnacity, during the half-dozen years she lived with us. She was the acting mother in our home.

My own mother had died early in 1902, leaving my father with two small boys of five and six. Until then, my grandmother, as the widow of a clergyman, had been living comfortably in the back farming districts of York County, Maine. In this section, though it is thinly populated, she had an ample supply of fond adversaries by kinship, propinquity or business. Moreover, she had leisure to feud happily with them, for she had inherited a modest income from her father, once a redoubtable country lawyer of those parts. However, on being called to preside over her son's bereft family, she resolutely put aside the pleasures of retirement and lit out for Bradford with a trunk solid-packed with her choicest possessions. Figuratively, too, she stowed away and clamped down in this trunk — which she never entirely unpacked during her time with us — all her purely sporting targets of attack, bringing forth for use only those she considered practical and workaday.

These, to be sure, were numerous. They included conspicu-ously: The Demon Rum and his procurer, Tobacco; cruelty to animals; misbehavior in church; suspected skulduggery on the part of grocers, butchers and others; inhumanity of man to man; and imposition upon the family under her charge by anyone soever. She also dealt vigorously with inanimate objects that pre-sumed to defy her — such as a stove that smoked or a pipe that froze — and if her battles with these often resulted in a double knockout, at least she always floored them, sometimes for keeps.

On advancing to any attack, she looked much like George Washington in the famous Gilbert Stuart "Athenaeum" portrait. Put a lilac-flowered bonnet on Stuart's Washington, draw his fluffed-out hair silkily close to the head, and you would have my grandmother in the instant before battle: the same icy-blue eyes under thin, half-lowered, hemispheric lids; the same high, deter-mined beak; the same ruddy, country-bred complexion; the same grim mouth all set to let off a low-voiced blast fit to lift you right out of your seat, curl your hair and make a Christian out of you — sincerely rueful, if temporary.

To see my grandmother's George Washington gaze come to rest on any miscreant was like the present-day experience at sports newsreels of watching a fast middleweight measure some blissfully inept opponent for the knockout punch. You know what the cavorting victim-to-be doesn't: that in a matter of sec-onds he will be flat on the canvas, toes up and dreaming of Jeru-salem the Golden.

Just so, Dicky Hathaway and I once watched my grandmother walk up to an itinerant peddler who was beating a horse stuck on a steep grade. "Gorry!" said Dicky, whom my grandmother had once socked on the nose for misbehavior in her Sunday School class, "that man better watch out." Instead, the fool dis-mounted and faced my grandmother with his hands — one hold-ing the whip — on his hips, and a silly grin on his face. There was a flicker of black bombazine, too rapid for the eye to follow. In the next instant the whip was in my grandmother's fist and working so fast the fellow collected a dozen welts before he could get out of range, which he did at high speed on an uphill course. My grandmother then led the horse right-about, mounted the wagon and drove the equipage down to the Square, where she interned it with Nick Banton, who was Chief (and half) of Bradford's police force.

Her usual or non-embattled expression was also Washingtonian, but with a subtle difference: she looked as Washington might if he had suddenly remembered an irresistibly funny experience while sitting to Stuart, and was trying to keep a straight face over it. To her, the world was full of quiet amusement. She was forever abrim with secret laughter.

This was the face which she turned almost invariably upon my brother and myself, though people who knew us all too well were at a loss to understand how she could maintain it. Other relatives on whom we were parked for even brief periods were accustomed to employ the hairbrush from the second day on, and my father, though naturally a mild, affectionate man, found himself obliged to develop the technique of bare-hand spanking to an extraordinarily fine point in order to exist under the same roof with us without taking total leave of his wits. Yet my grandmother, who never laid a hand in wrath on either of us for six mortal years, not only kept us out of reform school but even extracted from us prodigies of useful labor around the house.

Partly, this was because she loved us very greatly and, being greatly loved in return, found it easy to overlook our merely venial sins. Most of the others she sidetracked by ingenuity instead of by trying to suppress them.

She knew how to keep two active larvae on the move and out of mischief. In this she was aided by four very special characteristics: a surprising reserve of physical strength; a habit of poohpoohing difficulties; a weird, piebald knowledge of primitive mechanics and the gift of being both interested and interesting. She was also sustained in moments of trial, by the consolations of culture as manifest in the Fine and Applied Arts.

Her vigor and stamina were amazing in so slight a person. She could saunter up to a heavy-laden trunk, ease one thin, wrinkled hand beneath its strap handle and in a flash have it up-ended, ready to roll, baggage-man fashion, across the attic floor. She could walk the legs not only off a pair of small boys but off many grown men as well.

In her late sixties she traipsed over Europe with a crony of equal years, and there the two of them had guides begging for mercy in five languages and a dozen dialects. Going out for a stroll from Lucerne one day, they dragged a Swiss who had misunderstood their intentions or underestimated their capabilities clear to the top of Pilatus — a bush-league Alp, to be sure, but higher than anything in the east of this country. They descended in a snowstorm, ambling along in high-buttoned shoes, with their reticules flopping, and assuring the poor anxious guide that this was nothing to the snows on Mt. Washington.

This pooh-poohing technique made life strenuous for my brother and me. There was no such thing as being too tuckered to finish a job if she was bossing it — no such thing, even, as sitting down for a rest. She went at housecleaning — with us for skirmishers, infighters and moppers-up — in the manner of Grant flushing the Confederates out of the Wilderness. And though we and the house took as thorough a beating in the process as the Army of the Potomac and the forest lands of Virginia did, she always beat the eventual tar out of Disgraceful Circumstances.

Often, in the course of these operations, she had to move — or thought she did — some prodigious weight, such as a granite-slab doorstep or a cast-iron stove. Whenever one of these trifles was too massive to be snatched around with a Yo Heave Ho, my grandmother took swift thought of the basic principles of primitive mechanics, beginning with the lever and fulcrum, the roller, the inclined plane and so on, if necessary, to very involved contraptions of block and tackle with a jack thrown in for good measure.

She had first become a fan for these mysteries upon learning in young womanhood how the Egyptians had wrassled together the enormous stones of the Pyramids without other power than that of Israelite slaves. While still deeply impressed by these triumphs of mind over matter, she had picked up a copy of Luce's *Seamanship* at Edgartown, on the Island of Martha's Vineyard, where my grandfather had filled a youthful pastorate. This fat volume was intended to give shipmasters in the days of sail exact instructions for rigging tackle by which a handful of sailors at the capstan could jackass around incredible weights of masts, anchors, guns and chain cable. From Luce my grand-mother, though salty in no other respect, had picked up a considerable lore of slings, blocks, braces, purchases, whips, guys, parbuckles and preventers, and she could rig a double Spanish burton with the best of them.

In this art and science she reached her high point during the transfer of a great, round, cast-iron parlor stove from retirement in the woodshed, up the steep, narrow, angled backstairs to the hired girl's room — with only boy-power to move it.

Even so she would have failed, and the stove would be there yet, if she had not added resourcefulness in morale to ingenuity in mechanics. For my brother and I quickly grew exhausted at playing Children of Israel, and a change of rôle to that of Athenians building the Acropolis only served to wedge the whole contraption at the sharp bend near the stair top. Rigging a preventer at this point, my grandmother adjourned for brief study of a section of Luce she had hitherto neglected — one on the art of giving commands.

When she reappeared we found ourselves sailors before the mast, and under her shrill whoops of "Haul aft!" and "Sway away!" laid on at the end of a complex arrangement of block and tackle to such effect that presently, with a sound of crackling wood and falling debris, the angle of the wall gave way and the stove bounded aloft in a cloud of dust, bringing with it shreds of wallpaper, slabs of plaster, pieces of lath and a yard-long section of two-by-four framing wrenched from the very vitals of the house.

My grandmother dearly loved such proofs of the validity of Culture. She had been born and brought up in a great, flat-roofed Palladian house with fanlight windows over the doors and yard-wide pumpkin-pine paneling, in the southwest corner of Maine. There she had absorbed simultaneously the frugality and the classicism of Down-East New England. She could make soap and translate Horace with equal facility and mordant effect. She learned at one and the same time the art of drawing clear water from a well-sweep well in summer when water is very low, and the genteel female accomplishment of drawing pictures by copying fashionable chromos.

At this she was only passably fair, for she had no artistic talent whatever. But she had an eerie, unconscious gift for exaggerating some minor feature of each Work of Art she was put to copying, with astounding results. Given as model the picture of a lovely, innocent child holding a cat, she unintentionally bestowed on that cat such an expression of agonized ferocity as you would find only on a trapped panther. She once copied a landscape with weeping willows over a tomb by which two lovers lingered, and unwittingly gave the lovers every apparent posture and expression of Messalina and Don Juan about to leap into the near-by thicket of laurels for purposes which I am sure neither the original artist nor my grandmother intended.

Marrying out of this backwoods cultural milieu into the churchly towns of Massachusetts, she had lit neatly on her feet in Tuesday Afternoon Culture Club circles. There she had listened to innumerable Papers (and written her share) on Ruskin, Millais and Turner; Tennyson, Browning and Emerson. She had gazed upon God knows what phantasmagoria of lantern slides showing the Art and Architecture of the Old World, and had acquired a considerable collection of books on cathedrals, sculpture and painting, together with a number of ghastly plaster-cast reproductions of Greek medallions.

At the period of which I write she had long been released by widowhood from compulsory attendance at deliriums of culture. But, unable to shake off the habit altogether, she still took an occasional swig out of Ruskin or Philip Gilbert Hamerton, and went on benders in the Boston Museum of Fine Arts, then located on Copley Square where the Sheraton-Plaza is now.

It must have been on one of those occasions that she struck up an acquaintance with the lady representative of a firm which rented out fine-arts exhibitions to schools. These were not, you understand, original hand-painted pictures; they were cardboard-mounted lithographic reproductions of Great Masters, arranged in linked chains so they could be draped over the walls of schoolrooms or hung from steel-pipe frames between the aisles.

The lady, catching my grandmother in a debauched mood, persuaded her to sell the idea of an exhibit in the Pratt School to

Bella Barrie, its principal, and Bella, who had a weakness for such heady stuff, fell in with the plan.

This was all very well for my grandmother and Bella, for Wesley Mather, highflown and civic-minded editor of the Bradford *Monitor*, and for the several hundred females of the town who flocked in at ten cents a head to "Oh" and "Ah" before the Masters all day one Saturday. Bradford had never had such an orgy of Art. But the proceedings made no hit with the boys of the fifth, sixth and seventh grades, who had to put up the pictures under Bella's eye on Friday afternoon and take them down again early Monday morning, and less than no hit with me, for all my friends, suspecting my grandmother's hand in the business, took surreptitious pokes at me as we hung up endless strings of Raphael Madonnas, Corot landscapes, Landseer animals and the like. To this day I cannot see a reproduction of Rosa Bonheur's "Horse Fair" without the horrid fear that some justly outraged contemporary is about to pinch me in the fundament.

She was not above skulduggery to achieve an end she considered worthy. Once, in the interest of Art, she took a slingshot to editor Mather's buggy horse.

The occasion was a Sunday afternoon committee meeting at our house. My father had been appointed to a group charged with advising the Selectmen on a proposal that the town buy one of those standardized stone statues of a Civil War infantryman, as put out many years before by enterprising firms in the mortuary monument business. Bradford had never bought one of these. Hundreds of other towns had bought them and put them up, but ours had always declined on the grounds of individuality, strongly supported by frugality. Also there were many citizens who believed that the stock statues, considered purely as Art, were pretty awful. Now, however, the remainder of an old lot of such figures was being offered at close-out prices so seductive that frugality caught fire, individuality was strongly tempted and Art found itself in a tight corner.

What my father was doing on this committee I can't say. He knew little about Art. But then, most of the other members knew even less. To a man, however, they held strong opinions. And those opinions were evenly divided. Some, like Judge Dearden, scoffed at the stony figure, though acknowledging, as Union veterans themselves, that it was correct in every detail of uniform, arms and accoutrements. Others, led by Wesley Mather, were all for anything civic. Mather was no veteran but he was a powerful pleader, and as soon as he discovered that no one present was able to gainsay him, he assumed the position of the committee's Art expert.

My grandmother had, of course, been excluded from the meeting. But she listened to its proceedings from the adjoining sitting room. And as Mather unloaded one preposterous pontification after another, she began to sizzle at the seams and hiss at every pore. At anybody else's house, she might have barged into the meeting to set matters straight. But here hospitality restrained her.

She seethed in her rocking chair until she could stand it no longer. Then she got up and went outside for air. Coming to the front of the house, she saw editor Mather's horse and buggy standing across the street, facing downhill. Mather was one of the few people in town who, for business reasons, drove his own rig. His horse was a burly beast named Caesar. Caesar, for all his might, was unenterprising, so Mather was accustomed to let him stand untethered while he was newsgathering.

My grandmother, strolling and contemplating Caesar with distaste, stepped on a something in the lawn. It turned out to be my brother's slingshot. She eyed it for a moment speculatively, and then considered Caesar with particular respect to range and exposure. Then she picked up the slingshot, selected a sharp-cornered stone from the driveway and retired to a discreet emplacement among the hydrangeas. From there, with a nice eye for trajectory and a little allowance for windage, she Let Caesar Have It.

The stone, traveling fast, took him just where she had aimed — in a tender spot in his southwest area. And Caesar took off like a jackrabbit. Of course he made more noise, for his hoofs were enormous and there was the clatter of the iron-tired buggy to help him. He raised more dust, too, and may have traveled faster. At any rate, he was only a cloud in the distance by the time the alarmed committee poured out the front door.

Mather set out in pursuit, accompanied by my father as the spriest of the conferees. The rest sat down on the front piazza to wait. Here they were presently joined by my grandmother, inquiring what was the fuss. One explanation led to another, and soon the talk worked back to the subject of the committee's deliberations. So my grandmother sat down, too.

Half an hour later, when Mather and my father drove up in the rig — retrieved intact from the sanctuary of Mather's own barn — the matter of the statue was settled right where the committee sat, by a vote of seven to one against the editor.

And that is why the Town of Bradford, almost alone among Old Colony towns, has not, to this day, a monument to its Civil War soldiery.

2.

BACK-YARD TOWN

Bradford was a typical town of the Old Colony, which was (and still is) that southeastern sector of Massachusetts that liked to think of itself as the original, the genuine Colony whose thirty-odd towns had spread, by a natural seeding process, fanwise out of Plymouth, whereas Massachusetts Bay Colony ("so-called") was nothing but a promoter's Development around the upstart town of Boston. It didn't help any to remember that the brash Bay Colony had had the highhandedness to appropriate the Old Colony by annexation in 1691. Old Colony people had always said no good would come of being so close to a bumptious young place like Boston, and as far as they could see in the first 270 years or so, none had.

Their own towns had grown slowly and decorously, like box-wood trees. And, like boxwood, they were small, strong, fine-grained, close-textured, tidy, artlessly graceful and pungent. Old Colony people tended to take a lot of credit for this moderation, too.

Such smugness always put my grandmother's hackles up. It was not only that she deplored any conspuing of Boston — a city she warmly admired as the true seat and repository of Culture. Even more strongly she felt that the Old Colony was making a sour-grapes case for its own lack of gumption and ginger.

"If they'd had a mite of gumption," she said, "they would have declared their independence of Massachusetts, the way the State of Maine did in 1815. If they'd had a smidgin of ginger they'd have grown. But what have they got? Only one city, Brockton. The rest of 'em towns about the size of Bradford. Four thousand people! And there were three thousand here when Greenleaf [that was her late husband, my grandfather] was pegging shoes here and studying for the ministry before we were married. And not many more thirty years ago when I used to visit Arrie [that was her sister-in-law] while she was teaching in the old Blake School."

My grandmother considered herself entitled to lecture the Old Colony, not only because she had spent a good deal of her younger days in Bradford and near-by towns, but because the Leavitts had been among the region's early settlers, and we had relatives all over the place. Though a Down-Easter she felt a moral responsibility to her husband's country.

In truth the Old Colony was, industrially, commercially and almost literally a happy backwater: Its meandering streams had no force, no "head"; consequently it had no waterpower to speak of. So none of its towns had grown into roaring, tawdry mill cities. Perhaps these towns had once envied the seduction that befell their livelier sisters elsewhere in the Commonwealth. But by the 1870's they had made up their minds that if big-city capital wasn't going to betray them, they might as well relax and enjoy modest marriages with small but steady local providers who would know their places and recognize who really bossed the household.

That is to say, the Old Colony towns had taken unto themselves the kind of industries that had originally been handcraft shops — such as shoemaking or India-rubber goods. In time, of course, these providers became steam-powered and mechanized, and some of them grew to be very comfortable earners. But the towns took care — at least until the end of the Nineteenth Century — that their industries remained homebodies and didn't make public exhibitions of themselves.

In Bradford, for example, there were half a dozen small-to-medium-size factories. But they were so scattered around the town, anywhere along the elm-shaded streets, that to the outward eye Bradford was a residential community with a few accidental and immaterial factory chimneys sticking up through its trees.

Several of the shops were right among the finest residences, including conspicuously those of the men who owned them. One occupied the base of a triangular, park-like plot of ground; its owner's large house stood at the apex of the block. There was another factory — no longer operating in my day — which was connected to the many-gabled residence of its proprietor by an ell, the way country barns are often connected to farmhouses.

Nobody felt that a factory was an undesirable associate, any more than he gave a thought to the occupation of his neighbor. Just as Charlie Porter, owner of the Porter Works, thought it natural to build the biggest and finest house in town right across the street from the one-story dwelling of his own night watchman, so Mr. Beals, the town's leading merchant, saw nothing strange about living next door to Charlie Porter's factory. Indeed, it was on that side of his substantial home that he put up a summerhouse or gazebo, surrounded by rose bushes. Here, on a July afternoon, Mr. Beals would sit with his wife and daughter, eating cherries and passing the time of day with the men in Porter's shop whose benches happened to face open windows just above him.

Again, like other towns of the Old Colony, Bradford saw no reason why anyone shouldn't put up a store in his own yard, if he chose. So, you were likely to find anywhere in town a grocery store or a grain-and-feed store, or a fish market, standing neatly and apart in the grounds of its owner's well-kept house.

Typical of these comfortable, domestic emporia was the grocery store of Mr. Seaver, who lived opposite the Pratt School, from the student body of which he must have reaped a ringing harvest of as much as fifty cents a recess period, for penny candies, OK gum and pickled limes. His estate was about the size of a small ball park, with the house at first base. The store, matching the house in architecture and color, was in left field. A similarly matching stable occupied center field for the board and comfort of Mr. Seaver's horse Dolly. And where the pitcher's mound would be stood a well, capped by a comparable latticed and vine-grown summerhouse.

Grocery stores, in that lustily unsanitary era, had a fine, sharp, businesslike aroma to them, compounded of kerosene, molasses and coffee (always ground fresh while you waited, in a big hand-operated mill); of dill pickles, bran and licorice sticks; of cracked corn, brown sugar and yellow soap; of sage cheese, butter in open tubs, smoked codfish and cinnamon bark — all dug out of bulk stock as you asked for them, with no damned nonsense in packages. Mr. Seaver himself, however, was modern; he forbade his cats the old-time privilege of sleeping in the cracker barrel during business hours, and did more trade by hustling it in a delivery wagon than by waiting for it to come in at the door.

It was accounted a great privilege for a boy to be allowed to ride with him on his delivery-and-order-taking rounds and to hold the reins while Mr. Seaver was indoors parlaying with housewives. He liked to have a boy along, but not because there was the slightest danger of Dolly running away. She was a fat, sedate bay who would stand for hours if need be, yet at a cluck go into her decorous, unvarying clop-clopping trot over a route she knew as perfectly as Mr. Seaver. Rather, the merchant enjoyed company. And this was strange, because he never exchanged a word with his fellow passenger.

On your return, you and Mr. Seaver would split a bottle of Moxie, sitting grandly in his summerhouse and being saluted by passers-by along the street in front, yet still silent as two companionable sphinxes.

Most of Bradford's commerce, of course, clustered around the Square, along with two of its churches, its Town House and its Public Library. The Square itself was, like so many in New England, not a planned civic feature, but simply a widening-out of old road junctions, where Federal Street, slicing through Bradford on its way south and east from Boston, paused to pass the time of day respectfully with Orchard, Elm, Peabody, Pratt, Chase and Standish — streets that had been old when Federal was still the inconsiderable and little-used Boston Way.

Federal Street had little enough traffic in my day, though it was spoken of as the Highway. You could walk to Bradford the whole six miles or so from any of its neighboring towns, and see no more life along the white ribbon that lay between fair, sunlit fields, than an occasional hay wagon, a drummer's buggy or the cart of an itinerant tin peddler. Or perhaps, if it were a red-letter day, you might be overtaken by a horseless carriage, whirling along in its own cloud of dust at twenty mortal miles an hour and leaving behind it a glamorous trail of that exciting new smell we were coming to recognize as gasoline.

The Square we accounted hustling, with its traffic of delivery wagons, ice carts and doctors' buggies. Indeed, it made quite a prideful story in the local papers when Bottlenose Butterworth, the photographer, had to wait fifteen minutes for traffic in the Square to halt long enough for him to make a time exposure. People said that if teams kept on thickening at this rate the Square would have to be paved with stone in place of macadam, and one gloomy correspondent wrote to the *Monitor* predicting that the time would come when we should need more hitching posts in the Square.

Into the Square, on one or another of the streets that met there, came four trolley lines, connecting Bradford with its neighboring towns. Those were the days when, if you had a fistful of nickels in the summertime, you could voyage interminably and happily on the front seats of open trolleys, from town to town, changing at Squares very like Bradford's, and so from town to town again, humming between green hayfields, passing other trolleys like ships at sea, on the turnouts, and rolling with bravely clanging gong down elm-shaded streets into towns fascinatingly different from Bradford, yet so like it in every familiar trait of character that you understood them and felt at home in them, and knew what the people were talking of and thinking about as they sat in their platform swings underneath the apple trees or among the lilacs of their back yards.

You got an equally revealing and perhaps even more intimate view of Old Colony towns if you traveled by the railroads, whose close-woven network laced all eastern Massachusetts. Passenger trains chuffed busily over unnumbered branch and connecting lines (now, in the motor age, ripped out and forgotten). They trundled familiarly in and out of the towns between comfortable old homesteads that had been there long before railroads were even thought of.

Generations ago, prosperous and public-spirited people had ceded strips of their back yards to bring these tame little railroads into town, and their descendants had continued to live there, sitting out of doors in any pleasant weather and accepting the passage of trains just beyond their barberry bushes and dahlia-beds as simply and gladly as they welcomed the friendly passage of neighbors afoot — and altering their mode of life not one whit on that account.

So when you rode through this countryside on the steam cars, you passed, as it were, through an endless series of friendly outdoor living rooms inhabited by people you felt you knew — and sometimes did, in fact, recognize for friends — as they sat eating their apples or darning their stockings in the dappled shadows of horse-chestnut trees while their get played placidly in sandpiles, planning God knows what infantile outrages.

Of all countries in the world there is none to compare, for intimate, unpretentious charm, with the eastern New England that was. In all New England no land was more fair and friendly than the ancient, snugly settled Old Colony. And the heart of its charm lay open for all to see, anywhere and everywhere, in its back yards.

Bradford's back yards were superior, even for the Old Colony. They were neat without ostentation, though not without labor; in spring and summer the voice of the lawnmower was loud in the land and half a dozen mechanics in town conducted profitable businesses on the side, selling, sharpening and repairing lawnmowers. In fall, the air was horizon-blue with leafsmoke and sweet with the scent of burning leaves.

In those years, too, there was horticulture without frenzy. Many primeval oaks, chestnuts and sugar maples had been allowed to stand where they grew. Nearly every yard had fruit trees of some sort: fat, ancient, gnarled apple trees that bowed every year under their loads of red-striped and fragrant Astrachans, or yellow Porters, or juicy Russets; robust old cherry trees a foot or more thick in the trunk; Bartlett pears; plums and quinces. . . . It was a strange yard that did not have, somewhere in it, a Concord grapevine.

There were shrubs, too: lilac trees that had been old at the time of the Revolution; snowball bushes and wild roses in the taste of a bygone day. Of other roses, only the hardier, more prolific and more bug-resistant kinds were attempted, and these in severe moderation. Here and there you would see some curious waxy-leaved and strangely flowering shrub that nobody could identify, save that it had been brought back by great-grandfather's brother, a merchant captain. There were hedges of privet or of yew, liberally pierced with openings to walk through, for they were not meant as barriers any more than the fences. Of these there were few, and they were of a height planned for leaning-on and talking-across, or for the young to walk on top of, tightrope fashion. In some parts of town the lots were still divided by old stone walls, built solider than they looked, by colonial landholders, and now serving as sun-warmed seats for visitors and as the apartment houses of chipmunks.

I repeat, there was no excess of gardening. At the turn of the century people could take flowers or leave them alone. Women had not yet gone green-thumb happy — or perhaps it was their full length stays that nipped in the bud (if you will excuse the term) any intemperate longing to bend close to the earth. Men for the most part were paunchy and overweight, so even the most ambitious of them were content with a strip of dahlias, a peony or two, a cluster of poppies, a handkerchief-size bed of pansies and a small circular plot of geraniums.

No one in his right mind bothered to raise vegetables in Bradford, except, perhaps, for a discreet asparagus bed that had decorative value and was practically self-tending. Why should he? In season the groceries and markets were awash with fresh produce from the outskirts, and the streets rang all day long with the chant of Italian truck-gardeners anxious to unload upon the housewife more peas or tomatoes than a kitchenful of females could can on the longest and hottest summer day — for a quarter.

Some of the older and larger houses had stables in their back yards, but few of these, in my day, were tenanted by horses. Bradford people generally went afoot. Most people lived within a mile of the Square, and thought nothing of traipsing that distance daily to shop or get their mail. (There was not at that time any Rural Free Delivery, much less door-to-door carrier service in towns the size of Bradford. You went to the Post Office and if there was mail visible in your glass-paned box, asked for and got it with promptness and dispatch.) Similarly, men walked to work and kids to school. A few of the persistently sporting element rode bicycles.

Of course the trolley lines, which converged on the Square

along four of Bradford's principal streets, offered transportation to anybody fool enough to part with a nickel for a ride merely within the town itself. But those who squandered their money that way were looked at askance. Bella Barrie, principal of the Pratt School, was reprimanded by the School Committee for setting a scandalously bad example to youth because once, on a rainy day, she took the Brockton trolley into the Square, though she lived scarcely ten minutes' walk away.

Strangely enough, however, it was not considered profligate to hire a livery-stable rig, if you had business in the outskirts or if (like my grandmother) you liked horses and enjoyed driving them. Perhaps this was because the livery stables had made it generally unnecessary for people — even those with stables standing on their property — to keep horses of their own.

Consequently, the back-yard stable or barn, where it existed, was a storage space and a foul-weather playground for the young. (It was in the vacant lofts of these that juvenile shows were usually given.) Frequently, however, a portion of the barn was partitioned off for poultry, and a neatly wired henyard set off in back. Or a yard might very properly have an openly avowed henhouse, provided it was clapboarded and painted to match the dwelling. Often enough these were given the added touch of a gilt weather vane.

In the larger back yards it was common to find a summerhouse, and in nearly any yard an arbor, overarched with vines, in which people sat on sunny days. A sunburn was considered at that time in a class with ivy-poisoning, and a tan downright vulgar.

In the shade, too, were located the various swings and hammocks which were standard accessories in every yard. Some day, perhaps, a psychiatric-minded historian will explain why America, for so many years, had a compulsion to rock itself in chairs indoors and swing itself in various devices outside, and how this oscillating equipment all but vanished like the whooping crane and the once-innumerable buffalo, when folks took to auto-riding.

You rarely see, these days, a platform swing, yet there was a time when no back yard was complete without one — a contraption of two double facing seats suspended from a folding framework and connected by a latticework floor-piece. By pushing on this floor-piece as you sat, the seats could be set in motion, and when manned by small fry they were customarily swung to the violent limits of their arcs. But four adults would occupy a platform swing for hours at a time, solemnly gliding a foot or two back and forth like so many chimpanzees in a zoo, and scarcely more communicative.

Hammocks, too, were much in fashion, though they had obviously little to offer anybody but spooning couples, since they were uncomfortable to sit in, more so to lie in, and into the bargain commonly smelled of mildew. The only satisfactory thing you could do with a hammock was to get a friend in it and see if you could swing it so far up toward the zenith that he would fall out on his face. This was easier with a particularly villainous kind of hammock made of barrel staves strung railroad-tie fashion on two ropes. I haven't seen a hammock of this model for years, but I know several people I would like to get in one.

If there was any room left after all this furnishing had been put in a back yard, it was taken by a croquet set. Nowadays croquet, in so far as it survives, is largely a small-fry sport. And of course in my sprathood it was played, during daytime, only by the shriller-voiced citizens. But in those leisured summers, the lengthening of shadows and the falling of sunlight in long rays across the sward marked the hour when the short-pants and pigtail elements were wise to get the hell off the croquet course in favor of their elders and betters. For the adult generation had played croquet when it was the fashionable outdoor sport of what would now be country-club circles, in the 1870's and 1880's. And not a few still-handsome couples could trace the dawn of love to his refraining from blasting her ball out of the lot, or to her pretty dependence on his masterful split shots on the day they had drawn each other as partners.

Most men were home by a few minutes after five. There was time for a quick game before the universal supper hour of five-thirty. And afterward, there were hours for playing in the sunset and the twilight and even into the dusk, shooting for wickets marked with bows of white ribbon while the fireflies flashed applause. Adults played, of course, in the old style, swinging the mallet sidewise like a putter, instead of vertically between the legs. No lady in those days had legs, nor did any gentleman intimate that all human beings had them, by standing astride his ball.

But do not suppose that croquet, even as played by grownups in this hampered style, was a tame pastime. There were at that time few or no other outdoor sports that offered opportunity for a buck to subdue his doe, much less for a doe to make a fool out of her buck. Golf was a distant millionaires' amusement you read about in the magazines, and that only occasionally. There were only three tennis courts in town, and on those the only women that played were the ones young enough to make thunderous headway against the hobble of an ankle-length, starched linen skirt. Bicycling had gone out of fashion as a coeducational pastime. For wiry, active women with an itch to sock, and for men who wanted to contend against them, there remained croquet alone.

So Bradford summer evenings resounded with the smack of mallet on ball and with the outraged howls of players who got bad breaks or (as dusk deepened) suspected dirty deals. In our yard, the howling was mostly masculine, for my grandmother was a formidable opponent, with a billiard-shark's nice eye for angles, a whipping, full-arm swing and a wicked wallop when she got a chance to croquet some male coeval's ball. She was, moreover, not above clipping an opponent on the shin with her mallet, pretending to swing it absent-mindedly while looking in some other direction. It was thus dangerous to stand behind her, or to let her walk in front of you, as George Swan found to his cost one evening in early June, 1908. Ten years later he showed me that the scar was still there, though it had worked around a little to the inboard side of his leg.

In Bradford, then, back yards were the scene for the exchange of amenities and for a great portion of the year's living. If you were visible in your yard you were At Home, and neighbors or strolling friends dropped in, stayed as long as they felt like and wandered on again without the formalities of a card-laying call. People were welcome to pass through, too, on their strolls, and all proper back yards were considered to be in the public domain for sub-teen-agers.

Our street was named Maple Street, for the good and sufficient reason that it was planted with oaks, whereas the parallel Hollis Street was gay all fall with the yellow, red and orange of sugar and rock maples, and Elm Street, beyond, was really over-arched with elms. In this, as in many other matters, the town of Bradford and its people had too much good sense to allow themselves to be pestered by the obligations of mere logic or consistency.

For Bradford people were, like their yards, simple and natural. They were cultivated, but artlessly so. They supported two weekly papers in one small town. Their speech was at once Bay-State-careful and Old-Colony-provincial. They were generally respectful to grammar and construction and to all consonants in pronunciation except the letter "r." (In eastern Massachusetts, and particularly in the Old Colony, that letter is carefully elided when it comes in the middle of a word like *horse*, but always tacked on to a word ending in a vowel when that word is followed by another vowel: "the idear of.") They pronounced the word *yes* "ayah," but were not abashed to use in ordinary conversation vocabularies that would be hooted in derision anywhere outside New England. They had a great inbred respect for accurate knowledge, for a broad background of information and for genuine learning — and none the hell for affectation of any kind soever.

3.

SOFT TOUCH & SONS

Bradford's luxuriant unpretentiousness added greatly to my grandmother's troubles. For in it, the highly intellectual simplicities of my father flourished happy as brambles in a thicket, while underneath this cover my brother and I scurried about our natural iniquities as uncatchable as rabbits in a briar patch.

My father was a research scientist in natural history, employed as collaborator in the laboratory of a wealthy dilettante in the next town. He was a slight, spare, active man, with a reddish beard and a high, balding forehead fringed with curly hair. He looked somewhat like Shakespeare in the Chandos portrait. But he had sharper, more penetrating gray eyes than the Bard and a famous high arch of a nose.

A natural athlete, he moved with a springy, easy, long-striding gait. He always ran upstairs two or three steps at a time and habitually vaulted fences whenever he came to them. In his youth he had been a noted shortstop, and at Harvard an intercollegiate champion pole vaulter. Tangible evidence of these feats cluttered our home. In the family strongbox — a japanned tin affair that could be picked at will with a bent wire — there were numerous gold medals heavy with incrustation of wreaths and chain-appended bars. Throughout the house were dozens of lesser trophies in the form of engraved pewter drinking mugs.

Since my father neither smoked nor drank, these mugs lacked convivial employment. But because they had glass bottoms they made handy filing places for specimens of the innumerable kinds my father brought home to the study he had set up in the ostensible parlor of our house. You were likely to find in them anything from an Indian arrowhead to a live, but forgotten and very hungry field mouse — one of which refreshed himself, when discovered, with a bite of my grandmother's exploring forefinger.

My father was equally absent-minded about himself. He cared

little what he ate (barring a great fondness for apple pie with sage cheese, especially at breakfast), and his dress, despite my grandmother's best efforts, was incorrigibly untidy. This would not have been so bad in Cambridge or Boston, where the general getup of a scarecrow was the accepted badge of well-to-do intellectuality. But in Bradford it was no distinction at all to wear mismatched coat and trousers. The most she could make him do was to carry his books to work in a green baize, drawstring bag, but even this was apt to come home full of frogs.

When aroused, my father could show the most lightning-brilliant flashes of sharp, incisive reasoning, and on such occasions he was a formidable opponent in argument. But he preferred the friendlier pleasures: old, well-proved jokes; simple, time-dried aphorisms; familiar New England stories. For he liked people.

He liked them so well, and was so ready to believe good of them, that he was a natural-born pushover; a fall guy; God's own gift to confidence men, amateur or professional, particularly if their pitch was intellect or piety. He was forever getting nicked in his meager bank balance by second-hand Brahmins with mining interests, or by rolling stones who showed up at church long enough to borrow money to attend unspecified theological schools.

He was likewise the perpetual gull of the illusion that he could start and run a farm or any fraction thereof, as an avocation. He spent his summer vacations proving this to the exasperation of everybody but himself, on the old family place in southern Maine. Undeterred by annual defeat there, he wooed Demeter in his spare time at Bradford.

Here, too, she proved a bitch, aided and abetted by my brother and myself. He tried pigeons that laid eggs and died; and he tried hens that lived but didn't lay eggs. Probably both these phenomena were traceable to the fact that he had to depend for the daytime care of his livestock upon my brother and me, than whom two more unreliable farmhands never left a door swinging open or forgot to fill a watering pan.

We must have made more money out of his poultry than he did. For we not only got twenty cents a week apiece out of him for practically worthless labor, but in one year when he laid in a bale of stripped tobacco stalks as louse-repellent nesting for pigeons, we did a handsome business in the weed, which we sold to our friends at one cent for a fistful with no ends sticking out.

But my father's utter, innocent trustfulness of human beings and growing things had its violent compensation.

He was possessed of a compelling distrust of inanimate objects and forces, and of germs.

The first of these drove him to a weird, intricate forehanded-ness in averting accidents which were at best exceedingly un-likely to occur. Two very early instances typify unnumbered others across the years:

One calm, moonlit June night in 1900, the family (including my mother, who was then alive) took the night boat from Boston to Portland. Few less perilous voyages could have been arranged. But it was only a year and a half since the great winter storm of 1898 in which the steamer *Portland*, on the same run, had put out into a snow-blinding hurricane, in which she was lost with every soul aboard. So on this enchanting summer evening, my father put us all to bed in cork life-jackets with our clothes, neatly made up into corded bundles, tied to our wrists. Just in case.

Later, in my grandmother's day, we were invited to visit in Boston with my Aunt Kate and Uncle Billy, who were staying at the Bellevue, a hotel on Beacon Hill, and a skyscraping one for those days. Our rooms were on the tenth floor. Discovering this, my father went down to the waterfront along Atlantic Ave-nue and bought enough Manila rope to provide each one of us with a means of escape in case of fire. This must have decimated his working bank balance, and it was no small task for a 130-pound man to carry a 500-foot coil of 3/8-inch line half a mile uphill on a hot summer's afternoon. But I am sure he felt well repaid for both pence and perspiration by the fact that we es-caped being burned to so many crisps in a fire that never happened.

Greater and more constant than his maneuvers to circumvent accident were those directed at the frustration of disease. On this subject he knew just enough, as a naturalist, to envision bacteria crouched in every crevice, to hear in every inadvertent cough the approaching footsteps of pneumonia, and to suspect in any flush or fancied paleness the first symptoms of some disease all but unknown to science and certainly unrecognizable by the local medicos.

On this account, too, he all but drove a succession of family doctors to angry forswearing of their Hippocratic Oaths. He was much given to interrupting their examinations with suggestions, and with criticisms disguised as queries. Not infrequently he countermanded a doctor's orders before the clop-clop of the professional's receding buggy-horse had died away in the distance, and often as not substituted for their pills some external treatment of his own, such as sweating, chest-plasters, liniments, or the application of hot flannel cloths.

This last was the basis of his attack on croup, an ailment which, in my earliest years, I developed half a dozen times a year, usually in the dead of night. The cure was worse than the disease. At my first squawk, my father would arrive on the run, with a bottle of camphorated oil, a small table oilstove, a flat tin pan and an armful of flannel cloths — scorched yellow-brown from previous use and smelling accordingly. In a matter of seconds the cloths would be heating while my chest was getting rubbed with the oil. Now came the undermost and hottest cloth, clapped to my skin. The agony and indignity of this were heightened by the fact that — croup being croup — I couldn't at first yell with any loudness. But as cloth succeeded cloth the croup let go my vocal cords and I was able to make increasing noise. When my bellows had reached a satisfactory volume the croup was judged over and the hot cloths stopped.

The reward for this came next day, when I was kept home from school. This irked my brother. It was bad enough to have had his sleep murdered by my yelps. To see me reaping all the profit was more than he could bear.

He was younger than I by sixteen months, and brighter by about the same margin. So it wasn't long before he began coming down with entirely convincing attacks of croup of his own. They were lighter cases than mine, from which he recovered after a mere three or four hot cloths. But they worked. As soon as this was established, he made it a point to have his croups on the same nights I had mine, thus saving my father a good deal of work and insuring that the two of us would be out of school together.

This was approximately four times as pleasant as being home alone, for he had all the admirable qualities of companionship, including a heart brimming over with sunny deviltry, a gift for willing conspiracy and a face of such brown-eyed innocence that it alone would get the two of us out of any trouble in which we were not actually caught red-handed. On that face the very traces of crime itself — such as the smears of a stolen blueberry pie — took on an air of harmless mischief that often as not earned acquittal for both of us. An invaluable ally.

He was, morerver, generosity itself. And not only in the sharing of property or plunder. For example, he had the unusual gift of being able to pick up the words and music of any song on a single hearing. In this way he mastered a prodigious store of ribald ditties that used to be sung by Old Man Dunbar and other reprehensible characters in town. These he painstakingly taught to me, and we sang them happily together without being more than dimly aware of their meaning.

Again, he shared with me his case of measles. Inspired no doubt by gratitude for the croup, he went to really considerable lengths to climb out of the room in which he had been segregated and to reach mine by way of the shed roof. In return, I shared my chicken pox with him, and would have done likewise with my German measles except that he came down with them of his own accord.

Each of these, of course, meant a layup that was not unpleasant in itself, once we were restored to bedding in the same room. For we interpreted "bed" to include all the surrounding territory of floor and outlying suburbs of closet and — in decent weather — open windows from which we could taunt our school-bound friends.

Furthermore, each layup was followed by a prodigious period of No School, for convalescence. My father was no man to take chances on exposing us to new contagions, unsuspected by medical science, until we had been fortified by weeks of fresh air. So in the first year of our collaboration we spent more time out of doors than in school.

In the next year and part of another, he kept us out of school altogether — a feat he could manage because he was on the School Committee. He maintained our healths were delicate. As thoughtful sons we did our best to strengthen him in this faith. To be sure, during the daytime while he was out of town, we did more than our share of tree climbing, fire-engine chasing, wrestling in the mud and wading in ice-studded slush — all with no perceptible aftereffects on our persons. But at night when he was at home, we remembered to have interesting symptoms such as coughs or lamenesses or — when we judged it imperative — a spasm of concerted croup. We knew a soft touch when we had it.

4.

THE HOUSE
WITHIN A HOUSE

Our home was in a two-story-and-attic yellow house with brown gingerbread trim in the fanciful geometry of the 1880's. It had eight generous-size rooms, including a kitchen ample to swing a cat in — a fact which I confirmed one rainy afternoon by rigorous scientific experiment, with the loudly reluctant collaboration of Richard, the family cat. It also had, after the manner of its time, a prodigally wasteful front hall, a large, unheated one-story ell or shed at the back, and one pint-size bathroom fitted with an elegant diamond-shaped window in amber, red and blue glass. This afforded an interesting view of the neighbors or, conversely, cast on you a fascinating mottled pattern that discouraged a waste of time on soap and water.

You entered our house, if you were company or a fool, by the front door (also featuring vari-colored glass) which gave upon the slippery, varnished, front stair hall. On your ordinary occasions you came in either by the back door through the shed or, more usually, by the side door that opened directly into the kitchen. This had the tactical advantage that it put you instantly within snatch of food or, in cold weather, right next to the purring kitchen range. It had the disadvantage, however, that the kitchen was liable to be populated by one or more people who would demand, "Where in the world have you been?" From this there was quick escape by the narrow back stairway which opened immediately at your left. For discreet, unobserved entrances or exits, you used a lattice (ostensibly reserved for a trumpet-flower vine) that led directly to your upstairs bedroom.

This was the largest room of four (plus bath) on the second floor. My grandmother used to call it, for reasons I could never fathom, the Rats' Nest. Its principal item of furniture was a

monstrous folding bed in the semblance, when closed, of an upright piano, but such a gargantuan and oaken piano as never
was. To open this bed was a task-force operation, involving first
the clearing out of accumulated playthings and furniture from the
beachhead where the bed would land, and then the combined
forces of an adult to haul, plus a boy to climb on the top of the
unfolding section and give it weight for the descent. When finally unlimbered the business was supposed to be locked in its
open position, lest it fold up again of its own accord during the
night and smother you as you slept. The lock was required to be
snapped into place to my father's satisfaction when he came in
to hear us say "Now I lay me," or there would be hell to pay. He
was no man to take chances on the mysterious intent of inanimate
objects.

This room was the principal base of our civilized or non-
concussive operations. Here we deployed armies of Rough Riders
against British Guardsmen; here we ruined all clockwork-driven
toys in reasonable par — which is to say in two days after
receipt.

Here, too, we spent endless hours drawing pictures. Our Uncle
Billy, a paper manufacturer, kept us in unlimited supply of drawing paper on which we set down our innocent childish fancies of
Indian massacres, military carnage, railway disasters, naval battles distinguished for fire, explosion and the drowning of all fore-
ground characters, and frontier saloon manslaughter liberally
furnished with Forty Rod Likker, gunsmoke and gore. A few
months ago, helping to clean out a family homestead, I came
upon a stack of these morbid works, weighted down with a copy
of the Reverend John Keble's *The Christian Year* (1827) in which
it says:

> The heart of childhood is all mirth,
> We frolic to and fro,
> As free and blithe as if on earth
> Were no such thing as woe.

Our less-inhibited indoor hours were spent in the attic, a capacious and well-windowed apartment reached by a staircase

through the hired girl's room. The attic contained three strata, so to speak, of three anthropological epochs.

Deepest and farthest back in the corners were the implements and artifacts of the aboriginal inhabitant — a dentist, an amateur photographer, a pigeon fancier, a breeder of rare squirrels and a spectacularly unsuccessful taxidermist.

Of his professional equipment he had left behind numerous obsolete but fascinating items: notably an old-fashioned, foot-power drill with flexible cord and a box of worn bits. With these it was readily possible to perform prodigies of hollowing out and inlaying pieces of chalk, using a paste of ink and chalk dust for the filling amalgam. We got so good at this that Ward Trumbull brought us his sister's outsize Christmas doll, on which we did a spectacular pseudo-gold inlay job with a paste of yellow chalk stolen from the schoolroom. The last time I passed through Bradford that girl, now a frosty-headed dowager, snatched her grandchildren in off the street and locked them up for safety.

The dentist's photographic leavings included a great number of glass negatives, fascinating enough to look at in their horrid inversion of black-for-white, so that a pretty woman's face appeared to be a black skull with glowing white eye-cavities. But the plates were even more fascinating to prop up and shoot at with a slingshot. By the time we had shattered the lot, our marksmanship was so good that no cat in the neighborhood was safe, and few sparrows. There were also a dozen jars of chemicals, caked and hardened but not, happily, altogether inert. One of them, when treated with a teacupful of reagents that included some of my father's formaldehyde, the fag end of a bottle of iodine and a generous dollop of kitchen ammonia, gave off a perfect geyser of foam that rivaled Old Faithful, but was yellow and smelled worse.

Of the dentist's taxidermic relics the most appalling were half a dozen stuffed squirrels that looked somehow like ducks, and a duck that looked much like a squirrel. All were badly motheaten. But there was also a box of glass birds' eyes of all varieties and colorations, including a handful of owl-size ones in staring yellow and black. It was possible, if you were sprat-size, to fit a pair of these into your eye sockets, monocle fashion, and thereby to startle a hired girl practically out of her wits.

Off the back of the attic opened a small antechamber which — on structural and olfactory evidence — had served the dentist first as a dovecote and then as a darkroom. Being illuminated only through a faint square of red glass in its door, this served at one time or another as the secret meeting room of the following organizations: The Bradford Boy Sleuths; The Medicine Lodge of the Ogillalah Tribe; The Holy Grail Pilgrimage; The Sons of Captain Kidd; and The Secret Six. I forget the ritual of all these but the last, which revolved around giving two cents per member per week, to Four-Eyes Belcher. I remember this because, in view of our providing the Secret Cavern, my brother and I had to pay only a cent a week apiece.

The secondary stratum of deposits in our attic was that laid down by my own elders. It included a stovepipe hat, vintage 1889 (with narrow, smartly curled brim), unworn since my father's graduation from Harvard. My cohorts and I found it could be made to fit by padding the lining with paper, and so would do for the part of Gentleman Jim Corbett, conqueror of the immortal John L. Sullivan. In this act were included a set of enormous, tattered, chamois-covered boxing gloves — also relics of my father's college days — and a pair of knee-high bicycle shoes somebody had once mistakenly given my grandmother.

The accumulations of my family also embraced a considerable number of books of less than current interest to adults in the early 1900's, since they dealt with subjects like the Civil War, the Philadelphia Centennial Exposition of 1876, the Chicago World's Fair of 1893 and One Hundred Great and Memorable Events of America's First Century. But these books were all thoroughly illustrated, so we read them from cover to cover.

Much of this study was carried on with the nourishment of apples (a barrel of which always stood in the back shed) and to the accompaniment of an old Regina music box. The Regina had been the Gay Nineties' brave first step toward the incomparable blessings of the phonograph, the radio and TV. On it, revolving zinc discs, changeable like phonograph platters, plucked out resonantly tinkling music. The box could be set to repeat the same record over and over until the clockwork ran down. Perhaps for that hideous capability our Regina with its dozen or so records had been banished to the attic. The first book I ever read from cover to cover was *Blue Jackets of '61*, which I got through with the aid of God only knows how many sustaining rounds of the "Marseillaise."

The final deposit in the detritus of our attic was that of my brother and myself. Our heavier and more shin-breaking toys were all limited in use to the attic — a wise provision in view of the fact that the trains, wagons and ships of that day were made of cast iron. We had a ponderous rolling model of the armored cruiser *New York*, with a cast-iron figure of Admiral Sampson that could be plugged into a slot on the bridge. This redoubtable man-o'-war like to pitched Mrs. Buzzell, our hired woman, down the attic stairs head first when she tripped over it. And a set of baked tile building blocks — German-made with very precise angles — extracted from my father the nearest thing to an oath I ever heard from him, when he trod upon them in the dark, going barefoot into the attic to locate a noise that turned out to be chipmunks. Our train, like others of its day, had no tracks; it rolled on the floor — with a fine rumble as of a real train — on the bare boards of the attic.

This train had as accessories two cast-iron and dimly human figures — presumably railroad men — that could be fitted into slots in its various cars. They were about two inches high and enameled respectively red and blue. The red one became my brother's Man and the blue one mine. And during year after year, when they got worn smooth and bright from long handling and long carrying around in pockets, they were distinguishable by the faint specks of enamel in their crevices as My Little Man or *My* Little Man.

They were prodigious on sandpile diamond and gridiron, valorous in battle among a hundred anthills. They slew horse-chestnut buffaloes uncounted, and with toothpicks harpooned the hell out of a bathtub whale which proved to be, in all repentant reality, a salmon that had been tenderly brought on ice to my grandmother by George Swan, all the way from Maine. In the darkness before going to sleep we would dream out adventures for them.

For *My* Little Man I constructed secretly a romance in which he saved Lily Merrill, the prettiest little girl in Bradford, successively from runaway horses, Chinese kidnapers, sharks, Indians and the persecutions of Bella Barrie, sixth grade teacher, with whom Lily was having geography trouble.

He was in fact the real hero of my first venture into print, though that venture was about as abortive as any author-publisher's in all the history of literature.

It was prompted by the Christmas acquisition of an Excelsior printing press — a present from our Uncle Billy. This came with cases, both upper and lower, a complete font of type and a can of ink. There was also a book of directions, of which my brother and I could make nothing. My father was less than no help, for while he approached the problem of assembling the outfit with all the wariness of a farmer setting up a high-speed sausage-meat grinder, his mechanical skill was never on a larger scale than that required to chauffeur a microscope, and shortly he got the whole works jammed. My grandmother, being called in as consultant, saw, or thought she did, that all we needed was a mite more pressure. Applying this with a pick handle for a lever, she succeeded with no effort at all in cracking a vital casting clean in two.

There remained, however, the type, the cases and the ink. With these, printing of a soul-satisfying blackness was still possible. All you had to do was find the letter you wanted, in its appointed division of the case, pick it up in your fingers, touch it to a rolled-out film of ink on a stovelid, impress it on paper and replace the type. In no time at all I got so I could print as many as thirty characters a minute, with almost as few errors as fingerprints.

Having thus mastered printing, I set about publishing, or rather about authoring-and-publishing at one and the same operation. I composed my piece, in the classic manner of the country editor, right out of the case as I went.

It was to be an adventure tale. Furthermore, it would be woven of everything. Bravery, prowess and Congregationalist rectitude should be its warp; its woof would present an ever-changing pattern of gunplay, touchdowns, gales off Cape Horn, detecting, home runs, fur trapping, desert-island resourcefulness, the leading of charges sabre in hand and getting all A's at school.

I judged it wise to hint at these possibilities in my opening chapter. So, on an ominous May morning, an observer ("had there been one") might have seen a lonely horseman setting forth from the Charlestown Navy Yard for the campus of Porter Hall (a fun-loving preparatory school, all of whose graduates went to Harvard), his saddle-bags loaded with pemmican, shin guards and epaulettes, his secret-service badge concealed beneath his mackinaw, his trusty six-shooter at his side. His stern, manly, yet open visage belied his twelve years, and small wonder, for the sands of the Arabian desert . . .

All this I laboriously printed out, letter by letter, while my types got stickier and stickier with thickened ink and I kept getting the o's mixed with the i's in an adjoining box. And as I went I became aware that I was haunted by a problem which all my description was only postponing: my hero had no name.

So he was forced to stop and put out a fire, in the course of which he carried down a ladder a beautiful ten-year-old girl with a red hair ribbon (Lily's favorite color) while I tried to think of a suitable name for him. In vain. John and other respectable names lacked zing; Montmorency had a fine coat-of-arms glamour but didn't go well with the sobriquet of "Rattlesnake" which I had already decided upon. Our hero had to go on, stopping presently to dive off the Cottage Farm Bridge and re-rescue the ten-year-old beauty (this time with a yellow hair ribbon, Lily's second-favorite color), to the cheers of a passing Harvard crew, who little foresaw how one day . . . Still no satisfactory name. The shades of night fell and a desperate band of opium smugglers lay in wait. And as far as I know they are still lying there, waiting for a hero to be named.

The back shed opened off the kitchen. It housed a bin for kitchen stove coal; an insatiable rack which we were supposed to keep filled with kindling; two oil cans, of five and one gallon capacity, for the service of the household lamps; and various barrels of grain, cracked corn and bran for the nourishment of our poultry. All these were detested symbols of servitude. On the other hand, the shed always had its apple barrel which my father, though feckless in many other respects, never allowed to become empty, and it was the abiding place of the family refrigerator. Putting that tempting quarry in so exposed a spot was as trustful and simple-minded an act as though Daniel Boone had hung his choicest venison outside his Kentucky stockade with a sign saying, "*Not* intended for Indians."

The shed was likewise the storage place of various tools my father bought, fondly fancying he would get to use them before they got nicked as so many clamshells or lost forever in the near-by woods. It was also the garage for our sleds and double-runner (bobsled to outlanders) and for our skates, hockey sticks and other ice-bearing equipment that was contraband inside the house proper. Here, too, in a corner reserved to herself, my grandmother kept her private and impeccably respected store of blocks-and-tackle, levers, inclined planes and other devices for defeating Newton's Law of Gravity and the Coefficient of Friction.

Other than the Rats' Nest, the attic, the kitchen and the shed, the rooms in our house were of no importance, being inhabited by grownups. They were furnished with pathetically mismatched tables, chairs and sofas of all periods from black walnut to blacker Mission. They were heated by a gargantuan and insanely erratic hot-air furnace in the cellar, a limbo reached, if you must, either by interior stairs or by the conventional slanting cellar-door entrance from outside the house. And they were lit with kerosene-oil lamps.

Of the oil lamp as a factor in American hardihood much has been fondly written, but nobody I know of has done justice to its early accessory, the sulphur match. This was an invention of sheer fiendishness. Sulphur matches came in cards of wood, semi-separated like the teeth of a comb so that you could split off a match or matches as you needed them. The cards came in tissue-wrapped packs about the size and shape of a poker deck. The tip of each match bore a touch of red phosphorus which lit when you scratched it on the seat of your pants. The phosphorus also had the merit of glowing in the dark when damp, or if licked and drawn in lines on your eyebrows and cheeks — an effect much sought for on Halloween.

Though the phosphorus tip of a match would light on anything, it didn't burn hot enough to light the wood of the match. So the next half-inch or so of the matchstick was coated with sulphur, which burned with a hot, almost invisible blue-green flame and gave off a choking reek for perhaps five seconds before the match itself got going. History abounds in tributes to the flint and steel tinder box, the carefully cherished coals in the fireplace, the pine knot, the spill pipe lighter and even the Boy Scouts' dry sticks, but where is the Whitman or Sandburg to hymn the old-time sulphur match?

Our house was set in a lot of perhaps one-sixth acre, with a dozen oak trees in the back, and along one side a row of pear trees of which the fruit had this singular property: that for weeks it was rock-hard and sandstone-grainy and then suddenly passed overnight into a state of putrescent jelly. The oak trees were nearly all too high-branched for climbing and the pear trees too tame for sport. There were also a few hydrangeas and lilac trees around the house and at the very rear of our land.

At one rear corner of the yard stood a structure that had been the dentist's squirrel-house, with a fairly large chicken-wire cage, enclosed at the top. It became our henhouse.

This property, with all its land, vegetation, minerals, buildings, structures, rights and appurtenances had become my father's for $2,500.

On moving into it he was able to send for and uncrate several big pieces of furniture that had been in storage for want of space in the smaller house we occupied during our first year in Bradford. So my brother and I came into possession of a number of large packing boxes, stoutly and honestly made of white pine, after the misguided fashion of the time. Of these we built a blockhouse in the back yard.

The blockhouse was impregnable for a long time. You could go in, pull the cover down after you, latch it with a wooden turn-button and be secure from molestation by neighboring Indians or discovery by chore-conscious adults. A dozen auger-holes admitted air and light in moderation. So the place gradually became a sort of retreat — a combination of the Hadley hideout of William Goffe, the Regicide, and the castle of Merlin the Enchanter, a man given to strange brews, deadly fumes and the study of ancient tomes.

The brews were various: sassafrass tea, malted milk, lemonade — all made hurriedly in the house when no adult was around to forbid, and stored by the gallon crockful in our retreat. Here they quickly acquired an interesting flavor through the growth of a scum of mold on top. Indeed, the whole interior of our packing-box castle was pleasantly moldy since the structure was set flat on the ground. In this atmosphere, thickened to taste with the reek of sweet fern or cornsilk cigarettes, or of dried sage smoked in a corncob pipe, it was great fun to read the works of H. Rider Haggard, or Dr. Kane's Arctic Explorations in two volumes, profusely illustrated with steel engravings, or that most prodigally and satisfactorily generous treasure tale, *The Swiss Family Robinson.* Such pleasures, of course, became practically ecstasies when heightened by the sound of distant hollering from an adult who wanted us to run an errand or to come in and have our pants mended. We were secure in our stronghold.

Or at least we were until my grandmother showed how to do what all the slings and arrows of twenty sub-teen-age Indians had never been able to accomplish. She dislodged us in no time at all, simply by taking a board and slamming the flat of it bang against the reverberating walls of our hollow blockhouse. After about three resounding belts, Merlin and William Goffe fought with ringing ears to be first out of that thunderous hellhole and surrender at discretion. Merlin won. I know; I was Goffe.

5.

LEVEE OF A GENTLEMAN

You woke early, in the manner of the young. But how early depended upon when it pleased Nature in her visible, audible or tactile forms to notify you of the waiting pleasures of a new day. That might be a function of the season, of the state of wind and weather, or of some other natural phenomenon such as Richard, the family cat.

Richard, of course, was a strictly contraband bedfellow, who had had to be smuggled upstairs under your sweater in deference to naïve adult superstitions about 1) germs, 2) the possibility of his suffocating you by going to sleep on your chest. This last just went to show how ignorant grownups were; Richard was no such fool; he spent his nights in wintertime burrowed under the bedclothes out of the way of drafts. In exchange for this shelter he was willing to serve as a superior sort of hot water bottle. The acme of symbiosis is a small boy curled up under an extra helping of blankets and comforters around a large, clandestine cat on a cold, cold night.

On the other hand, a cat, unlike a hot water bottle, knows what time it is, and as the hour of sunrise approaches, he stirs, stretches, yawns and worms sleekly forth from under the covers, demanding to be let out. You always hoped, against experience, that Richard would have learned that the way out was through the window and down the trumpet-vine trellis. But he always went perversely to the hall door where he sat, fluffed up in the chilly air, looking meaningfully back at you and getting visibly ready to purrow. There was nothing for it, then, but to hop out and, scorning the easy way of opening the door for Richard, to gather him up, ease him hind-end-first out the window, hook his foreclaws into the trellis and close the window in his reproachful face. This was a frigid operation when conducted in a nightgown, but it was full of moral satisfaction, for you invariably believed

the lesson would take this time. And it was followed by the
sensuous reward of a plunge back into your still-warm spot in
bed.

There you lay huddled till circulation was restored, then exposed an ear to listen in the silver stillness to the sounds of the
coming of day: the far-off whistle of a train among the hills, and
the tiny, distant growl of its many wheels rumbling clear through
the frosty air; from up the street, the creak of pung runners on
hard-packed snow as Mr. Leach, the milkman, approached on his
morning rounds; next door, the thumping explorations of Old Man
Linfield in his woodshed, not unmixed with soul-searing curses;
from your own back yard the adolescent crow of stripling cocker-
els and the crawking of hens; directly below you, the cheerful
clatter of the hired girl wrestling with the furnace. This was the
signal that you could shortly get up, for you had strewed your
clothes on the hot-air register, and very soon your flannels would
be piping hot.

You began with long woolen underwear. Of thick, scratchy
wool, speckled gray in color, it was heavier than your summer
husk of knitted cotton, but no wise different in cut or coverage.
The shirt, which buttoned at the neck, had sleeves that came
right down to your knuckles, so that they had to be folded back
in cuffs. The cuffs, however, were so loose that they came un-
furled whenever anything you did was violent (as it usually
was), and so remained to impede your breakfast or blot your
penmanship in school. The drawers were long, too. They bagged
picturesquely at the knees in folds that gave your legs a spavined
look, and their extra length, when turned up around the ankles,
made further knobby bulges under your stockings just above the
shoe-tops.

Over the undershirt, you put on a Ferris waist. This now-hap-
pily-vanished garment was a light, knitted, vest-shaped affair,
reinforced with up-and-down and beltwise tapes, on which were
many buttons to hold up your drawers and pants. To the tapes in
front were pinned the upper end of your inverted-Y garters,
which clutched the tops of your stockings just above the knees.

Your stockings were stockings; not socks, which were worn
only by small boys below the age of effective resistance, whose

fond mamas did them up in Buster Brown suits. Stockings of that era were invariably black, heavily and closely ribbed, and made by manufacturers grimly resolved to deserve in the sight of God and man alike such trade names as Ironclad or Holeproof. And, as a matter of fact they did; you could get a considerable gouge in your knee or shin without breaking a thread of these redoubtable garments. There were, however, some makes which had a fascinating weakness in another direction: if carefully water-soaked — as by your wading through a series of puddles — the dye would come out and stain your feet and ankles an interesting purple-black capable of resisting even the yellow soap of your Saturday night bath.

Next came your pants. These were invariable in style — straight-cut to come just below the knee, where they ended in a slit at the side, set off with three or four purely conventional buttons, like those on a man's coat-sleeve today. Shorts were unheard-of. Knickers were "bicycle-pants," worn by adult dudes or, if the pictures were to be trusted, by city boys. Small fry never wore long trousers. A normal boy, from the time he outgrew dresses at three or so until his middle teens, wore plain short pants. They were usually fastened to his person by the same waist-buttons that upheld his drawers, though some boys were allowed to wear suspenders chastely concealed by their blouses.

And these were blouses, not shirts, made to come outside, not tuck inside, your pants. They ended at the waistline in a drawstring arrangement of tape, of which the ends were forever escaping to get inadvertently tucked among the books in your desk at school, so that they pulled out and embarrassed you when you stood up to recite.

The great point of a blouse, of course, was its carrying capacity. Customarily, you stowed in it anything too large for your pockets, such as library books, or anything you fondly hoped would escape observation, such as a hatchet borrowed from your father's tool chest. But on occasion you could take aboard cargo almost as opportunity offered; I have known my brother to return from a foray among the orchards with a silhouette like the Ace of Spades, which being unloaded on the best bedspread, yielded no less than forty-four Bartlett pears by actual count after discarding those mashed in transit or judged on close inspection to be too far gone with age and mold for human consumption.

Your coat — worn over the blouse except in summer — was invariably of the same material as your trousers, and suits were, almost by definition, two-pants outfits. In fact, they were by unwritten law two-pants-bat-and-ball suits, for no boy in his right mind ever consented to be haled to a clothier so mean as not to give away a free bat and ball with each and every Little Gentleman Double-Breasted Cheviot, $3.95.

You had only two suits; that was all you needed, for the function of a suit was determined not by its cut or material, but merely by its age and state of dilapidation. Your Best Suit simply became in due course of time your Other Suit. That is to say your lounge, business, school, morning, afternoon, country and spectator-sports turnout, not to mention your football, skating, wrestling and tree-climbing uniform and the ever-reliable storage-place for all your portable articles of value. For since your suit was never pressed, its pockets were undisturbed, and you always knew exactly where to lay hands on your jackknife, or your spruce gum, or your collection of chewing-tobacco tags.

Your shoes were invariably black — or had been originally and were again after each visit to the cobbler; they were otherwise as innocent of polish as yourself. They were as lightly built compared to today's thick-soled, heavy, waterproof bluchers as a buckboard alongside a bulldozer. Yet they endured endless scuffing, wetting-and-drying, clamping-on of skates and other abuse, and by grace of occasional half-soling, or "tapping," were outgrown before they wore out.

Once shod and on your way along the upper hall, you considered the question: to wash or not to wash. On the one hand, there was the aroma of new johnnycake which caught your nose right by the bathroom door, calling you to make all speed below. Perhaps, if your father were not awake and listening . . . On the other hand, you knew all too well the acuteness of your parent's ear and his absurd obsession with hygiene. Usually it was best to run the spigots a while, violently. And sometimes you even brushed your teeth if the toothpowder in current family use were engagingly flavored

Arriving below stairs, you bargained with the hired girl for breakfast ahead of the adult contingent. In consideration of the *quid* of bringing in an extra hod of coal and an extra armload of kindling, you sat down to a soul-satisfying *quo* of well-sugared oatmeal and milk, browned codfish balls, fried potatoes and hot johnnycake dripping with butter. If you worked fast you could be well through this and at the departure stage before your later-arriving elders got around to asking embarrassing questions about your schoolwork. Further, you could pile up almost an hour to be out of doors before schooltime. For this you now arrayed yourself.

Removing your coat, you pulled on a sweater, first unobtrusively making sure that the former back side was in front, and that the former front side, with the hole you had torn last week while sliding sledless on your breadbasket down the frozen front walk, was in back. This was easy, since the sweater was turtle-necked, aping the varsity style.

Your headgear was a cap of the general cut shown in pictures of his late Majesty Edward VII of England — or in portraits of Harry Vardon and other golfing greats of the pre-plus-four days. It rode insecurely right up on top of your head — when you wore it. Often as not you removed it after leaving home and stowed it in your blouse. In wintertime you might wear black velvet ear-muffs with your cap.

You usually tried to get out without further encumbrance than this, no matter what the temperature, but were as usually halted and made to get into your overcoat. This you despised, not only on general principle but because, being two years old, it was too small, too tight, and pulled your coat, blouse and shirt sleeves way up your wrists. Furthermore, it was furnished with mittens sewed to a tape that ran up one sleeve, across the shoulders and down the other sleeve — a humiliating precaution against loss. Sometimes, too, your grandmother insisted on your wearing the wristers she had knitted for you in a hideous shade of lavender or rose.

In sloppy weather you were forced to put on rubbers. This was a sissy measure which you accepted only as a challenge. In self-respect you took pains to defeat it as quickly as possible after release, by walking through any slush-puddle that was over rubber depth. True, this was painful in the deed and made you uncomfortable for hours after, but it was a moral duty. We all performed it even when, one year, some conspiracy of parents put practically every boy in our part of town into rubber boots. In the woods back of the Pratt School there was a vale which, in winter, used to fill up with water and become a pond two or three feet deep. That year, on mornings when the pond was not too solidly frozen over, it was always full of boys by eight forty-five or so, wading in until the icy water just brimmed over the tops of their boots. New England's sons are born and bred full of the old Moral Moxie.

6.

DOUBLE PLAY: GRANDMA TO SINGER TO SATAN

I hope I have made clear that in turnout we young gentlemen of Bradford avoided with utmost care any point of getup or carriage that made us conspicuously distinct from one another. This was easy enough in matters over which we had control, or in those where parents, providing clothes, had the mercy to follow established style and fashion. But now and then some fatuous elder would foist upon his (or more often her) offspring an atrocity the wearing of which was a crown of thorns beyond human endurance: a snowy-collared Eton jacket or a sky-blue velvet suit . . . or worse.

This happened to my brother and me at the hands of our grandmother, and in a way that took its place among small-fry legends of Bradford, which agreed that there never was any sartorial outrage in that town — up to 1908, anyway — to compare with the dual one of the Leavitt boys' grandmother's blue serge suits.

My grandmother's ideas often took an unpredictably arty shape. But being of a practical mind and having an economical streak by inheritance and by training as the widow of a clergyman, she confined her self-expression to useful things. She would paint the door of a henhouse her idea of a Florentine blue — but only if the door needed paint. She would make dresses for herself, but only as she required them.

In the early months of the year 1906, my grandmother treated herself to a new sewing machine. First, she took it all apart with monkey wrench and screwdriver to find what made it tick. Then, reassembling it, she tried out all the attachments, and having mastered the science of using them, embarked forthwith upon a costume of vaguely Burne-Jones intent. This was built of burnt-sienna velvet with trimmings designed to call into play all the gadgets for ruffling, hemstitching, pleating and scalloping that the late Isaac Singer had invented, together with a couple of tricks my grandmother had discovered on her own by teaming up two attachments in tandem. True, when the dress was supposedly finished she had to call in Mrs. Noonan, the local dressmaker, for alterations so she could get into it, and these must have taken many days, for I remember that Mrs. Noonan, who prided herself on being Lace Curtain Irish, ate dinner with us so continually that my brother and I picked up a lifetime habit of declining a second helping in her words, "No I thank you; I have a sufficiency and more would be a superfluity."

Having thus solved dressmaking, my grandmother looked around for new worlds to conquer. Her eye lit naturally upon us, who were then aged nine and ten and one-half, seemingly broken to harness and growing out of clothes faster than we could abrade them. She went to Boston and there, at a mill-remnant sale in the woolen district, became possessed of a length of blue serge. It must have been part of a bolt originally made for the field uniforms of Major Generals in the Civil War, for it was fine-spun, woven extraordinarily close, heavy yet limp, and practically indestructible. She next procured at a clearance sale in Beals's venerable Cash Store a couple of sets of patterns for boys' suits of the Philadelphia Centennial era — a period whose vanished graces she held in loving memory. Laying these out on her cloth, she was agreeably surprised to find she had such an overage of material that it was possible to make the collars more generous, the coats fuller in skirt, the trousers forehandedly long against growth. So she went to work.

That fall was a period of much trying and fitting, during which my grandmother, who had been brought up on a farm and knew how to soothe restive horses under the currycomb, drove us nearly crazy with hissing sounds breathed out through a mouth-ful of pins. It didn't help, either, when she stuck an occasional pin right into us.

But the worst came with the final fittings, along in mid-spring,

when Mrs. Noonan was called in. I think that by then my grandmother had begun to have doubts of her own handiwork. Until
then we, at least, had not; the nature of the suits had been so
thoroughly obscured by pins, bastings, armlessness and the dis-
comfort of being clotheshorses that suspicion had not yet entered
our minds. Mrs. Noonan, who knew a good thing when she had
it, promptly transferred all doubts from my grandmother's mind
to ours by letting off a series of ecstatic squawks in praise of the
suits. I suspect they were the first male garments she had ever
had a hand in making, and the good lady was hard-put-to-it to
find language to express her delight. The words were ominous
enough: "drape," "style," "gather," "fetching." . . . But when we
got a look at ourselves in the bureau mirror, taken down and
propped up at an angle, we suddenly realized their awful import.
For the suits were the damnedest creations ever seen.

The jackets were long, in an age when store-bought suit coats
were short and "boxy." They were full-skirted, almost, as a pair
of miniature Prince Alberts, but otherwise cut as a sort of cross
between the Norfolk jacket and the Russian blouse. That is, they
had box-pleated vertical members up and down the front and
back, and belts (fastened with buttons) which could be worn
either very tight (giving a bundle-of-string effect) or very loose
(so that they hung down in a bight in front), but not halfway
between. And the coats buttoned clear up to the neck, where
they ended in great spreading collars of about the size and shape
of Eton collars, but made of serge as integral parts of the coat.
The buttons, moreover, were about the diameter of small saucers,
and darkly iridescent in hue. Worse still, my grandmother,
through some miscalculation in altering the patterns, had got
the buttonholes irregularly spaced — and by spectacular differences which were almost the first thing to hit the horrified eye
of the beholder. After this, it was only what you might expect,
to find that the coats had no outside pockets whatever, and that
inside them, where the store-bought coat's pocket was ample to
carry a slingshot, there were only little recesses about the size of
a watch-fob.

Not so the pockets of the pants. They were deep and narrow,
and their closed ends hung down almost to the knees. Yet because

their openings were located in front — riding-breeches style — the bottoms of these pockets were all but unreachable by the wearer, so that anything put into them could be fetched out only with acrobatic contortions. This was the more so because the pants had been inadvertently cut very tight indeed. On the other hand, they were long in the leg; the bottoms of them came just about halfway between knee and ankle, where they were finished off — by an inspiration of my grandmother's — in neat, flat, serge bows at the sides, just about the size of the bow on your hatband.

Each and every seam of the whole incredible getup was sewed and sewed again with row after row of stitches set to every variation of closeness and pattern that my grandmother's experiments among the Singer attachments could contrive.

It was a horrid fascination to gaze at your brother in this God-awful outfit, but even worse to look thence at your own reflection in the mirror and see that you — because you were on a larger scale — were more frightful still. But the worst of all came when at length we were forced into these hideous costumes and sent off to school.

We were late; there had been some difficulty about fastening the hooks and eyes at our collars. So we appeared at the doors of our respective classrooms like a couple of leading ladies making hoked-up entrances upon the stage. Nor did I ever hear, until years later when Jeritza flashed suddenly in a flame-colored gown before the audience at the Metropolitan in New York, such a single, great, ecstatic gasp from a multitude as rose from the fifth grade in the Pratt School when I appeared in their doorway. It was followed on the instant by the sound, from the fourth grade room below, of a burst of laughter exploding around my hapless brother. . . .

We rushed home, of course, at noon, just ahead of the yelps of our classmates, demanding our proper clothes. But my grandmother, foreseeing this, perhaps, had already given away our everyday outfits and locked up our Bests. Furthermore, we must go back to school that afternoon, on pain of her going right downtown to notify the truant officer herself — and we knew she would do it. . . .

Why go into the miseries of that day — or the next — or the entire week that followed? My father refused to intervene. Our erstwhile friends and companions at first chased us regularly into the house, then tired of it, and when we in turn got tired of isolation and would willingly have been chased, affected not to notice us at all. They would choose up sides on the ball field and, even if short a player a side, would have neither of us. We tried ruining our suits by getting them wet, by crawling in the mud, by getting them caught on barbed wire. . . . They were proof against all manner of mayhem. We debated burning them behind the gashouse, but it was still too cold for a next-to-naked return home.

I know now why men take to drink. For my brother and I took, not to liquor, but to tobacco. We would go to hell the quickest way we dared. Specifically, we went down to the Square on Friday noon and bought a corncob pipe apiece. As fuel for these we laid in a package of Union Leader Cut Plug and the only cigar we could get for our remaining three cents, which was a long, wicked, black stogie, crooked as the dried hind leg of a lizard and, I should imagine, of about the same flavor. We tried the pipes on the way back to school that afternoon, but had to quit when the bell rang. However, we carefully dumped out the partly smoked tobacco into the inside pockets of our coats. During recess we broke the cigar in half and experimented with its parts behind a lilac bush. But again we had to extinguish the fire and stow the partly smoked butts in our pockets.

After school we followed the crowd to Porter's field where, being unable to get into the ball game, we sat down in the shelter of a stone wall and recommenced our debauch with nicotine. This time our portions of cigar didn't taste so good, so we rubbed them out, stuck them back in our inside pockets and resumed the pipes. My brother soon began to show an abatement of interest in his; he let it go out and would have thrown it away except that I forbade him to waste so expensive an article and made him drop it into the depths of a pants pocket where it would be safe. Shortly thereafter he became violently ill. This obliged me to give over smoking — probably just in time — and to set about getting my brother home, for it looked as though he would die at any minute. Moreover, it was beginning to rain.

I spare you the details of our progress home across back lots and through the woods. It was so slow and agonized that we were wet to the skin before arrival. And I wish now that I could have spared my grandmother the anguish of learning, the instant we limped within smelling distance, what awful thing it was that had brought us back. For to her, tobacco was the younger brother and ally of the Demon Rum, and indulgence in it by a boy was the first, irrevocable step to a drunkard's fate, a life of crime, a death in the madhouse and burial in a pauper's grave. She could not have felt more disgraced if my father had been arrested for holding up the mail train.

By bedtime, I myself was prostrate with fear of damnation and with remorse for having caused my brother's downfall. And still was when I awoke the next morning, Saturday. But as I lay speculating upon life's lost promise and the miseries of existence in the gutter, my eyes lit on the chair by the foot of my bed. Over its back, neatly laid out and waiting for my levee was not the hated blue serge suit of the past week, but my Best — a gray tweed that I particularly fancied and one which had brought as premium a baseball bat of especially handsome grain. Come! I should at least start for hell in decent, respectable, even elegant garb. Just then my brother entered all aglow. "Guess what!" cried he, and held up *his* Best suit.

That day we were received back into the society of our fellows with no questions asked about our late, astounding suits, and only admiring comment on our affair with Lady Nicotine. And, the next day being Sunday, our Bests were indicated as a matter of course. But on Sunday night I went to bed with as heavy a heart as a condemned man whose stay of execution has expired. On the morrow . . .

But on Monday we *still* had our Bests. Could it be . . . ? And in time it did prove true: My grandmother was unable to expunge the odor of the Weed from our trick suits. This is not surprising when you consider all the tobacco and half-smoked cigars and pipe-dottles that had been in the pockets of them, and which had then been well juiced-up and soaked into the serge by a thorough wetting. Even the dry cleaners couldn't get it out — not to the satisfaction of my grandmother's white-ribbon nose. So the offending suits vanished; we got new Bests — with bat and ball, of course; our former Bests became our Other Suits while still new. Thus we were for some days among the toniest young gentlemen that ever climbed a horse-chestnut tree in the sap-sticky season.

I learned later that my grandmother had tried to give the blue serge outrages to a pious scrubwoman in great need, with a glass eye, a drunken husband and thirteen children shivering in near-nakedness. But her one remaining eye was enough to tell this deserving female that there were extremes of hardship, worse than those of poverty and cold combined, to which she would not subject her offspring.

So my grandmother, watching her chance at a box-packing shindy of the Women's Foreign Mission Society, sneaked our late habiliments into a chest marked for the Bushmen of South Rhodesia. And there they may still be, encasing on ceremonial occasions the reluctant limbs of little boys among the BaNyai or the AbeNanswa tribes, for I cannot conceive any thorns of Africa strong enough to tear their fabric, or any decay of the fetid jungle able to unloose my grandmother's valiant stitching.

7.

OLD COLONY TWIG-BENDING

Though we would never have admitted it, we enjoyed school, taking it as a whole ball of wax. At least we got there early and were making the neighborhood shiver with decibels long before there was any decent need for it. Unlike Shakespeare's snail-creeping schoolboy, we usually came on the gallop. One day in fourth grade punctuation exercises, Miss Wyman dictated, "Roger, do you walk or ride to school?" "I run," said Roger Sanford, and was kept in at recess for being fresh. But the fact is that Roger did run every day the mile and a half from his home on the easterly outskirts. There was a lot going on at the Pratt School that neither Roger nor any other intellectual-minded boy would willingly miss — such as fights and pigtail-pulling and the chance that some friend would fall or be pushed into the school pond. And, to be fair, school was often exciting inside.

Bradford, being only a small town, had only three main school buildings, with a few outlying one-room schools for rural scholars. The town school system comprised nine grades of primary and grammar school and four of high school. The grammar grades would teach you, among other things, how to spell — a task considered unworthy of today's Progressive Education. The high school would make a competent bookkeeper or stenographer out of you if you wanted or, if you chose, would put you into any college in the country. And that in an era when you had to take at least eighteen hours of examinations for admission, and might be required to show a proficiency in Greek, Analytical Geometry and the History of English Literature, in addition to Latin, Algebra, Trigonometry, Physics, Chemistry and a couple of modern languages. Otherwise, our schools were laughably primitive. You would go to them one hell of a long time without learning Morris Dancing or getting a grade in Adjustment on your report card.

Ridiculous, too, were Bradford standards of accommodation

and pedagogy. Forty-eight head of pupils in a room were considered a mere handful for one teacher, and she was expected to beat into every head an honest passing knowledge of the three R's, Grammar, Spelling, Geography and History, together with such incidental lore as she happened to possess and had a mind to impart. She did all this in six hours a day with no study periods and — in the grammar grades — no home work. On the other hand, a teacher got her six hours' hack at us solid and undeflected by manual training, self-expression, domestic science, rhythms, library research, the dramatic arts, assembly-hall lectures or gymnasium periods. For all these our school system was as innocent of facilities as a horse of petticoats.

As you might expect, the schoolmarms who performed such miracles in the Old Colony were redoubtable characters, robust, resolute and resourceful. Likewise, they were imperturbable, by a process of natural selection, for any woman who couldn't, single-handed, suppress incipient riot without the displacement of a hair in her pompadour would shortly be carted off to the state loony-bin in Danvers.

The first grade, in our part of town, was taught for years innumerable by a stubby, muscular little female named Becky Stackpole. She was the only woman in town who, in my day, still bicycled in bloomers and calf-length laced boots. Becky was commonly reported, as a girl in the 1880's, to have ridden an old-fashioned high bicycle. All I know is that in the year 1920 she was zipping around corners and blithely missing pedestrians by a hair's breadth, on an Indian Twin Cylinder Motorcycle. Becky commonly received the decanted small fry of our area when they were four years old. At this mature age most of them could already tie their own shoes and button up their own pants after a visit to the facilities — sciences now considered to demand at least a year of kindergarten. Becky, who had originated on the Cape, was at pains to point out to Bradford's puling offspring that the Pilgrims first landed at the Cape's Provincetown, and only later at the Old Colony's Plymouth. She was to the end of her life a defiant foreigner in those parts.

I missed most of the grades between first and fifth, since my brother and I were kept out of school a good deal of that time for delicate health imagined, almost unaided, by my father. But somewhere along the line I must have put in an appearance at some grade long enough to learn " 'Come, little leaves,' said the wind one day," still one of my favorite songs, along with "God damn his soul, O'Reilly," which I picked up, elsewhere, I suppose, about the same time.

The fifth grade was presided over by Flossie Hunter, an ample and extraordinarily handsome brunette with whom all the boys were in love, secretly or openly according to temperament. She was prettier than any of the girls (Lily Merrill always excepted) and had much more sense. Flossie could, on occasion, sock a baseball out of the lot, and sometimes would do so for boys who stayed after school to clap the chalk-dust out of erasers.

(We always spoke *of* teachers by their familiar handles, as "Flossie" or "Granny," though never *to* them except respectfully as "Miss Hunter" or "Mrs. Fuller.")

In the sixth grade I came under the influence of Bella Barrie, principal of the Pratt School, a gay, iron-gray extrovert, built like a tackle and possessed of a sales manager's passion for Getting Something Organized. We sang defiantly antiphonal part songs, boys against girls; we had a no-holds-barred spelling match every day; we were encouraged to debate all the headline issues in the newspapers, with an equal allowance of time to the pro's and con's.

This last arrangement ran on a rock when the execution of Charles L. Tucker for the murder of Mabel Page became a *cause célèbre* in Massachusetts. An unfortunate young woman had been robbed and murdered by stabbing while alone in her home in Weston. For this crime Tucker, a twenty-four-year-old drugstore cowboy from Auburndale, was arrested, tried and convicted on abundant and perfectly matching items of circumstantial evidence. Chief among these were the bloodstained fragments of the blade of a hunting knife which had belonged to Tucker. He had broken it in pieces and attempted to hide it. But when discovered and reassembled it proved exactly to fit the wounds in the body of the victim.

As the day of Tucker's engagement with the electric chair approached, several Boston newspapers set up a sentimental and circulation-getting howl for his pardon, on the ground that no man should be fried on circumstantial evidence alone. Other papers upheld the jury, the courts and the Governor, and (also with one eye on circulation) published enormous halftone pictures of the knife blade. This shortly became as well known to Massachusetts eyes as the State House dome itself. In no time at all, the entire population of the Bay State was ranged on one side or the other: either Tucker was a murderer or Governor Guild was about to become one.

In the sixth grade the issue, once Bella had allowed it to come before the house, was debated daily. For every innocent tot of us had a profound conviction about the anatomical and mechanical details of the butchery and was anxious to be heard upon his or her theory. The only trouble with this was that practically all the class came from homes that took in the Pro-Pardon or Bloody-Handed-Guild newspapers, and among them they were entitled to no more total time than could be claimed by Butter Holliday and myself shrilling for the death of Tucker and brandishing about full-page newspaper diagrams of the corpse, with the sub-surface course of its gaping knife-wounds traced in dotted lines. Bella gave us our full time, which we used though hissed frequently, for we were hard-to-shut-up brats. Everybody breathed easier when Tucker finally sizzled, and we returned peaceably to the study of the works of John Greenleaf Whittier, that good gray poet.

Bella's other organizings were happier in outcome. In the fall we went to the Brockton Fair, riding grandly in a chartered open trolley-car; studying Natural History in the five-legged-cow tent, Anatomy before the runway of Zuleika, the Queen of the Harem, and Anthropology in ten-cent looks at Kyko, the Wild Man of Borneo ("He Eats 'em Alive"). We likewise watched, very knowledgeably, the trotting and pacing races. Afterwards we returned by the same car, melodious in the sunset despite a surfeit of red popcorn and Simpson Spring Strawberry Tonic. ("Tonic," I should explain to non-New Englanders, is the Brahmin designation for what is elsewhere called soda pop.)

That winter we had a moonlight hayride in the enormous double-runnered four-hourse sleigh which normally brought hides to the local shoe factories. I suppose Bella had some idea of encouraging the sub-adolescent to "spoon," for we were encouraged to share soapstone-warmed blankets with the girls. But this didn't take very well, at least among the boys. True, there was hardly a one of us who was not secretly in love with at least one girl, and very likely two or three. But at that age the only expression of affection for a girl that wouldn't get you derided by your equals was to give her a good push. Preferably into a snowbank. So while the girls were more than willing to bundle, the boys had to be ushered into blankets with them by Bella, much in the manner of one inserting a cat into a coal bag, which is an experiment you ought to try some time, if you never have. My coal bag turned out to be occupied by a little blonde girl named Elsie, a newcomer to town who didn't know many of the school songs we sang. So I showed off how well I knew them, though I had not then (nor have now) any more voice than a screech owl. I felt pretty good at being such a great, big, knowledgeable man-about-the-Sixth Grade.

We wound up the year's outside activities with another trolley-ride excursion — this time to Brockton's Prospect Amusement Park, where we rode on roller coasters, gawked at a small, moth-eaten zoo of foxes and black bears, peered into penny-in-the-slot stereopticon machines purporting to show the shooting of Stanford White by Harry K. Thaw, and I gave to Lily Merrill the brass ring I snatched on the merry-go-round.

In Bella's classroom I was a teacher's pet, being allowed to sit in the back row between a fat beauty named Eleanor and a tall one named Nellie. For my position, within covert pinching range of either belle, half the boys in the room would have traded a bull's-eye lantern just like that of Raffles, the Gentleman Burglar. It never occurred to me that this and other favors Bella showered on me were not due to a winning personality and a heart of gold. Bella may have liked me well enough, and indeed I returned her kindness by deserving the "A" in deportment she gave me every month, and by doing my erratic best in studies. But she was certainly not blind to the fact that my father was a hot-shot on the School Committee.

The next year, I landed in Granny Fuller's seventh grade, and was put right down front where that formidable lady — who leaned over backward to favor nobody's offspring — could keep a sharp eye on me. Yet by that year's end I loved and admired Mrs. Fuller and, it gives me pleasure to believe, was regarded with affection by her — if not with any noticeable admiration.

Granny Fuller was then in her sixties. The widow of an officer killed at Spottsylvania, she had been teaching school for forty years. She was a large, well-upholstered woman, who always wore a black dress — and it may have been the same black dress — that dated from the 1880's: very full and pleated in the skirt, tight-bodiced and with one row of close-set buttons grandly serpentining up to a cameo brooch at her throat. Above this, and set off by a thin ruffle of some crinkly white stuff, Granny's face was pale and placid. Her eyes, large and gray behind gold-rimmed spectacles, were bland-seeming — and saw everything. They had, furthermore, the capacity of taking it easy when nothing of importance was going on, but of blazing into action when the game was afoot. Granny's voice was that way, too: normally calm, never raised, yet in the clutch vibrant, somehow, with a terrific thrill, a soul-stirring urgency, as of something inside Granny coming right out and directly into you. She had, supremely, the gift of communication that is the mark of the great teacher.

She could make you see the Civil War and smell the dust that hung over the sweating columns piling along those roads that led up to Gettysburg. You heard the clatter of the reapers in the wheatfields and the crash of great fir trees echoing across mountain valleys, and the sound the sea makes plashing under the bow of a Grand Banks fisherman. You felt on your cheeks the tingle of the air in the high Pyrenees, and beneath your fingers the rough texture of old Flemish tapestry. You became aware, startlingly and headily, that words set one after the other in one order would sing aloud — while in another order the same words would stumble and stammer like a milkman at Town Meeting. You caught an exciting glimpse, even if you were as blundering and uncertain at arithmetic as I, of the beauty and perfection of numbers, and the way curves and shapes and patterns had relationships in the strange and strict yet limitless world of mathematics. . . .

It was in arithmetic, too, that Granny Fuller showed a pawky humor and a decisive resourcefulness when she dealt instantly with a phenomenon that later drove every other schoolteacher in the nation crazy. This was the unbearably comic significance of the number 23.

Some time about the years 1906 or 1907, there appeared in our language the imperative verb "skidoo," roughly equivalent to the later "scram" but connoting a belly-busting alacrity and indignity of gait and manner and facial expression on the part of him who was supposed to comply. Skidoo first appeared by itself, as vaudeville slapstick. In this form it was worked into innumerable sidesplitting dialogues, and into uproarious songs such as that (sung to the tune of "Marching Through Georgia") which began, "Hurroo! Skidoo! And paddle your own canoe." Unsupported, skidoo might have palled quickly and vanished like the expression "Wouldn't that dot your shirtwaist!" But late in the spring of 1908 skidoo got allied with, and equated with, the number 23, in the expression "Twenty-three, skidoo!" This was not merely twice as funny as skidoo alone, but four times as funny. And almost immediately, by some occult mathematics, it became eight times as funny to say, "Twenty-three for you!"

As a result, the chance occurrence of the number 23 anywhere, in any connection, was enough, for a year or so, to throw anybody in the bulldog-toe and mandolin-pick set into hysterics, and to plunge the short-pants and pigtail element into convulsions. Families who had lived in dignity and righteousness at 23 Anything Street since house-numbers were invented, suddenly became the laughingstocks of their towns. No merchant dared price even the choicest cuts of meat at 23 cents a pound. In church, any minister who called for the Thirty-third Psalm took a long chance on the self-control of his congregation. It was as much as a teacher's sanity was worth to assign a lesson on page 23 of any book soever. And if she gave a problem in arithmetic, say, to which the answer happened to work out to 23, why then all hell broke loose. Children whooped and hollered, fell out of their seats and rolled in the aisles, helplessly fighting for breath to squeal, "Twenty-three! Skidoo for *you!*"

This contagion swept the country; at least it was rife in the mid-Atlantic state to which my family moved the following fall, and was still claiming victims near New York in the year of Halley's Comet. But in Granny Fuller's seventh grade, it lasted just over one hour.

The first explosion came at noon on a Wednesday, when it developed that Havana was in Lat. 23°N. This outburst could not have taken Granny altogether by surprise, for the town was already Twenty-three-stricken. But she affected well-bred astonishment. Then her eyes went bright as two ice ponds on a sunlit winter day, and she shooed us out of the room, boosting the last exhausted stragglers with the soft sole of an elastic-sided shoe.

When we came back at one, Granny was ready for us. We were due for a pleasant afternoon of reading, penmanship and other non-taxing studies, beginning with a consideration of the poems of William Cullen Bryant.

The smartest-pants boy in the room was Chester Gifford. "Chester," said Granny innocently, "what page shall we read from?"

"Twenty-three!" crowed Chester. "Skidoo!"

Pandemonium!

Granny let the gale blow itself out, busying herself calmly with totting up some figures on a large sheet of paper on the desk before her.

"Very well, Chester," she said when the uproar had subsided to whiffles, "you may come up to the blackboard. . . . And now you may multiply these four numbers by one after the other, in this order."

And she wrote four longish decimal numbers on the blackboard, copying them off from the sheet on her desk.

"I will tell you in advance, Chester," said Granny, kindly, "what the answer will be. But you will have to work it out right, because I am going to check every figure you put down, all the way through. Class, do you want to know what Chester's answer is going to be?"

Uncertain nods, and murmurs of "Yes, Mrs. Fuller."

"This," said Granny, and wrote on the blackboard while look-ing at us — a trick any experienced teacher can do — the follow-ing number:

$$23.23232323232323232323232323$$

At the first two digits we were off again, but this time our laughter was short and nervous, because it had become aware of a something on its heels — a something like a big cat that had maneuvered a mouse into the middle of a bare tennis court fifty feet from the nearest mousehole.

Granny finished writing out the answer. "It *is* funny, isn't it?" she said. "Now you may all take pencil and paper. . . . And you may multiply the same four numbers as Chester, but in this or-der," and she wrote them down again, top for bottom. "I think you might as well start now, because everybody has got to get it right before he goes home. And even those of you who are pretty good at arithmetic may want to wait for the slow ones and per-haps do the same example again, but multiplying the numbers in another order still. There are many possible orders. We could have fun with this for days."

Well, if Granny had really kept her class waiting till Chester and I got our examples ungrubbed and correct in every digit, we would all be right there in the room today, for Chester's arith-metic was nearly as bad as mine. Promptly at four, however, Granny called it off.

"You may go," she said, "but remember that if tomorrow or the next day anyone sees anything funny in the number twenty-three, he can have a good long laugh for himself, at the black-board after school." She threw open the door. "Now," she said, "skidoo!"

We folded our tents like the Arabs and silently skidooed away.

Supplementing the efforts of the grade teachers were two peri-patetic females who taught, respectively, Art and Music.

In the cause of Art, a small, strawberry-colored woman named Northbridge covered every room in each of the grammar schools twice a week, which must have taken considerable hotfooting. You were supposed to be ready for her appearances with a suit-able object to paint: according to season a wild or domestic flower, an autumn leaf, a sprig of evergreen, an apple or an orange. If you failed to bring such a natural object you weren't allowed to paint gaudily in water colors, but were condemned to penciling the likeness of a wooden cone, cube or cylinder from a stock carted around by Miss Northbridge for just such as you. If, however, you had brought your gentian, or had a cent to pay to Four-Eyes Belcher for one from the extra supply he always had (or, in winter, to rent an apple from him), then you got served out to you on a china palette three delicious dabs of water color squeezed from tubes: red, yellow and blue. With these, one brush, one jar of water and one sheet of paper, you went to work, painting in the most excruciating and minute detail the flower or whatever it was, twelve inches from your nose. The more detail you got in, the better, for Art according to Northbridge was synonymous with Accuracy, a word she loved passionately and never tired of writing on the blackboard, together with its Latin derivation. Imagination was so much mendacity, and any accidental finger painting would get you a wigging.

The singing teacher was a strung-out, chinless lady named Hoot Shute. She came at less frequent intervals, for any grade teacher was expected to teach music — including both the reading and emission thereof — with the aid of a pocket pitch pipe. Hoot's principal job was the whipping-up of choral effects for the massed small fry of the schools to let off on civic occasions. In the later stages of preparation for these we generally had a mass rehearsal in the Town Hall.

It was at one of these that a certain short-pants soprano who shall be nameless literally stopped the show and all but brought down the house. This was the more remarkable because he was not a soloist, but only one of a flock of fifth graders bunched at one side of the hall. From this nest of emulous canaries, shrilling up to the climactic note of a chorus, he shot for a High C and hit a note about one-and-a-quarter tones above that shining mark. La Shute, with great presence of mind, instantly smote all the piano keys she could bang with the flat of her two hands, and thus cut short the hideous dissonance before the Town Hall ceiling should crack and fall in slabs upon several hundred of

Bradford's young. But I can still feel upon me those hundreds of accusing eyes. I may have had no more sense of pitch than a screech owl, but I had a lusty pair of lungs and a larynx ground to a sharp point by frequent bouts with the croup.

8.

FLESHPOTS AND
PLEASURE-DOMES

In the opening years of this century an important part in the life of youth — and of adulthood itself — was played by that noble institution, the candy counter, and by its amateur auxiliary, the back-yard confectionery and cake fair.

It was not that we were unable to stoke up for free, either at home or on the town at large. It was a poor household that wouldn't yield, knowingly or not, maple sugar or Baker's Caracas Sweet Chocolate or currant jelly or, at a pinch, Horlick's Malted Milk by the tablespoonful.

You could even get chewing gum for nothing. If you cared to go into the woods after it, there was spruce gum. And very good it was, too, after you got the chips of bark and the embedded insects chewed out. Failing this, there was tar. In Bradford, most of the sidewalks were made of a tar-and-sand composition which had the attractive property, when new, of softening in hot weather so that you could leave a Crusoe's Friday footprint in it. When old, it cracked badly and had to be resurfaced. Consequently, there were usually tar-sidewalk men operating somewhere around town, with their fragrant boiling kettles from the edges of which they would let you pick off semi-congealed gobs to chew. As gum, tar wasn't very satisfactory; it was stiff, and its astringent flavor endured forever. But it would do if you were out of funds.

In that era you were funded, for fleshpot purposes, if you had one cent. On two cents you were affluent; on a nickel you could be a regular Coal Oil Johnny and treat all your friends. For the candy counters of Bradford — or any town of its time — knew no larger denomination of purchase.

Such counters were an essential working part of every home-stead grocery store like Seaver's or Fitts's, of which there were half a dozen around town. And of course they were a principal department of drugstores, like Meekins's on the Square.

A candy counter consisted of a series of glass showcases, conveniently low for the inspection of the youngest young and opulently curved down along the front edge for the ease of investors' elbows and the comfort of investors' noses. In these were disposed a great number of trays. Each held some one kind of confection with a price tag showing how much or many of it you could get for a cent.

There were highly flavored sucking pieces such as peachstones, wild cherry or horehound or checkerberry drops or peppermint lozenges. . . . There were variously shaped sugar pieces, including everything from Necco wafers to candy corn—the latter constituting a sound buy since it was cheap and being in small bits lasted a long while. . . . There were gumdrops and jelly beans. . . . There were chocolate creams, considered costly at three for a cent, and chocolate-marshallow rats that looked like a bargain because one of them made a small bagful for a penny. The bags, incidentally, in which self-respecting candy was always sold, were printed in thin vertical stripes of purple and red. There was licorice in a variety of forms: in the black as shoestrings, door-bolts and pickaninnies; in sugar-coated balls; in brownish fluted sticks of heavily licorice-flavored sugar; in twig-like sticks of the natural root with its bark on. . . .

There were prize packages with valuable jewelry inside, irresistible to girls but avoided by boys who figured that no gold ring was worth anybody's cent. . . .

Before a half-acre of choice among these delectables a short-pants citizen with only a cent to spend was often bemused with ecstasy, so that the merchant waiting for him to make up his mind had to teeter from foot to foot for five full minutes or more.

An even better bet for the purchaser came now and then when girls held fairs. Girls could make candy at will — the only quality for which boys openly envied them. Nobody, of course, wished to be a girl on this account, any more than he wished to be a sparrow so he could fly; in fact, one patent proof of the inferiority of girls was the fact that, being able to concoct fudge or taffy whenever they pleased, they did not incessantly do so.

(Boys were never successful at home manufacture of any kind of candy, save under the supervision of adults, which rendered even candy-making scarcely worth while. An exception was an afternoon of candy-pulling put on exclusively for my brother and me by Miss Hetty Hatcher, the maiden-lady organist at our church and a crony of my grandmother's. Miss Hatcher, who, I think, had designs upon my widowed father, laid herself out to provide the makings of a beautiful satin-white taffy which we would pull and take home with us. I remember to this day how snow-pure it looked as it came out of the bowl ready for pulling. But when my brother and I got through manipulating it with our cute little hands, it was the color of old pewter.)

As I started to say, girls had fairs in one or another's back yards. Here each girl had a booth, contrived out of a packing box and decorated with fringes of tissue paper. At this she sold her own fudge, penuche, taffy or vinegar-candy, for prices in-tuitively calculated with respect to her own drawing power. I.e., a girl who could count on many admirers gave less candy for a cent than one who knew all too well that her only physical at-traction was the tempting handiness of her pigtails. But even the prettiest girls, like Lily Merrill, gave such abundance that you could get for a fistful of pence as much carbohydrate in various forms and colors as would slay a hyena. The only difficulty with girls' fairs was that you never knew when they were coming. Consequently, they were all too likely to catch you insolvent.

In fact, Lily Merrill's own fair caught me just that way, and I still blush hotly to remember it. Coming home from school one Friday she told me that she was having a fair the following after-noon, and asked if I would come. Grandly, I assured her I would, putting hand in pocket with a lordly gesture as of one who has a whole nickel — maybe even a dime — to squander upon pretty women. There was, as it happened, nothing there but my jackknife, a cigarette card of Cy Young and the slightly fractured skull of a mouse. But I had twenty-four hours to raise funds. Unfortunately, I forgot all about this until Saturday noon, when my father and grandmother had left for a visit in Boston.

My only possible banker then was Mrs. Buzzell, the hired woman, a Down-Easter of whom I shall tell more later. She was closer than tin on a pieplate and tougher than dried-out rawhide, and I couldn't wring a cent out of her. So I didn't go to Lily's fair, but instead stayed home and knew for the first time in my life the pangs of jealousy, picturing Dicky Hathaway buying fistful after fistful of Lily's luscious fudge.

Grownups had back-yard fairs in our town, too, and it was in connection with one of these that my grandmother perpetrated an outrage:

I have said that there were few ambitious gardens in Bradford. There was, in fact, only one among the largest estates that even affected a gardener. This was the rococo pleasure-dome of a rubber manufacturer named Barstow. The house was remarkable enough, combining, as it did, the more spectacular features of the Taj Mahal with the fanciest taste of the Rutherford B. Hayes or early Pullman-car period. But the gardens were very special. They boasted not only a fine constellation of flower-beds shaped like stars, half-moons and comets, but a collection of statuary unsurpassed in those parts, if, indeed, in New England.

There were, of course, the conventional cast-iron deer and fountains cunningly contrived in the semblance of two 1860-style tots under a cast-iron umbrella. To these had been added carven-stone immortalizations of several of the more affecting Rogers Groups and a few chastely draped classic figures.

Common report had it that these works of Art had been added, one by one, to soothe the frequent tantrums of Mrs. Barstow. She was a notable virago, fondly caressing as long as she got her way, but expert in the hurling of Lowestoft plates against Dutch tile fireplaces when balked. Common report added that this skill had been perfected in the Nevada hash-house where she was a waitress until Mr. Barstow had discovered her charms, and from which he had brought her east in the expectation — hers at least — that she would become the reigning queen of Bradford.

For reasons she could not understand, this didn't take. People were friendly to her, but obstinate about being queened over. So she frequently failed to be chosen chairman of the Tuesday Afternoon Club's lecture committee, or awarded first prize for costume at the Chemung Club's Patriots' Day dance.

Every time she got such a comeuppance, she threw a fit of high pressure vapors. And every fit Mr. Barstow soothed with a new statue. This had been going on for quite a spell of years when our family arrived in Bradford, so that Mrs. Barstow's garden was, as Wesley Mather put it in the columns of the *Monitor,* "a veritable Versailles, but with virtue in place of vice."

In this garden, in the late spring of 1908, our last year in Bradford, Mrs. Barstow finally got to be hostess for the annual cake fair and lawn fête of the Tuesday Afternoon Club. This orgy customarily began with an invocation and speeches of welcome, followed by musical selections, vocal or instrumental, loosed by gifted females and culminating in a choral number by all the members, gifted and not-so-gifted. This was supposed to soften husbands and escorts for the kill. Thereupon the gentlemen were steered forcibly and unashamedly up to a series of booths, festooned with crêpe paper and lit by Japanese lanterns, at which the handiwork of members was brazenly offered for sale: cakes, pies, cookies, jellies, preserves, candied fruits or confections, each in a booth of its own. About nine o'clock the booths were shut down for another hypo of entertainment. This time there was less noise and more intellect. Songs and piano solos were interspersed with readings. The climax of this frenzy came with the awarding of the Tuesday Afternoon Club's annual prize for the Year's Best Poem by a Member.

The idea governing this Annual Poem was such as only a women's culture club would dream up, and that only for festival purposes: Each fall a subject was chosen by a committee of former prize winners, no longer eligible to compete, who would also act as judges, come spring. The subject was a general one, such as any member might go to town upon in her own way: "My Home," "Memories of Last Summer" or "My Daydreams". . . . Contestants were supposed to do epics on this subject in such a way that when the winning poem was read aloud without revealing the name of its author, people would have difficulty in guessing who wrote it. Yet the offering was supposed to contain so many legitimate clues that everybody would say, when the name of the successful poetess was finally announced, "Why, of *course!*

How clever of her!" It was all very involved, and placed a premium on ingenuity typical, perhaps, of Old Colony women in
that age.

Mrs. Barstow had never won the prize. In fact, there had been
many years when she didn't even finish her poem in time to
meet the deadline, owing to getting stuck for a word to rhyme
with "moon." But this year she was determined to get the award
and thus win a Daily Double never before recorded in Bradford
history, which would put her, Nevada notwithstanding, at the
top of the Old Colony class for bluestocking mares. She was the
more anxious to win because this year's subject was "My Husband," and Mrs. Barstow, though she put Mr. Barstow through
the meat-chopper regular as clockwork, was as proud of owning
him as a cat is of a well-chewed mouse. If necessary, she would
get help in the final polishing of her verse, from somebody who
could think up a rhyme for "moon."

I don't know why Mrs. Barstow picked upon my grandmother
for this difficult task. Though a member of the Tuesday Afternoon
Club, my grandmother never entered its poetry contests, rarely
read a paper at any of its meetings or put in more than an
astringent sentence or two at its discussions. Furthermore, she
steered clear of Mrs. Barstow on all other possible occasions,
choosing neither to be bossed nor to be patronized, and not wish-
ing to be forced into a fight to avoid either. The nearest she had
ever been to the gardens of the Château Barstow was to take
some visiting friend on a walk past them for the laughs. And
needless to say, Mrs. Barstow had never come calling on common, ordinary people like us. Yet one afternoon in May, there she
was at our front door, calling cards in one hand and tentative
manuscript in the other, while her pair of bays sneered down
their noses at the all-too-evidently little-used hitching post that
was moldering with dry rot in front of our house.

Mrs. Barstow graciously overlooked the fact that my grandmother entertained her in the sitting room, the parlor in our house
being impiously occupied by my father's desk, working library and
microscopes. She got the amenities quickly over and came to
business. Her poem, for a wonder, was complete, or practically
so. All it needed was a little polishing. "You know: like Felicia D.

Hemans, with elegant rhymes like 'coast' and 'tossed.' "

My grandmother's first impulse, of course, was to tell Mrs. Barstow politely to go to hell, or such words to that effect as were proper to the relict of a clergyman and a disciple of John Ruskin. But when she took a look at Mrs. Barstow's effort she was seized by a wild temptation.

"Why," she said, "this is quite a little gem as it stands. All it needs is a change of a word here or there. Just leave it with me. I'll get it back to you on the day the contest closes."

She then counseled Mrs. Barstow to give her friends the impression of being in a perfect incandescence of literary composition, and at the same time to throw them off the scent by asking for rhymes to such words as "onion," "piazza" and "pickerel," or any other words that occurred to her, and ushered her out. (In the event, it proved that Mrs. Barstow had been so industrious in carrying out these instructions that one-third the members of the Tuesday Afternoon Club guessed she would rhyme "hubby" with "tubby," one-third with "stubby" and the remaining third with "grubby." All of which fitted Mr. Barstow.)

My grandmother next carefully read the poem as Mrs. Barstow had written it. It started off like this:

MY HUSBAND
My husband is the Treasurer of a Mill.
And he does not do it ill,
Because he has brains more than muscle
And also likewise plenty of hustle.
He wears a black alpaca coat
To keep the dust off his sleeves and also his throat . . .

My grandmother read on to the end, and meditated a while. Then she went and got a sheaf of paper and a pencil. She sharpened the pencil very exactly with the keenly whetted jackknife she always carried in her pocket.

Then she licked the point of the pencil, and a light came into her eyes, as of Elizabeth Barrett dreaming of Robert Browning.

And this, if the files of the Bradford *Enterprise* are to be trusted, and if the photostatic camera is not a liar, is what my grandmother wrote — and what won the prize that year, for Mrs. Barstow:

was awarded for her entry which the ████████ is privileged to reproduce for its readers.

MY HUSBAND

All day he labors at his mill,

Nor e'er forgets to hustle

Dollars with his mental skill

Instead of bone and muscle,

Wearing morn and afternoon

Engaging black alpaca.

Aiming straight at his spittoon

Refreshing chewed tobacco.

Then at eve when he's at ease

He dearly loves his supper.

Every dish he licks till he's

Plumb stuffed from nose to crupper.

After, as he wields his pick,

Neglecting not a denture,

Thoughts to me come fast and thick:

So happy, life's adventure!

At the evening's conclusion an elegant collation was served by ████████'s justly popular caterer, ████ ████████, which the

Looking at the clipping now, I suppose it was my grandmother who put Bancroft Gill, editor of the *Enterprise,* up to using such big, black capital letters at the beginning of every line.

9.

WAYS AND MEANS

When I was very small — during the first years I lived in Bradford — I was greatly puzzled by the economics of grown-up life. Fathers and other male adults, I knew, went to work, but I took this to be just another symptom of senile decay, like having whiskers or not seeing the fun of throwing stones at cats.

Working had obviously little to do with getting money: my own father went daily to work in a near-by town, but I knew very well that he got his money in Bradford because I used to see George Swan giving it to him through a hole in a window (irrationally enough installed indoors), in the First National Bank. Again, many of my friends' fathers worked in factories, where they got money on Fridays. Only an hypothesis of doddering eccentricity could explain why they went there on other days.

Another evidence of lunacy among grownups was observable in barbers: They labored diligently to cut people's hair off short, then immediately set about defeating their own ends by dousing it with stuff out of bottles to make it grow long again.

But the grownup who troubled me most was Mr. Beals, owner of Beals's Cash Store on the Square. Here was a man with limitless supplies of things like air rifles, toy locomotives, express wagons and magic lanterns which were all his for the taking, without a cent of disbursement. Yet he had not the wit or enterprise to carry them home, as I well knew for I had followed him a dozen times, to see. Often I used to lie awake at night, speculating what I could do with his store and my good sense.

With the passage of time, some of these mysteries were partly resolved. By early 1904 when I was eight, going on nine, I had discovered that there was a more or less causative relation between work, commerce and spending-money.

This relationship was, to be sure, tenuous, and continued agreeably so as long as I lived in Bradford. Boys did occasional work without pay. Sometimes it was under compulsion from their parents in such matters as raking leaves; sometimes it was for sheer glory in the holding of livery-stable horses or the accompanying of grocers upon their rounds. On the other hand, a good deal of money could be had without work at all.

Most of this unearned income was obtained by arguing for it. You put the bite on your father or your grandmother for two cents or three cents or a nickel, according to your need, your estimate of what the traffic would bear and your best judgment of the cogency of the case you could present. Thus, a plea for funds to buy candy at the stores would be wisely limited to a matter of pennies, while one for the same purpose, but to be spent at the girls-next-door's fair could be confidently stretched to a nickel.

For day-to-day needs, a nickel was amply sufficient; there was almost nothing in town of a consumable or expendable nature that couldn't be bought for five cents. Larger appropriations, as for a Spalding's Junior League Ball (20¢) had to be negotiated with an eye to the tactical situation, in which the major element was a fellow's own recent behavior — not, of course, in the eyes of God but in those of his elders. If you had been detected spatting the rump of the hired girl with a shingle, it was wise to defer your application until you could manage to be seen carrying out the ashes. This fact developed in us a quick eye for the favorable break; I well remember the one phenomenal month when I got a good report card from Bella Barrie. Though surprised almost to stupefaction, I rallied by the time I got home, and swiftly parlayed the wonder of wonders into a pair of Winslow's key-fastening hockey skates.

A more regular source of income without work — though in smaller increments — was knocking down a portion of your Sunday School collection money. This was considered highly ethical, even morally obligatory. You never would have dreamed of holding out on your parents in change from errands to the grocery store, but you would have felt disgraced in the eyes of your fellows if you were seen putting your Sunday dime intact into the basket. Getting the dime split before the basket came round was therefore a social as well as a fiscal problem.

Of course if your parents were out of dimes and had to give you two nickels, you were set; you could even oblige a friend who had a dime — always, however, holding the dime in escrow yourself for later settlement. On the other hand, if you were stuck with a dime, you either had to skin out of the house early enough to stop by Meekins's drugstore and invest at least a cent of your money, or you in turn were dependent upon the fortunate position of a friend.

Most friends were honorable enough about this, for we all recognized the working validity of the Golden Rule and its converse, You Just Wait. Furthermore, it was customary in such cases to change the dime immediately after the services by purchase of candy at Meekins's, and your friend had a moral claim on one piece of any two-for-a-cent item or half of a one-cent bar. But if all friends failed you, there was always Four-Eyes Belcher.

Four-Eyes was the somewhat older boy who on weekdays played by preference with kids safely below his own age, in whose ball games he could be a big star. He was, moreover, able to engineer window-breaking and pear-stealing operations with greater safety to himself when in company with smaller, slower and less prescient companions, whose capture delayed pursuit and insured his own getaway.

On Sunday mornings Four-Eyes was always on hand at the church early, and always provided with a pocketful of nickels and pennies. His standard or opening rate of exchange was nine cents for a dime, but if you came late, or if the demand looked as though it might crowd the supply, Four-Eyes would give you only eight cents.

Again within the realm of unearned income were the occasional windfalls which came our way whenever an affluent uncle arrived on a visit. In our case, my brother and I rejoiced in not one but two uncles of substance. Uncle Billy, chunky, chipper, alert, humorous, wise and infinitely good, was to prove all his long life a benefactor to us, no less generous with counsel and encouragement than with money. At this stage, however, he was a luminary whose ordinary light came from afar in the shape of

handsome birthday and Christmas presents, supplies of paper to
draw on (for he was a paper manufacturer himself) and thoughtful packages of the funnies section of the New York *Herald* —
a month's accumulation at a time. He came our way in person
only once or twice a year, but when he did he was good for fifty
cents apiece, and the knowledge that he was due would send us
out for a week's window-shopping and counter-browsing at
Beals's and at Behan's sporting goods store.

Our other cyclic benefactor was, strictly speaking, a great-uncle.
Uncle George was a moderately big shot in one of the steel
companies Carnegie absorbed. He was a large, paunchy, ruddy,
burnside-whiskered man, with eyes like a Saint Bernard's absently
staring off into the distance from above a pair of magnificent
purple pouches. He had a throaty voice, a majestic gait and a
great fondness for good living. On his annual visits with Aunt
Arrie he would arrive in a hack from the station with an armload of choice edibles personally selected in Boston. There was
always an immense, tender and juicy steak, cut from some ele-
phantine steer. There were usually, too, hothouse vegetables and
fruits out of season, and once a novelty until then never seen in
our household, if indeed in our town: grapefruit, which he taught
us to eat by separating the sections and peeling off their transparent skins.

I presume, too (in the light of my own adult experience), that
Uncle George carried a pint of good bourbon on his hip when
he came to visit a teetotaling family such as ours, and that when
he got discreetly locked in the bathroom to wash his hands before
dinner he took himself a good, honest slug of it, for it was upon
his reappearance that the largesse for my brother and me came
forth.

Uncle George was a handsome giver — alas, too handsome, for
the crisp pair of dollar bills he handed out were invariably
marked down by my father's eye and extracted from us after
Uncle George had left. From this transaction we got only a
quarter apiece in cash, the remainder being salted away to our
account in the savings bank where — in our view — it was as good
as destroyed. Consequently, we rated Uncle George at a precise
half of the value of Uncle Billy.

Between sheer windfalls and the proceeds of actual labor and commerce, there was a twilight-zone form of income without work which could occasionally be picked up in small install-ments. At ball games, boys might sometimes by arriving early get good seats along either base line, and often later-arriving adults would pay them ten cents for their places. Mrs. Bancroft used to keep Boxer Parton, who lived next door, on retainer and occasionally to bribe his friends as well, not to run through her privet hedge.

As a matter of fact, now that I look back on it, I am afraid various kindnesses of well-to-do citizens to us boys were ac-tually (without our realizing it) a species of Tribute to the Barbary Pirates. As racketeers we were for the most part un-witting ones, which was perhaps just as well. I recall, indeed, only one case of downright extortion upon adults and this, I blush to say, is my own. I have in my archives a bill to accuse me of it, and it is in my own juvenile handwriting:

R. G. Leavitt, Ph. D.
49 Maple St., Bradford, Mass. — Dr.

To R. K. Leavitt, Son
49 Maple St., Bradford, Mass.

For keeping still while riding. . . .06

PLEASE REMIT

Silence, as the feller said, is golden, and the schoolbooks had taught us how to make out bills.

Later, of course, when we got to be ten or twelve, most of us achieved the dignity of allowances, in consideration of which certain chores were supposed to be done with approximate regu-larity, passable thoroughness and a minimum of reminding.

These, God knows, were lenient standards enough and the pay was handsome, often running up to ten cents a week for the mere keeping of a kitchen supplied with coal and kindling, and doing the dishes on the hired girl's night out. Indeed, during my last years in Bradford, when my father kept first hens and then pigeons, the earnings of my brother and myself from the ostensible care of this livestock rose to a princely twenty cents a week each. So it was practically impossible to get us to do such seasonal chores as rug-beating or sifting ashes, notwithstanding an offered rate for the latter of ten cents a barrel for re-usable coal, picked over and clinker-free.

In fact, the only extra-pay household chore we did without squawking was to kill flies at the standard rate of ten flies for a cent. This was partly because of the sporting nature of the occupation; you stalked your wary game with a rolled-up issue of the Boston *Herald* and annihilated him with a whack loud as a pistol-shot. But even more, fly-killing flourished because you collected from your grandmother cent by cent as your account was rendered, and could thus quit at any time and light out for the fleshpots of Meekins's, Fitts's or Seaver's candy counters to enjoy the usufructs of your enterprise.

Most boys in Bradford had a fling, one time or another, at door-to-door selling for some out-of-town corporation. *The Youth's Companion* had a habit of issuing, annually, a number swollen by many pages cataloguing a fascinating assortment of steam engines, skates, mechanical trains and other yearnables. Each of these could be gained by selling so-many subscriptions or, failing that, by sending so-much in cash.

No young reader of my age, of course, ever had the cash. But nearly everybody was tempted to take at least one hack at selling subscriptions to the *Companion*, especially since he could start on the spur of the moment; he didn't have to make prior arrangement with the publisher, or agree to get twenty subscriptions or die in the attempt. He just started. Naturally enough, he started at home. Sold. One down and only nineteen to go.

But as soon as he got out around town, he found that practically every other boy-or-girl-inhabited home had already become a subscriber by the same process. The market was saturated, so he let the matter drop.

Net to the *Companion*, one subscription without any commission whatever. No hard feelings, though; the *Companion's* annual Christmas Goods number alone was worth the price of a year's admission, so that its other weekly issues, while not up to the standard of *St. Nicholas*, were so much velvet.

Similarly, most of us took a crack, sooner or later, at peddling

Mr. Curtis's then puny and little known *Saturday Evening Post*. On signing up to be Mr. Curtis's agent, you got a bravely lettered canvas newsboy's bag, for which, if memory serves, you paid. Or ought to have, anyway, for nobody ever sold any *Posts* to speak of, and within a month our fathers were customarily deep in correspondence with Mr. Curtis to get us out of our contracts. This always worked, for Mr. Curtis was a merciful man. But it cut him to the quick (so his letter said) when we let him down by not becoming Alger boys in his image and with the opportunity he had furnished us.

But there was a soap company operating briefly in our area that was troubled by no such weakness. Its contract was so drawn that even Judge Dearden could only advise parents who had underwritten it to continue taking in and paying for box after box of Whoozit's Soap, until the date of expiration freed them. Fortunately, my brother and I, having an antipathy to soap, never got our father into this one. But I do not doubt there are homes in Bradford today whose cellars are still richly stocked with Whoozit's Soap, colored like a dissecting-room cadaver and smelling like the Eleven Thousand Virgins of Cologne.

10.

FREE ENTERPRISE

As I have tried to intimate, I and my fellow *insecta* in Bradford were far from being industrious little bees or ants. In fact, we made extremely unsatisfactory employees, partly because of natural depravity, but largely because we didn't like working under anybody's orders.

We preferred Free Enterprise of our own — even at a dubious or non-existent profit — to the bondage of labor for others at any rate of pay. We would rather venture grandly if inefficiently on our own for a whole day, or intermittently for weeks as the spirit moved, than swink for an hour at a task supervised or specified as to results by our elders.

Such independent operations, taken one with another, certainly yielded a minor part of our incomes, but in terms of time consumed, of pants torn, of scratches, abrasions and bruises incurred, of danger risked to life, limb and fundament — and of sheer, rapt fascination — they were the largest part of our money-earning lives.

These enterprises had another characteristic. They were almost without exception conducted in company, as Gentlemen Adventurers, with financial arrangements more or less loose as the operation warranted, but with moral, social and tactical obligations to one another that were never disregarded.

There were numerous reasons for this. In the first place, we rarely conceived a project except by chemical reaction upon one another. Individually we were not people of Vision. But in a group, consulting early in the morning upon the proper employment of a fine day, ideas would generate by a species of spontaneous combustion. Sometimes those ideas were merely inspired by the season — "I know what let's do; let's go blueberrying." At other times the ideas would be the gifts of an all-wise Providence.

I remember a very successful circus (admission two cents; children — under four, that is — half price) which germinated when Mrs. Tenney's blue Persian cat, Omar, came trustfully fawning and purring among us just as I was boasting that my father owned a real barber's clipper for his beard. My coadjutors, being naturally gifted mathematicians, instantly saw the equation: 1 cat + 1 clipper = 1 lion. An undersized lion, to be sure, and probably a rather uncooperative one, but on the other hand, a lion capable of being manually operated through the hoops. Furthermore, a lion of striking and distinct coloration. Come One, Come All and see Omar, the Man-Eating Blue Lion of Abyssinia. Educational.

Omar's color scheme proved (on application of the clipper) to be even more remarkable than we had hoped — something on the order of a badly raveled, gun-metal-colored silk stocking worn over a mosquito-bitten leg. When word of this got around the neighborhood we had a flash-flood audience of estatically squealing hired girls, several of whom had at one time or another worked for Mrs. Tenney. It was a profitable operation, and would have been more so on a repeat performance warranted by popular demand, except for Omar's premature escape under the tent wall after his climactic Leap for Life Through the Flaming Hoop.

It will be evident from the foregoing case history (not, in its essence, unlike those from which the Higher Principles of Business Management are taught at the Harvard University Graduate School of Business Administration) that another reason for associational enterprise was the need of moral support. You never could tell when a perfectly legitimate operation would be interpreted by the Authorities as in contravention of The Law. In such cases, it helped to know that while you were serving a day's sentence in bed (my father's wholly correct idea of a sentence even more dread than a vigorous larruping with a strap) your associates were at least going around nursing black-and-blue posteriors.

But even when there was no risk of parental displeasure, we sought cooperation for moral support of a more practical nature. We had a keen awareness of the fact, learned by soul-searing experience, that work of however agreeable a kind is beyond the capacity of the human boy to endure for very long alone. He needs the moral support of company. He may conceive himself capable of standing up singly in armed combat with savages by the score or desperadoes by the dozen, but he knows better than to face unsupported a two-quart berry-pail at that appalling stage when it has got about one-third full and refuses for seeming hours to show visible evidence of getting any fuller.

Another reason for association in business venture was that most of our enterprises required the participation of outside capital. Boys assemble capital not by asking investors for money to buy equipment, but by directly borrowing the capital equipment in kind. Thus, if you decided to give a Magic Lantern Show it was necessary, in order to attract paying customers from your household and adjoining property (all too familiar with your own scratched and cracked slides) to borrow relatively fresh slides from all over town. This involved cutting in the lenders, at least to the extent of deadheading half the house. In some other forms of enterprise the extent of investor-participation was by unwritten law terrific.

One such business was lemonade-standing. A lemonade stand usually started when you found yourself in possession of a sizable chunk of ice, by courtesy or inadvertence of the iceman. You then had to assemble lemons, sugar and utensils. Each one of those usually meant cutting in some friend for a piece of the undertaking even before you could discover whether his family's kitchen was both stocked and unguarded. Once started on this, you had to keep on until you had assembled the necessary equipment and supplies, even if that meant a dozen shareholders who thereafter hung around all day, declaring themselves frequent dividends out of stock, to the financial if not the esthetic ruin of the business.

Associational venture was sometimes necessary for tactical reasons. For example, the best raspberries in our part of town grew around the foundations and cellar-hole of a long-since-vanished house that belonged to and adjoined the homestead of a notoriously close-fisted farmer named Pettingill. This man, out of sheer dog-in-the-mangerism, used to chase boys with a horsewhip if he caught them in his abundant thickets. In such a tactical situation, an experienced group of boys, and one not hampered by the presence of juniors, could usually manage the escape of all its members unharmed, by the judicious interposition of ever-fresh decoys between Pettingill and his quarry of the moment.

One day we chanced by such maneuvers to lead him into his own apple orchard, just then abundant with green apples of ideal throwing size. The colorful sight of Pettingill, a full-blooded man by nature, getting redder and redder and hotter and hotter, as he pursued one after another of us through the leafy green orchard, and the melodious "thump" of apples on his tightly overalled figure, proved so esthetically satisfying that ever after, when we went back there, it was only ostensibly in search of raspberries.

In fact, after several such expeditions, we abandoned our encumbering pails and went armed with long, limber, birch sticks, sharpened on the end. A green apple, impaled on the point of such a stick, can be thrown with approximately the same range and terminal velocity as a well-driven golf ball. And while long-range shooting with such weapons lacks pin-point accuracy, a volley from half a dozen boys, aimed at, say, a man on a two-horse mowing machine, has a fair chance of ringing up some sort of hit.

It was sheer accident, of course, that directed a fine, hard, green apple from one such salvo to the exact top of Pettingill's bald and gleaming scalp. The yowl that went up from our enemy, and the purposeful way he leaped from the mowing machine, grabbed his whip and started for us, warned us on that day to go quickly thence. So, having perhaps 150 yards' start, we retired to the more populous districts, where we spent the rest of the morning in gleeful argument about whose apple it was that had scored the bull's-eye. . . .

Needless to say, such overhead activities cut into the profit of our berrying operations, but we still felt they were worth while. The spiritual values of the Free Enterprise System far outweigh its material gains or losses.

The greater part of our activities were conducted along traditional lines. The ritual procedure of circus-giving or lemonade-standing, or berrying, or dandelion-green digging, or chestnutting, was well understood; we had for models the techniques of older

boys after whom we in our infancy had tagged along, or the
observable operations of adults. Indeed, I remember only one
undertaking upon which we ventured with insufficient data. Commercially, it was a flop, but intellectually and historically it was
a wow.

One November afternoon, exploring the recesses of a deserted
cowshed under the leadership of Davy, second oldest of the
Ogilvie boys, we came upon a bundle of a dozen rusty muskrat-
traps. The Wild Surmise of stout Cortez' men was nothing to ours
as we looked at one another on beholding these keys — ours for
the taking — to the untold wealth of John Jacob Astor and the
Hudson's Bay Company.

We knew that the banks of all the water courses around town
teemed with muskrats, and that gray squirrels dwelt in all the
trees. There were so many red foxes in those parts that it was the
expected thing for any Nimrod to slay a few to make a muff and
neckpiece for his wife or his best girl. We had even heard it said
that there were mink in the waste land up toward North Bradford.

But it was late in the day to go so far afield. So we set our
traps (baited with hastily abstracted scraps of meat from the
nearest venturers' home ice chests) along a circuit of stone walls,
thickets and disused barn cellars between Davy's house and the
Pratt School which most of us attended.

The arrangement was that on the next noon, after a swift dinner between morning and afternoon sessions of school, we would
meet for a rapid round of our traps, and harvest our crop of pelts.
("Don't forget your knives, everybody.") And then . . . well,
everybody knew that furs were valuable; we would be on the
way to wealth measurable only in terms of a pony apiece.

When the time arrived, we met: not the original half dozen, as
the unacquainted-with-boys might expect, but twenty or thirty
strong, as would be natural with a whole morning (including
recess) for everybody to tell his best friends, and for hangers-on,
including very small boys, to have horned in on the expedition.

We started at the thicket just back of Davy's and drew blank.
So we continued unrewarded (except by one of my father's
Rhode Island Red pullets in the location east of our house) until

we came to inspect the trap that had been set in Mr. Blanchard's barn, almost down to the school.

Here we knew, even before we had entered the doorway in back, that we had struck what would now be called the Jackpot. But it had never occurred to us that skunks, too, were among the fur-bearing animals of our locality. Skunks lived trustfully and companionably among us, inhabiting our cellar-pits and the underpinnings of tool-sheds. We used often to meet them on our forays, particularly in early summer, when mother skunks with broods of young would be out digging grubs and beetles, and on such occasions would pass them by, undisturbing and undisturbed. A skunk, when not annoyed, is far less perceptible to the nose than a pretty lady in $25-an-ounce perfume; you can stand within a yard or two of him and perceive no fragrance. But the skunk in our trap in Blanchard's barn was Annoyed.

This posed a puzzling problem. Entering and remaining respectfully at the door end of the barn cellar, we could see the vivid white streak of our quarry's back, far in the darkness of the distant end. Humanity and avarice alike (for we now remembered that skunk pelts were supposedly valuable) forbade leaving him there to suffer. Yet we were in our school, or everyday, clothes. And clothes exposed to skunks, said popular report, had to be buried for a month before they were again wearable.

At this juncture, Davy Ogilvie's eye lit upon a small boy named Waldo Prescott, one of the uninvited members of the party. Now there is — or was, anyway — an unwritten law among boys concerning the function of small boys among middle-sized ones. They were guinea pigs. It did not matter whether they were little brothers sent along by parental fiat or tag-alongs as Waldo was in this case; if you were in doubt about the depth of a spring-thaw puddle or the slipperiness of a wet roof or the taste of an unknown kind of caterpillar, you talked a small boy into making the experiment and judged from his reactions whether it was safe for his elders and betters.

Waldo was one of those six year olds whose mothers would have dressed them in Little Lord Fauntleroy suits if it had been a generation earlier. Now, in 1907, the nearest thing was Buster Brown. So Waldo was done up in an Eton-collared brown suède leather suit that consisted of a sort of long-waisted Norfolk jacket, belted with green leather, above a pair of very baggy above-the-knee knickerbockers. Below, Waldo's chubby legs were encased to mid-calf in white socks and his feet in strap pumps of black patent-leather. Above, Waldo's snowy collar was tied with a fluffed-out bow of green silk, and his page-boy-trimmed blond head topped by a sailor-hat of brown suède bound with a green ribbon stamped U.S.S. OLYMPIA.

"Waldo," said Davy, "what are we going to do about that old skunk?"

"Kill him!" said Waldo.

"I haven't got the heart to," said Davy, "and I bet there isn't a feller here that has."

"I have," said Waldo. "I'll kill your old skunk for you. You just give me a gun. . . ." (This was obviously foolish; nobody had a gun.) "Or a bat. Or a rock."

"Why Waldo!" said Davy, "you wouldn't dare."

"Wouldn't I!" said Waldo, and grappled with a large flat stone from the disintegrating foundation of the barn.

We all helped Waldo poise the heavy slab on his infantile shoulder and started him off in the right direction. We even guided him for a few steps. In fact, we were able to go quite close and watch the actual dispatch (which, thanks to the weight and size of the rock, was quick and merciful).

This was possible because of a surprising phenomenon: the more concentrated skunk-odor is, the less noticeable it gets. Indeed, once it has passed a certain threshold of acuteness, something happens to the olfactory nerves so that the smell becomes rather pleasant than otherwise. Then it ceases to be perceptible at all. The nerves have passed out.

Not realizing this, we took the apparent vanishing of skunk-odor as most remarkable. We drew long, deep, healthy breaths and cross-questioned each other to see if we smelled anything. Not a thing. Not a sniff. We couldn't even smell the skunk himself when we picked him up and passed him from hand to hand.

All the way back to school, led by Davy, swinging the skunk by the tail, we talked about this unusual circumstance. We arrived late. Davy laid his skunk far back on a coatroom shelf and we dispersed for our various classes, tardy but righteous with the important nature of the interesting discovery in Natural History which we had just made and were ready to report.

Now, you suddenly insert into each of four separate classrooms a half-dozen or more boys who have been associating with a late skunk, and you produce quite an effect. To us, in the innocence of completely stunned olfactory senses, this was most surprising. We were, of course, all sent home at once, and the windows were opened for a thorough airing of all rooms. But no amount of airing seemed to do any good. The minute the windows were closed — Mercy! All over the building!

It did not at first occur to our puzzled teachers to attribute this to any other cause than our momentary but powerful presence. Not until the Pratt School had been dismissed for the afternoon in all its six grades did Grandaddy Wilson, the janitor, and Bella Barrie, the principal, discover the unwitting, black-and-white cause of it all, lying forgotten on a shelf in the coatroom, nestled in the folds of Miss Barrie's best blue umbrella.

11.

THE MAKING OF A TOSSPOT

My grandmother was a distinguished semi-pro in the battle against Alcohol.

I take it that this must have been something acquired, not inherited, for her father had been a fancier of things that came in bottles — if I can trust the evidence of the lower strata in his Down-East desk drawers which my brother and I used to explore for stamps on our summer vacations.

At any rate, on becoming the wife of a parson, my grandmother accepted, as in duty bound, the post of chief hell-cat of the W.C.T.U. in whatever town she landed. Somewhere I have a picture of her, seated among a dozen other buttoned-up and bosomy ladies and looking grimmer than any of them at the mere thought of the Demon Rum. And in the town of Bradford her only steadily organized activity, apart from church, was in the ranks of the militant White Ribboners.

She persisted in this despite a spectacular defeat which she suffered at the hands of John Barleycorn in one of her earlier years in Bradford. This rout was the more humiliating because her adversary contrived to achieve it by the agency of my grandmother's trusted ally, Water. It came about in this way:

An invariable feature of Bradford's Fourth of July parade was the section devoted to floats. The D.A.R. always had one; organized labor another, the press a third, and so on. In 1903, when a close local option vote loomed in the offing, the W.C.T.U. entered a float, and appointed my grandmother to design it and superintend its execution.

Starting early, she pre-empted the biggest dray from Kelly's Lumber Yard, with Kelly's two big white horses to draw it. Upon the dray she persuaded Deacon Talbot to build a mountainous framework culminating in a platform at the top. Rounding up her fellow priestesses of prohibition, she hovered over them while with needle and thread they trimmed the whole business in flounces, ruffles, ribbons and bows of gleaming white. From among these harpies she then selected half a dozen of the grimmer sort to sit, clad in classic robes of white, around the base of the pyramid. They were labeled with ribbons across their bosoms: Purity, Thrift, Piety, Charity, Prudence and Respect for Law.

This left the summit or apex of the float to Temperance. For this stellar rôle, to which a less arty director might have assigned the grimmest of all the White Ribboners, my grandmother decided to cast a type that should embody the very essence of goodness, innocence and purity in such a way as to melt the heart of even the hardest toper along the line of march. Accordingly she drafted Lily Merrill, a spectacular beauty even at six years of age, to whom the affections of every male in town were ardently attached. Lily was to stand at the top of the whole business, behind a gigantic glass punchbowl filled with pure water, and to hold aloft in her beautiful little hand a crystal glass of the same invigorating beverage as an example to all who had an eye to see and a heart to be melted.

The float took its position: the harpies mounted to their posts; the punchbowl was filled; Lily, in a short, fairy-like tulle dress, was given a glass and boosted to her lofty perch; the band struck up, and they were off.

Unfortunately, my grandmother had not had time to rehearse Lily very thoroughly in the Business of her rôle. She had merely instructed the little girl to hold her brimming glass on high and smile at the multitude. But Lily, a natural-born actress, could not resist throwing herself into her part. If she was going to dramatize water-drinking, she would drink water. So she did — glass after glass of it as the parade wound through the streets and the float jolted over the pavements. This went on for quite a while. Until, in fact, the W.C.T.U. float, rolling into the Square, came exactly abreast of the Judges' stand. At this moment an expression of sudden consternation overspread Lily's face. And the next instant it became apparent to a thousand fondly watching eyes that Lily was only in one sense Dry.

In after years Lily, who was a gal of great spirit and humor as well as beauty, used to make quite a story of this, but my grand-mother never got over it as long as she lived. Years later, hearing a crowd of men suddenly guffaw, her face would darken with recollection and she would exclaim, "Miserable toads!" She pro-nounced "toads" in the Down-East, York County fashion: with the vowel sound as in "tawds" but the whole word short as "tods." "Miserable toads!" It was her term for incorrigible sots.

She drew nice distinctions, however, among topers.

She could close her eyes, in ordinary contacts, to the sinfulness of men like George Swan and Major Capen, who drank moder-ately but honestly and openly. To be sure, she would quarrel violently with them whenever they appeared in the capacity of advocates of the licensed sale of drink, but off the field of battle she was friendly enough with them, though not above taking an occasional dig at them in the same spirit that you taunt a good friend across the bridge table with his addiction to the wrong party in national politics.

She could accept the support of lip-service drys whom she sus-pected of secret tippling. So long as she had no proof of their hypocrisy, she figured that even dubious allies were useful in a great cause.

She could go so far as to tolerate the existence of confirmed guzzlers if they were quiet about it, though she pitied them.

One of these was her own brother, a physician in a small city in eastern New Hampshire. Doctor Charlie was a stout, florid man with a piercing, humorous eye, a curly gray moustache and a breath you could light with a match. As long as he lived, he practiced medicine, and as long as he practiced medicine, he did so in a benign alcoholic mist. And if he occasionally got his pills mixed up and gave people the wrong medicine, why the health records of his town show he got as good results as physicians who gave people the right medicines, but for the wrong ailments.

He always felt good; he never had a grouch to take out on patients by ordering them to have every tooth in their heads yanked for a sprained ankle. Because he liked people and knew they came to him to be doctored, he gave them whatever medi-cine was handy, instead of booting them out with orders to stop smoking, eat green vegetables and get lots of rest. On this amiable therapeutic system, he may have given an occasional patient a terrific if not fatal jolt, but he eschewed the practice — still prevalent in this day — of opening them up with a cleaver out of cold-sober curiosity to see what was inside of them.

Doctor Charlie was a Knight Templar, and loved nothing better than to go around to the conclaves and other gatherings of his order. He had been to every major city in the land, and to many towns as well, and had found himself at home even in the most austere of them, for he carried a prescription pad in the lining of his hat.

On these jaunts, he sometimes dropped in to visit us. And on one such occasion he was accompanied by his bosom friend and traveling companion, Lorenzo Gerrish. This happened during one of my father's absences on a specimen-collecting trip, so my grandmother was forced to take them in and entertain them (if that is the word for her frigid reception) with no stouter support than that of my brother and myself. This didn't faze her; she feared nobody. But she was visibly and grimly on the defensive from the minute she let them in the front door.

For Lorenzo was the one type of tosspot she couldn't abide. He was a real miserable toad, famous in our household long before I ever laid eyes on him. A ribald old reprobate, he not only drank all day long, beginning at the moment he swung his legs out of bed, but gloried in it, and was forever offering old ladies like my grandmother swigs out of a pint he carried on his hip with the neck of the bottle sticking out through the slit in the skirts of his frock coat. He was likewise addicted to pinching them on the bustle, and his conversation (which was airy and incessant) was lively with such similes as "hotter'n love in a haymow." He sang songs, too, in a cracked old voice that kept getting off the key and then back on again. And these songs were all too deplorably out of the camps of the late General Sheridan's cavalry.

He proved to be, on arrival, a shrimp of a man, with monstrous white moustaches flaring out, wild and tangled, from either side of a prodigious, hawk's-beak nose. His eyebrows, too, were white, bushy and undisciplined. They arched up from the bridge of his nose in perpetual astonishment. Beneath them, he had a pair of wickedly swiveling dark eyes that were apt as not to fix on you — askance and staring out of the corners of his lids — like a brace of blue-steel pistols. When he took off his hat (which on this evening he hung insouciantly on my father's best compound microscope) you could see that his head was high and bald as the State House dome, but pink and topped off with a Kewpie-like wisp of white hair swishing up and back off the peak of it.

He was talking as they came in, and so continued with scarcely a break right through the entering formalities, which consisted of Doctor Charlie kissing his sister and shaking hands with us, while Lorenzo Gerrish gallantly offered to salute my grandmother and she avoided him by skittering around the cast-iron dictionary stand.

The burden of this running discourse, as best I can remember it, was that the Great Sea Serpent had not really given up haunting the coast of New England, where he had not been reported since the year 1851, but only that the visual acuity of mariners and observers on shore had been impaired by the inroads of the mid-century Washingtonian Temperance Reformation, and the habit — which, he said, infected even Admiral Farragut — of serving out coffee to sailors in place of grog.

I have forgotten what other national calamities he ascribed to the same lamentable cause during the next hour or so of practically uninterrupted monologue. And I remember all too few of the instances he cited in which this Republic had been saved by the grace of good likker in the nick of time.

Of course he brought in General Grant's well-known diet of whisky and in fact named the brand, which he said he had communicated to Lincoln in response to the President's widely publicized request. He also referred to the whisky flask that Sheridan had drained at the foot of Missionary Ridge and then flung up the slope, following it instantly at the head of his men.

"Liquor?" he cried. "Let me invite your attention, Susan, to the fact that we hoss-soldiers first got the upper hand of Jeb Stuart at Brandy Station, Virginia, and ran him to earth finally at Yellow Tavern, in the same state. Jeb Stuart!"

My grandmother sniffed.

"Don't snort!" cried Lorenzo. "Stuart was a great horseman, a magnificent swordsman, an incomparable leader, a brave man and a very handsome officer. He had everything, in fact, except brains. Why, do you know what he did, one time?"

Lorenzo laughed wildly at the mere recollection of what he was about to impart, and unconsciously stretched out a hand, in the practiced narrator's manner, for a swallow of drink to wet his throat. It wasn't there. He made as if to reach for his hip pocket, but thought better of it. Leaning back, he fixed my grandmother with a steady eye and resumed.

"You know what Stuart did? He figured out, one time, that if he could get around behind that old fool, Johnny Pope's army, he could burn down a railroad trestle on Johnny's line of supply at a place called Catlett's Station, and so he could force Johnny and his whole army to clear out of there. It was a wonderful idea, and it would have worked. Lee saw it on the map and told him to go ahead.

"Well, to get to that bridge and burn it, Stuart would have to ride and fight thirty miles around our flank, through a country stiff with Union troops. In fact, right through Johnny Pope's own headquarters. And back again."

Here Lorenzo laughed once more.

"Well, sir," he said, "Stuart picked fifteen hundred of his best men and finest hosses, along with a battery of light guns. He turned 'em out and fell 'em in. . . ."

At this point, Lorenzo interrupted himself to give, in a lively falsetto, a whole series of bugle calls beginning with "Boots and Saddles," "First Call" and "Assembly" and ending with "Fours Right, March," "Trot" and "Gallop."

"All night," he said, "they rid and they fit. They fit and they rid. Right through ten thousand flabbergasted Union boys. They took three hundred prisoners. They even chased Johnny Pope right out of his headquarters and captured his hat and coat."

He laughed again. "Complete with rooster-feathers and brass buttons. Also some very choice hosses.

"Finally," he resumed, "they got right up to the bridge they were supposed to burn. Tantivy, tantivy, tantivy!"

He shrilled the bugle call for "Charge!"

"They broke through the last line. They got to the bridge. There it was, theirs to burn. And guess what?"

Nobody said a word. My grandmother's face was stony.

"Guess what!" he demanded.

"Well, what?" said my grandmother.

"They'd forgot to bring along the matches!"

"Stuff and nonsense!" snorted my grandmother.

"Fact," said Lorenzo.

"I don't believe a word of it," said my grandmother.

Lorenzo sighed. "You don't have to," said he, and reached — decisively this time — for his hip pocket. The one thing that could shut him up was to have his veracity questioned.

He set his pint bottle of whisky down gently on the desk at his elbow and looked around for something to use as a tumbler. The only thing in sight was a graduated beaker among the row of glass-stoppered bottles of specimens and preservatives at the back of the desk. Rising, he secured this and poured into it about four fingers of rich brown bourbon, which he then diluted somewhat from a bottle that had caught his eye, labeled "Grain Alcohol." And he sat down again with an air of dignified, patient and greatly wronged virtue.

For as it happened, Lorenzo's tale was as veracious as makes no difference. Barring a little over-simplification here and there, it checks with the account which I discovered, to my astonishment, years later, in Douglas Southall Freeman's historical works. It wasn't matches Stuart had forgotten to bring, but it was something nearly as elementary: the wherewithal to destroy the bridge if the surface of it happened to be dampened (as it was) by a seasonally expectable August thundershower. You will find the story in Freeman's *Lee's Lieutenants*, Vol. II, pages 68-73.

Of course, none of us had any idea of this at the time. So we let Lorenzo subside into the dignified contemplation of his glass, while my grandmother and Doctor Charlie seized the delayed chance to inquire after one another's healths, families and friends.

As long as this continued, nobody noticed Lorenzo. But finally, in a pause, we heard the faint flat sound of his putting down the empty glass. And for some reason everybody looked at him.

He was gazing benignly upon my grandmother.

"Susan," he said, "you may not have much of a profeel, but I always did say you had the prettiest figger on God's green footstool."

My grandmother jumped up, her eyes blazing. "Go on with you!" she said. "It's time for your train." And without another word she ushered the two of them out the front door.

But I noticed as she closed (and locked) the door behind them that there was a telltale little half-moon dimpling across her upper lip just beneath her nose. It always appeared there when she was trying hard not to laugh.

Ironically enough, it was no miserable toad that first taught me to relish the taste of hard liquor. Nor even an appreciative tippler.

If I am a tosspot, it was my grandmother that set me to toping. And if I live to end my days a drunkard — which seems unlikely in view of the present price of strong drink — I can truthfully say that my grandmother herself planted my infant feet upon the path to the Keely Cure.

When she returned from her cultural jaunt to Europe, she brought back incredible quantities of loot. Most of it was artistic in nature: photographs by the ream from Rome and Florence, laces from Valenciennes and Alençon, carvings and cameos and candlesticks. . . .

But among the lot were two bottles of Medicine. And not medicine merely, but medicine prepared by Clergymen. Of course the clergymen were Romish, but that was inevitable in France, and besides, they were only Monks, not priests. There were two kinds of this medicine, green and yellow. And whenever my brother or I had a cold, she would give us a big slug of whichever kind was handy, easing it into our upturned fledgling mouths out of a brimming tablespoon.

It was wonderful medicine — with a sweetness and flavor delightful to the palate, a pungent fragrance that lingered in the nostrils, a warmth you could feel worming gratefully all the way down to your gizzard, and an aftereffect of sheer beneficence. I could not then — nor can I now — tell which I liked the better, the green or the yellow. But Oh! I wish today's gin-mills, which serve their cordials in stingy little thimble-size glasses, would sometimes give me as generous a slug of Chartreuse as those my grandmother used to pour down the innocent, eager throats of my brother and myself when we were nine and ten.

12.

SUDDENLY SLEUTHS

The foraging operations of us free-sample-size citizens may not have been very profitable to ourselves, and no one of them could be counted on to produce anything of value to anyone else. But taken all together, they contributed a fairly steady flow of seasonal produce to the local merchants: dandelion-greens to Atherton's; berries and chestnuts to Cassidy's fruit store; fresh-water fish to Wyman's fish market (where, in winter, pickerel caught through the ice brought as much as five cents each); crabapples to DeVito, the wagon-peddler, and so on. . . .

Certain curious businesses in Bradford even depended measurably upon the likes of us. There was a shrewd old lady named Appleton (but always known among us as Annie Applesauce) who did a nice business in herbs and simples bought from country wives and who, whenever she ran short of sassafras-root bark, would collar us and by artful exhibition of shiny new coins would spur us to prodigies of digging in the woods. (I presume that hers may have been one of the most ancient trades in the Old Colony; many years later I discovered, browsing through the history of the island of Cuttyhunk — the earliest, but abortive, settlement of the English upon these shores — that the very first cargo ever sent back to the old country from America consisted of furs and sassafras bark.)

Another minor factor in the town's economy relied very largely upon our industry and in fact rewarded it so generously that we served it more eagerly than all the rest put together.

This was the Junk Yard, a tidy establishment just south of the railroad tracks run by an amiable Pole named Zelinsky. An important part of his operation was the collection, sorting and sale to distillers' supply companies of used whisky bottles. The law did not at that time prohibit the sale and re-use of empty liquor bottles. So Zelinsky paid well for such glassware in good condition.

Quarts were good for one-half cent each; pints for a quarter cent; half-pints for one-eighth cent. Once in a coon's age we would find a two-quart empty — worth a whole cent. These prices, however, applied only to bottles without blown-in-the-glass trade marks. So we detested not only brands with distinctive bottles, like Blake's, but the people who drank them, whom we regarded as deliberate old meanies, to be marked down for special attention, come next Halloween. The sole exception to this rule was a certain proprietary medicine, at that time about 40-proof by alcoholic content and in great demand among the righteous. The bottles in which the estimable preparation had come were worth one-third cent each.

In the point-of-discard collection of all these, and delivery to the Junk Yard, we were Zelinsky's ardent acolytes and, I suppose, his biggest source of supply.

I doubt if any of our parents at first realized that liquor bottles were the principal commodity of an operation we conducted in spur-of-the-moment syndicates under the innocuous name of "junking." They supposed we were only picking over people's rubbish piles or at worst helping ourselves to lead pipe, lead flashing and other parts from abandoned tumble-down houses in the outskirts, with peril only to our necks, not our souls. So they contented themselves with advice to be cautious, when we sallied forth with our carts early on certain mornings.

In truth we did occasional highly profitable strokes of business in the disembowelment of empty houses. To say that they were all abandoned would be to say that every golf ball is lost when it stops rolling, but after we got through with them, they were certainly in a fair way to tumble down. But our bread-and-butter business was in liquor bottles.

For this, a good roomy cart ("express wagon" to the prissy) was the principal operating equipment of any junking syndicate. Perhaps for that reason my brother and I were consistently members of junking parties. Our cart (the yield of a certain memorable Christmas) was a superb example of the carriage-maker's art, complete with paneled maple sides and heavily shod wheels.

I think it is safe to say that this cart, in its time, carried as many bottles as would have put under the table every Colonel in Kentucky, with enough left over to sozzle a convention of Elks. It would have carried more, except that it — and we — retired from junking in the year 1907 and in a blaze of glory. This, if you will let me tell the story in a kind of roundabout way, is how it happened:

In the eyes of the law, and of its more churchly citizens, Bradford was a "dry" town. Though the proposal to license liquor sales was annually on the ballots at Town Meeting time — put there by George Swan, the town iconoclast, and others of the openly drinking sort — it was always overwhelmingly voted down by the Best People. My grandmother, along with most of the other redoubtable old pillars of the W.C.T.U., believed this meant that the Best People didn't drink and that the miserable toads couldn't. We knew different.

The unregenerate drank handsomely if unostentatiously in all the livery stables, at the Odd Fellows, the K. of C., the Masons-and-Shriners, the Veteran Firemen's Association, and in the back room of Mills's Hay, Grain and Feed Store. Such genteel establishments were our first ports of call when cruising for empty bottles.

The livery stables and Mills's were dependable for a steady supply of pints and half-pints, probably because Samaritans operated there for the relief of the improvident, who bought for on-the-spot consumption. They were the easiest places to harvest, because their bottles were customarily tossed down through trap doors into the cellars as emptied, and the cellar doors always stood wide open.

The clubs assayed higher in quarts, for a club member didn't have to drink his bottle all at once, but could keep it on the shelves, marked with his name or initials, for consumption at leisure. Club contributions were set out on schedules based upon the habits of their janitors, which we knew as precisely as fisherman know the habits of fat trout.

Our next calls were made at the homes or offices of the few unabashed citizens who drank and didn't care who knew it. George Swan, of course, was first among these; he used to set out a quart bottle defiantly on his front steps every Sunday morning. Major Capen, chief ornament of the G.A.R., was equally dependable, but on Mondays and in the modesty of his back yard. There were two or three others of similar substance and courage whose ash barrels could always be hopefully inspected. Morally, Judge Dearden was among these, but junkingly he didn't count; the Judge drank port, Madeira and sherry, for the containers of which there was no market.

But most of the home drinkers were secretive about it — or so they thought. Wesley Mather, orotund and pious editor of the *Monitor*, Bradford's conservative paper, and principal mouthpiece of the temperance party at the annual voting, regularly buried four empty pints a week in his ash barrels, from which we as regularly abstracted them. Mr. Beals, another pillar of civic virtue, though addicted to unmarketably bottled California wines, was often good for a pint concealed (as he fancied) in the excelsior and other packings from his store. Deacon Talbot, our church's most hell-roaring layman, drank Jamaica Ginger (a stimulant ranking for sock, in case you don't know, with Demerara Rum) in half-pints, of which he emptied a prodigious quantity, throwing them afterward into the vacant lot adjoining his austere residence.

But most supporters of no-license were careful to carry their empties (wrapped in newspapers) to some near-by refuse-dump. Since the newspaper used for this purpose was usually the *Monitor*, which bore the names of its subscribers at the upper right of the front page, we grew familiar with the names of many of our unwitting contributors: Jethro Safford, the real estate agent, who intermitted his mortgage collections only for salvation-howling at Thursday prayer meetings and for plate-passing at Sunday services; Mason (known as Mazie) Sleeper, the Sunday School superintendent; Mr. Tucker, Treasurer (which, in New England, is to say Pooh-Bah) of Tucker's Shoe Factory . . . and many another whose annual chant at voting time was, "Let's not have *that* sort of thing *here*."

All these gentlemen belonged in their capacity as Best People to the Chemung Club. Architecturally, this was an ancient, white, flat-topped, cupola-crowned mansion, standing elm-shaded at the corner of Hollis and Standish Streets. It was not only hedged but fenced-in from the gaze of vulgar eyes.

Since, however, the fences were rotted along their bases, it was possible for boys to crawl under them at will and to observe the early pat-ball game of tennis, as played on a mossy court by young men in flannels and Gladstone collars and young women in long, starched skirts. For us, watching from under the outlying lilacs, the high point of tennis came whenever one of the young men would coo, "Thirty-love!" However often a love score was called, it never failed to send us into muffled hysterics.

Culturally, the Chemung Club went in for Musicales, Readings and Stereopticon lectures. Recreationally, the Chemung (except for its half-dozen tennis players) relied upon billiards, whist, euchre and the then-new-fangled game of Bridge. Socially, it was Bradford's home-sewed version of the Colony, Piping Rock and Union Clubs, with full-length merino underwear.

Politically, the Chemung controlled town affairs by astuteness, assurance and a heavy reliance upon the bland highhandedness of Joel Pettingill Todd Joslin, a lawyer who could now and then in a critical year be elected Moderator of Bradford's Annual Town Meeting.

This Joslin was a thin, greasy-mannered man with a high-pitched, crooning voice like a coffee-mill and as transparent a dishonesty as I ever saw on the face of mortal man, but he always managed to get things voted — or counted, anyhow — the way the Best People wanted them. There had been the time when it was a close thing in the vote on liquor licensing. . . .

Now it had never occurred to us, in our capacity of junkers, that the Chemung Club might be a source of empty quarts and pints. As easily conceive the president of your local Woman's Club operating a house of call. But one Thursday afternoon three of us, exploring the outside of the premises on The Help's afternoon off, chanced to look through the latticework under the big back porch. And there, piled up tier on gleaming tier, was the wealth of Golconda, the treasure of Monte Cristo, the Klondike itself in glass. Pints and half-pints, quarts and two-quarts; whisky, brandy, rum and gin beyond the elocutionary Dream of Avarice.

We were not, at the moment, on a junking expedition; we had no cart. Nor, if we had had one, would a single cart have sufficed to carry away that wealth. We held a swift council of war, ticked off orally the list of all trustworthy companions who owned really large carts — and lit out to mobilize our forces.

An hour later, with a convoy of six carts of prime merchandise, each cart stacked as high as boards stuck in the sides could make it, we trundled out the service gateway of the Chemung and headed through the Square for Mr. Zelinsky's. It was then about four o'clock of a pleasant May afternoon.

In the Square we were overtaken by George Swan, on his way home from the bank.

"You boys got a likely haul," said George.

"Ayah," said we.

"Looks to me," said George, "as though you might have been to a certain place I was once a member of."

"Well . . ." said we.

"Nice-looking bottles," continued George, picking one off a cart and examining it. "Good condition. Labels and all . . . Wait!" he said. "*This* looks like a bottle I'd kind of like to buy from you myself."

Now this was puzzling, for George, as we very well knew, was able to provide plenty of empty bottles for himself if he needed them. But there is no accounting for grownups' eccentricities. We came to a halt.

"And this," said George, picking up and squinting at another bottle . . . "And this one . . . and this . . . I tell you what I'll do: If you just stop around back of my house on your way to Zelinsky's so I can look over your load, I'll pay you a *cent* for every quart and *half a cent* for every pint I can use."

It was as though Allan Quatermain, emerging with a hodful of diamonds from King Solomon's Mines, had found the price of stones miraculously doubled. Marveling, we followed in George's train, all six carts rumbling down Chase Street and across the tracks. There we hauled around into the driveway behind the house where George lived in bachelor solitude.

George went swiftly to work. He overhauled our entire stock, passing by not so much as a half-pint. He set aside perhaps fifty

assorted bottles. What he was after — what was the criterion of
his choice — we could not make out. At times it seemed he was
assembling a collection, a set of rarities. Yet he retained many
seeming duplicates and discarded such exhibition pieces as a two-
quart Hunter. Again, he would replace one specimen with another, seemingly better in his eyes — yet of an entirely different
brand or size.

His remarks were no help, either: "Button Gwinnett, where are
you . . . Button Gwinnett Chemung Joslin, I got to have *you*, or
it's Hamlet without the melancholy. . . . Damn! Where *are* you?"
At last, with a yell of triumph, he found whatever it was he
sought.

"Before you boys go," he said as he counted out the money,
"I'd like to get some photographs of the whole kaboodle of you."
And fetching his camera, he lined us up against the sunny wall
where he took snapshots, from two or three angles, of us with
our stack-sided carts.

"What in time," we asked each other as we went away, "d'you
s'pose George was after?"

"Maybe," said Newton Ballou, who collected stamps and knew
a great deal about Varieties, "maybe he collects labels and Type
I is worth ten dollars if you can spot the secret engraver's marks."

Well, George *had* been looking pretty closely at the labels,
now that we came to think of it. We took a look for ourselves
before turning them over to Zelinsky. But there was nothing
different we could see. Only just a lot of people's names written
on them.

It was, as George had said, quite a haul. We netted over fifty
cents apiece — the price of a first-class catcher's mitt or a Little
Giant Electric Motor or practically anything short of a bicycle
that a boy might desire all in one piece. But it was not until the
following week that even we realized the magnitude of our ex-
ploit. On that week we found ourselves hailed in the public
press as so many little Horatio Algers.

Wednesday's weekly *Monitor* appeared with our picture right
on the front page, over an article about Bradford Boys Exem-
plify Thrift. There we were in the picture, carts and all. It wasn't
a very good picture, and you couldn't make out what the carts

contained, but it was us, all right — including me with a hole in the knee of my stocking. And our names were printed, too — right in printing type. But that was not all. In the article it said that we were the Business Men of Bradford's Future.

Move over, Mark the Match Boy; relax, Ragged Dick; take it easy, Tattered Tom . . . Bring on the Banker's Imperilled Daughter. Even the teachers in the schools pinned up the clipping on their burlap-covered bulletin boards, and all our friends paid us boyhood's sincerest tribute of forced and envious jeers.

There was one peculiar thing about it — though in our infatuation with our new rôles this did not greatly arouse our curiosity: By some strange omission the person — presumably George Swan — who had given Mr. Mather the picture and told him about us so he could print the story, had not mentioned bottles — just said that we collected junk.

This was a relief to me, for while my father was abroad collecting botanical specimens and so was beyond immediate shock and reaction therefrom, my grandmother, acting head of the house, would likely throw a conniption fit if she saw us blazoned in the newspaper as tools of the Demon Rum. So I was glad to let it go at home, as well as in public, that I was practically Mr. Alger's composite hero incarnate. What was good enough for the *Monitor* was good enough for me. But there was another paper in town.

On Friday, when the *Monitor's* brash young rival, the *Enterprise,* came out, we found ourselves presented in a guise beyond our wildest dreams of glory: "Boys Expose Secret Sots; Toping at Exclusive Club Revealed as Industrious Lads Unearth Hidden Cache of Rum Bottles." I well remember coming upon that enchanted page. The picture was better than the *Monitor's:* it showed all the bottles and it did not show the hole in my stocking. In fact (I thought, as I scanned it a second time, with the implication of the headline seeping blissfully into my consciousness), I looked a good deal like Young King Brady himself, the detective (though in short pants, of course). Or perhaps Sherlock Holmes at an early age, for I was already beginning to acquire an eagle beak. I went and got a cap pistol, slipped it into my hip pocket and prepared to read further.

There was no mention of the Chemung Club by name. It was merely "a certain whited sepulchre not ten miles from the Square," whose members' voices were "oft heard uplifted in not-so-muted threnody, condemning the wisdom of Isaiah, Zachariah, Judges, Samuel, Ecclesiastes, the Proverbs and the Apostle Paul who should, according to these sad ululators, have said, 'Use a little tea for thy stomach's sake.' " This was academic, uninteresting. I wanted to get down to whatever it said about the Boy Sleuths.

Presently, there it was: "On Thursday of last week, a handful of our young hopefuls, among whom no doubt are the Great Detectives of this nation's future, rummaging among the decayed underpinnings of this shrine of hypocrisy . . ." Great Detectives of this nation's future! I rose again, to search out and appropriate one of my father's magnifying glasses. Henceforth it should be ever in my pocket and used not for counting pollen but for confounding peculators, predators and poltroons. I read on. . . .

". . . Tomorrow, Saturday, there will be on exhibition in the show-window of James Behan, Esq., Bradford's justly popular dealer in hardware, sporting goods and bicycles, also agent for Ford's Horseless Carriages, a complete collection of the above-mentioned liquor bottles, each and every one bearing the signature of a former owner. That is, of one of our staunchest advocates of No License. The signatures have all been examined and pronounced genuine by Mr. George Swan, Cashier of the First National Bank."

I figured that all this powerful publicity for a great deed on the side of righteousness would so far outshine my having engaged in the liquor trade that not even my grandmother could raise much of a ruction. But I watched her closely as she read the *Enterprise* under the lamp that night. She didn't say a word — just looked more than ever like George Washington trying to be grim in spite of the recollection of a disgraceful anecdote out of the mouth of that old reprobate, Franklin.

That night I hardly slept. Certainly not more than ten hours. "Elementary, my dear Watson," I was saying, or "Put up your hands, all twenty of you."

Next morning I was up and out before anyone else in the

house, and early in front of Behan's window. But not earlier than
my fellow sleuths and not as early as a crowd of grownups,
through which we could hardly worm our ways to examine the
display. There were the bottles — a windowful of them grouped
around a pasted-up clipping of the *Enterprise's* article. Each and
every one — as promised — was turned so that every eye could
read the signature of its quondam owner: Mather, Beals, Talbot,
Safford, Sleeper, Tucker . . . Names Spencerian or crabbed, names
signed with a flourish or with Old Colony brevity and reti-
cence . . .

And right down in the front, next to the clipping, was a quart,
with initialed pencil-marks on the edge of the label to indicate its
successive levels of authorized consumption and thus to guard
against nipping by The Help. This magnificent autographed
piece bore the careful, ever-so-precise signature, Joel Pettingill
Todd Joslin.

All this we gathered only a glimpse at a time, as we wriggled
beneath the elbows and between the hips of our rubbering elders.
"Gorry!" they said, and "Gosh!" "Who'd ever 'a thought that
dried-up old goat . . ." "Can you picture old Wesley . . ." "And
the Deacon! Well, I always thought . . ." "But that Joslin! Do
you remember . . ."

They were too busy and too excited even to see us, the origina-
tors of it all, the sleuths who with unerring instinct and at the
peril of their lives had ferreted out The Evidence. This hurt.
Pose conspicuously as we would, nobody took the slightest notice of us. I wondered whether it would not help to go home,
rummage around in the attic trunks and come back wearing the
deerstalker cap which had been part of my father's getup on a
honeymoon tour in Europe. . . .

I could visualize the sudden coming-to-consciousness of the
citizens, perceiving at last the prodigy in their midst; the plaudits; the eager questions; the snapping of still more photographs.
I could even see those pictures, printed in some magazine of the
far-distant future: "Famous Detective's First Case . . . Robert
Leavitt, the fearless sleuth whose exploits in bringing to book
the dreaded Bowery Gang of Chinese Counterfeiters are still

ringing in every ear, gave early evidence of his acumen and nerve. . . ."

From this agreeable contemplation of practically assured glory I was rudely awakened. A cold, clammy hand inserted itself at the side of my blouse collar and an unseen force snatched me flying right out of the crowd, to the curb. A vibrant, crooning voice, rising to frenetic pitch, said, "You whelp!" and I looked up to find myself in the wrathful possession of Joel Pettingill Todd Joslin. Then he began to shake me and there were two, six, a dozen Joslins vibrating before my eyes.

Now I could not know at the time all that had wrought Mr. Joslin up to such a pitch. Years later I learned from Judge Dearden how a committee, headed by Joslin and the doubly incensed Mather (who had been neatly victimized by George Swan) had gone to the police station the minute it opened, demanding our immediate arrest and dispatch to Reform School as common thieves, and the simultaneous jugging of Bancroft Gill, publisher of the *Enterprise,* for criminal libel.

There they were met by the Judge (previously alerted by George Swan), who assured them that it was their privilege to prefer those charges but gave them furthermore his solemn promise that if they did so they would find themselves in the hoosegow before we were even rounded up. He had before him a complaint already drawn and ready to be lodged against *them.* It seemed there was on the local statute books an ancient, long-disregarded and all-but-forgotten ordinance, providing a thumping-good jail sentence for Unlawful Possession, the interesting definition of which he was prepared to read them.

"It was touch-and-go for a minute," the Judge said, "they were so awful mad. I could see Joslin was scared 'most to death, but I was afraid he would recover and realize the old Blue Law wouldn't stand up. Then it broke: the Deacon snickered; Old Beals burst out laughing, and the rest of them just melted away."

Of course I could not know this. Indeed, I couldn't know much of anything except that I was getting such a shaking that my teeth clicked and my heels clattered on the pavement. I was no longer the boy-wonder detective; I was just a boy getting rattled damn near silly by a grown man.

Then all of a sudden I was standing, dizzy but released, on the sidewalk. Between me and my late captor a slight, black-clad figure was interposed. As my eyes came back to focus and my senses settled into place, I saw that it was my grandmother.

She had a high, thin, clear, true voice with a carrying power — even in hymns at church — surprisingly beyond its volume, and with a cutting edge, when she was roused, like that of a butcher's skinning knife. And she was using it.

"Todd Joslin," she said, "I knew you when you were a smutty-nosed little boy pulling the legs off frogs. I knew you when you were a sneak of a tattletale in Mr. Trufant's school. I knew you when you were a skulking young coward that wouldn't stand up for his own sister. I knew you when you were thrown out of Senator Durfee's office and when you were fixing to steal Squire Brigg's law practice. I knew you when you had a wife and couldn't keep her. But this is the first time you ever got right across *my* path. Now, see here: from this minute, if you don't cut and run every time you see me coming, I'm going to lick you right out of town with the nearest horsewhip off the handiest wagon, buggy, dray, hayrack or dumpcart I can see. And that begins right now."

My grandmother ceased and cast an appraising eye around the vehicles tethered on the Square. But Joel Pettingill Todd Joslin was gone. "Come, Robert," said she.

All the way home, I could see that my grandmother was simmering, seething and occasionally popping steam with her feelings. I took these, naturally enough, to be the ire I had hoped averted. Now that I had had the Young Sleuth shaken out of me, I could see all too plainly the disgrace I had brought upon my family through dealings with the Demon Rum.

But about a hundred yards below the house, she turned to me, and I could see that she was at the exploding point with pent-up laughter. "Robert," she said, "you run ahead and get after feeding those hens. I've just plain got to stop and rest." And the last I saw of her as I scampered into our yard, she was sitting on the Duttons' horse-block with her face in her hands, rocking from side to side like a pacer in the home stretch at Brockton Fair.

13.

DOCTRINE AND DOCTRINAIRES

Bradford was a churchgoing town. But it was old and mellow enough to take its piety in moderation. There were no orgies of revival; no morose, red-eyed suppression of dancing or cards or laughing on Sunday.

We had five churches in town, of which the most fashionable, by reason of its architecture and location, was the Universalist. There is a Natural Law about such things: Martyrs may die, dogmatists sweat, theologians argue themselves hoarse, pastors bellow, and vestries employ all the artifices of floating a bond issue — but in any small-to-medium-size community, the sect that gets the Carriage Trade is the one that happens to own the biggest, gaudiest and most centrally located church.

Bradford's century-old Universalist church sat like a sleek, white mother hen, at the head of a green or common abutting on the Square. Rather a large hen, George Swan used to say, considering its ancestry: by Bulfinch out of Wren. But George was a Congregationalist, and an irreverent one at that. The Universalist church was undeniably handsome, and proud with its gilt-domed belfry rising above the tops of the spacious surrounding trees. From this lofty vantage-point you could look out over all the town. And wherever you saw, rising from the greenery, a roof that was plumper than its neighbors, there was a Universalist — a millowner, a lawyer, a fashionable doctor. . . . Not only Lily Merrill, but the *second* prettiest little girl in town were to be observed on Sundays going to the Universalist Sunday School — a circumstance that raised grave, secret doubts in my infant mind whether God did actually love the Congregationalist church better, as alleged by my elders.

Whatever *our* church lacked in smartness, it more than made up in self-assurance. For Congregationalists knew themselves to be the spiritual, and in most cases the lineal, descendants of the original colonists. Ours was the solid, respectable denomination, not a mere heresy of light-minded apostates whose tenets didn't even go back to the Revolution. And while we were liberal and no longer believed (as our grandfathers had) that these apostates and all their get would certainly fry in Hell, there was a general feeling that in Heaven the Universalists would find themselves, in retribution for their worldly extravagances, living on the Wrong Side of the Railroad Tracks.

Meanwhile, in terrestrial Bradford, our own Congregationalist church building was itself as near as could be to the wrong side of the tracks.

Though it fronted on stately Federal Street, the great through-highway to Boston, its after end was forced to associate with the New Haven's Old Colony Division tracks and locomotive round-house, which had impudently pushed their way in there seventy years before. This was a trial to our long succession of ministers, each of whom had to learn to store up a reserve of breath for competition with the 11:34 Sunday local when it came rattling, screeching, hissing and dang-danging into town.

On the other hand, the roundhouse served the boys of the congregation as a kind of ameliorating annex to the church. We used regularly to adjourn to it during the entr'acte between church and Sunday School, and there pick up (along with smudges and smears of grease) both a sound knowledge of the anatomy of a 4-4-0 locomotive, and a useful fluency in speaking of the members of the Heavenly Hierarchy. For the roundhouse was administered by a faculty of engine-hostlers, oilers and fire-men whose conversation showed an easy familiarity not only with the Holy Family but with all the seraphic host and the live-lier Prophets, both major and minor.

In my earliest years of attendance at this academy, I was much impressed by the helpful knowledge I picked up there, and not having learned that conservatives are allergic to new information, attempted to share some of it with my teachers on return to Sunday School. My first disillusioning experience with the Closed Mind came when I contributed to Miss Violet Upham's Infant Class the helpful gleanings that the Son of Man had a middle initial, H., and that the Creator's full, legal style was Sylvester Aloysius God.

I had, I am afraid, been a trial to Miss Upham since my very first day in her class — the first time I ever went to Sunday School. I remember it very clearly because when they passed around a shallow basket with pennies in it, I took only one (for even at four I had polished manners) and politely said, "Thank you" as I had been taught. On my second Sunday, Miss Upham had substituted for the basket a cast-iron mechanical bank representing Jonah and the Whale. You put a penny in Jonah's hands and pushed a plunger. Thereupon Jonah took a swan-dive into the mouth of the whale, and when he came out again, your penny was gone. It was great fun but not, I thought, quite so nice as the earlier system.

In addition to its handiness to the railroad, our church had another distinction. Its belfry served as emplacement for the two-thousand-pound sockdolager bell that was part of the town's fire-alarm system. The Selectmen had put this bell in our steeple simply because that was the most solidly constructed one in Bradford. Happily unaware of this structural consideration, we Congregationalist boys assumed that the bell had been placed there in recognition of our church's doctrinal pre-eminence, and used so to argue when at grips with our Universalist, Methodist or Catholic friends.

As against this was the contention of the Methodists that in all the history of the town no Methodist had ever been struck by lightning. This remarkable fact had been dug up by Wesley Mather, editor and publisher of the Bradford *Monitor* and principal power among the Wesleyans. Examination of Annual Town Reports all the way back to the early 1700's and comparison with church records showed that while fate in the form of "Vapours in the Head," "Griping of the Guts" and "Gallant Combat with a Wolf" had carried off Wesleyans as well as unbelievers, lightning, well known to be reserved for the impious, had smitten down adherents of every sect *except* Methodism.

I will not say there was not a conscious gap between the Catholics and the Protestants of Bradford, but only that it was not a *self*-conscious gap. It was more like the cleavage between

Giant and Dodger fans — a matter forgotten in all ordinary affairs of life and referred to, when occasion arose, with hearty good nature: "You dirty old Protestant," or "You bigoted old Mick." For Protestants and Catholics were amiably intermingled in every aspect of Bradford: residential, business, professional, political and social. And on practically every question they split along non-sectarian lines. Father Reilly, as an ardent prohibitionist, was more beloved by the Better Element of the evangelicals than he was by certain of his own spiritual children. The White Ribboners and Civic Do-Gooders were forever lionizing him at Chemung Club teas and musicales, to which they pointedly did not invite the topers from their own denominations. In School Committee policy the torch for the classics was borne by an alliance of Harvard and Holy Cross intellectuals against a Typing-and-Bookkeeping coalition from both sides of the Martin Luther line. The Ball Team and the Fire Department were happily inter-denominational, and so were the livery stables which served as our dry town's Oases and the centers of its philosophical and speculative life.

Of the clergy in Bradford, I remember only two, other than those in our own Congregationalist succession.

Father Reilly was, as I have indicated, a town character. He had been all his clercial life in Bradford; St. Mary's was his first parish. Now, in his seventies, he was a part of Bradford's fabric, and its fabric a part of him. He was an authority on town history, in which he had done a great deal of scholarly research. Perhaps it was in the course of this that he had picked up certain old-fashioned New England traits — among them a high regard for the principle that a penny saved is a penny earned.

Whenever he went on the train to Boston, it was his custom to tuck his ticket between the leaves of his prayer-book, with about a sixteenth of an inch of its end sticking out. Then the good man would open the book at another place and lose himself in liturgical reading. If the conductor, coming by, failed to recognize a new passenger in this settled-and-absorbed old priest, why that wasn't Father Reilly's fault. On the other hand, if the conductor, after looking doubtfully at him, mustered courage to interrupt his devotions, then the good Father simply glared and waggled the end of the book (with its sliver-end of the ticket right there for the taking) as much as to say, "Imbecile! I've been trying to give it to you ever since I got aboard."

The only other non-Congregationalist clergyman I remember was Dr. Carver, of the Universalist church, and him I recollect principally in the rôle of father of my friend Johnny. He was a patient, kindly soul with a dry sense of humor, always making jokes with us that were a little over our heads, and I think intended to be. Once, coming into the darkened living room of the parsonage just as we were about to start a magic lantern show, he volunteered to deliver the accompanying Lecture and did so *ad lib,* for he had seen practically none of the slides assembled for the occasion by borrowing up and down the street.

Remembering that Lecture, I realize now that Dr. Carver was having the time of his life burlesquing the then-popular type of traveloguist who infested church entertainments. But on that day this went past me, and I was merely concerned to find my friend's father imperiling his immortal soul by telling (in ignorance, I hoped) a series of awful whoppers about Niagara Falls, German village costumes, whaling in Arctic waters, the Flags of All Nations and equally unrelated subjects. I wish I could remember his marvels, but they have all vanished except the allegation that the Great Stone Face in the White Mountains of New Hampshire was accustomed to hail the appearance of an utterly honest man by singing "There'll Be a Hot Time in the Old Town Tonight." God, I figured, could not overlook that one, even out of the mouth of a Universalist parson.

Our own Congregationalist pastors were full of no such nonsense. In fact, that was the main trouble with them. They were good men, earnest and sonorous in their calling. But they had no juice in them, or at least none that percolated through to the young.

Though we were exposed to them for an hour and a half each Sunday morning, it was like taking so many cats to a symphony concert, each with its head sticking out of a drawstring bag. Yet it could not have been altogether our own natural depravity that made us deaf to most of those interminable sermons:

There appeared once in our church, in the capacity of supply preacher during an interregnum, or a vacation of the regular incumbent, a little old man of humor-loving aspect. He did not preach; he talked to us. What he said I do not remember, but only the pleasure and the thrill and the comfort of it, as he led us on in his quiet, mellow voice. Now it was calm, lucid, and inviting to follow as the course of a meadow brook. Now there was a purr and a ripple to it, so that you had a quickening awareness of beauty glimpsed afar. And now there came into his voice (though he did not raise it) and into what he said, that which made your scalp stir with the splendor and the triumph of it, as though the sons of God were right beside you, shouting for joy. And now, at the end, there was just a feeling of All-Rightness, as though God Himself were among us, comfortably and familiarly and lovingly in the sunlit morning town of Bradford. . . .

I do not know who the little old man was. Probably he was a famous preacher, for there was a great crowd that day, and the people pressed close around afterward to take his hand. But in my simple mind, I thought there was a chance he might have been God Himself, come among us for a little, in that homely, natural form. And for years afterward, I hoped He would come back. But He never did; all other parsons were unmistakably and sometimes distressingly human.

In fairness, it must be said that our workaday ministers at the Congregational church had an exacting bill to fill. For our membership included people with every shade of palate for preaching. We had at one extreme a sprinkling of old-time orthodoxologists and at the other a group of intellectuals, including my father, who was as near as could be to a Unitarian. Between, were two intermittently warring factions: the adorers of the memory of the late sainted Henry Ward Beecher and the iconoclasts who at the drop of even a very small hat would haul out and triumphantly read aloud extracts from the published (1875) records of that famous theologian's trial for administering more-than-spiritual comfort to a fair member of his flock.

Of these the leader, and the most eloquent and entertaining, was George Swan, who was church treasurer by virtue of being cashier of the local bank. George was a bachelor, an unabashed tosspot, a sardonic commentator upon the foibles of humanity, a lover of practical jokes and a very passable performer on the bass viol. On the other hand, he was an extremely astute financial adviser, relied upon not only by the church but by large numbers of its more solvent customers. This gave George at least a working veto-power in church policy, and especially in the selection of the parsons whom George would consent to endure. Since we had only a few communicants who (like my grandmother, as the widow of a Congregationalist clergyman) believed in giving a fair break to any poor devil in holy orders, our dominies were apt to be either temporary as performers at an Amateur Vaudeville Night or safe and solid as the Reverend Dr. Burton, the first incumbent in our church whom I remember.

This hard-plugging operative was a veteran of the Civil War, in which he had been a Captain of Infantry. I remember his appearance very well, for he had a pair of sweeping white moustachios calculated to strike terror into the heart of George Edward Pickett himself, late Major General C.S.A. and leader of the famous charge at Gettysburg. Of his spiritual equipment I remember only a whacking old Colt's Officers'-Model revolver which he used to hand over to his visiting grandson, Winfield Scott Hancock Burton, in order to get Winfield and Winfield's local friends out of the parsonage so he could compose his sermons in quietness. I always handled the weapon (when it came my turn to "Bang-bang" with it) in reverence, for I supposed it was Dr. Burton's last resort for dealing with Satan in case of a charge.

Dr. Burton was succeeded by the Reverend Mr. Dean, a man of greater glamour in my eyes, for he was reported once to have been a locomotive engineer, and while I knew familiarly many graybeards who had chased Rebels all up and down the valleys of the Blue Ridge, I never had met — even in the New Haven roundhouse — a genuine, throttle-nursing, mile-a-minute engineer. Whether Mr. Dean had in fact reached this pre-eminence in railroading, I don't know, but somewhere along the line he had lost the fourth finger of his left hand and as he preached I used to watch for gestures which would display Mr. Dean's romantic dismemberment, and picture to myself a hundred lurid scenarios for the loss of that finger. Now, in the instant before a head-on collision between the Limited and the Night Mail, Mr. Dean was leaping for his life and escaping, all but that finger. Now bandits shot it off as he drove the Gold Dust Special at ninety miles an hour across a blazing trestle in the last minute before the whole shebang collapsed. . . .

The only other aspirant for Congregationalist honors whom I distinctly remember (though there were several of them) was a young man named Williston, who was esteemed by some to be gifted beyond all expectation of his years, and by others merely to have swallowed the dictionary. He was fresh out of Harvard Divinity School, and correspondingly learned. His sermons were stuck full of gaudy, many-syllabled words that left his audiences at the end gasping, gulping, glassy-eyed and groggy as so many livery-stable plugs that had been chasing a county-fair pacer up and down the Great Blue Hills.

He was full not only of theological but of physical zip-and-vinegar. He had been gently nurtured behind fences in Cambridge, and his emergence into the Country, where grass grew high enough to need frequent mowing, and leaves fell thickly enough to be raked, threw him into a primeval frenzy. To this he added zeal for the material upkeep of the church establishment, figuring that it would make a hit with the elders to discover in their trial pastor one assiduous not only for the soul but for the soil of the congregation. He was forever starting bonfires he couldn't control and building trellises that fell down on the heads of deacons.

It was this diligence, and not his dreadful rhetoric, that proved Mr. Williston's undoing. In June of 1907 there was scheduled the annual Sunday School Picnic. The young pastor plugged it in his Announcements for weeks ahead of time, like a cheer leader whooping up a Big Turnout for the Crucial Game. Two days before this orgy, Mr. Williston went out to Glen Burnie Pond to peg out the courses for the races — sack, potato, three-legged and otherwise — and to make sure that the spectator space on the slopes overlooking the scene was smooth and clear. It was not, he thought, as neat as it might be; a fuzz of new-sprouting shrubbery had begun to encroach on the hillside. So next day he went out with a sickle and lawmower and in spite of his unfa-

miliarity with these implements, mowed the slope as close and
fair as a jowl shaved by Mr. Chadwick, Bradford's Tonsorial
Artist.

Now, it is perhaps natural that the city-bred Mr. Williston
should not have recognized the young shoots and creeping ten-
drils he cleared away right down to their leafless stubble. What
was unnatural was that he chanced to be immune from contact
with certain of these familiar country flora. Or maybe he was
rendered temporarily so by the Devil, designing to pull a dirty
trick upon the godly people of the Congregationalist church.

At any rate, neither botanical knowledge nor the usual swift
penalty for lack of it warned Mr. Williston; he played right into
Old Nick's hands by reaping away every telltale trefoil by which
any Bradfordian could have spotted from the extreme limits of
vision the presence of poison ivy. The hillside was neat as a
lawn, and only a little more prickly. Fat ladies and skinny ladies,
portly gentlemen and bony ones, innocent babes and rosy maid-
ens sat on it all morning, and rolled about in ecstasies of mirth
when the three-legged-race team of Ira Hardwick and Old Man
Peabody fell down right in front of the crowd and started slug-
ging one another in mutual exasperation. . . . Ah, Satan! Satan!
The serpent under the innocent flower, the ivy stubble in the
new-mown lawn!

The departure of Mr. Williston took place as soon thereafter
as a quorum of the congregation could rise from a strictly prone
position in bed and hobble down to howl in unison for his heart's
blood. Nevertheless, there were not a few who lamented his going. They had acquired a taste for his preaching, as slap-happy
pugilists are said to develop a craving to be knocked cold as
haddocks. "He certainly could preach," said they.

14.

GAMBOLS OF THE FLOCK

The practice of religion in Bradford was amiably diluted with sociability of a hearty, homely order and high calorie content.

Chief among these observances were the Church Suppers held at least three or four times a year by every denomination and more often yet by the Methodists. In these engorging-ceremonies, it always seemed to me that our church, the Congregationalist, had a slight edge on account of the superior fragrance of its specialty, roast ham with baked beans and brown bread. I considered myself a judge because I sampled them all.

The procedure of a Church Supper started with its customers lined up in the hall outside the Sunday School rooms, clutching their tickets or their twenty-five cent pieces and listening to the clatter and bang as the ladies of the church set the long trestle-tables for the imminent agape. The minute the doors were opened, you filed in past the pay-here table, found a place favorably located with reference to the kitchen doors, tied an enormous napkin around your neck and settled yourself to endure as best you could the inevitable wait for the appearance of food.

This was not easy, for your gastric juices were soon whipped into a tide rip by the aromas that swirled in through the doors to the church kitchen: the hearty steam of finally born brown bread, the bubbling savor of baked beans; the pungence of cloves, burnt-sugar and ham that told you the main dish was even now being carved. Interwoven with these, like minor airs in a symphony, were such themes as pickles, cauliflower, celery and, perhaps — when somebody opened an oven door for a look — that mingling of cinnamon and apple blossoms and browning crust that heralds the perfect pie. Over and behind and pervading it all was the wonder-fragrance of coffee.

It did not matter that in your capacity of small fry you never drank coffee; the smell of it was glamour and excitement enough;

it was the soul of the Church Supper. Some day I hope to live long enough to throw a lip over a cup of coffee that tastes as good as our Congregational coffee used to smell.

At length — when you were nearly dead of hunger and longing — there was a chorus of shushes; the diners stopped gabbling and fiddling with their forks; the cheerful clatter in the kitchen subsided (after maybe one last clang of an oven door to make sure the pies were doing all right); a hush fell upon the company and the Good Man asked the blessing of God upon our gathering and our fare. It was the only occasion on which anybody ever knew a parson of those days to be brief.

At the venerable man's "Amen," as at a signal-shot, the kitchen doors burst open. And from them emerged, like bullets out of a Gatling gun, a stream of fast-moving females in aprons, bearing aloft gigantic platters and trays and baskets and tureens of Food, together with washstand-size pitchers of coffee. (These pitchers had towels wrapped around the waists of them to guard against the chance of an inadvertent drip scalding the shaven neck of some newly barbered deacon.) Landing almost simultaneously upon all the tables, this blitz-barrage of provender was swiftly dispersed from platters to plates and almost as swiftly from plates to the interiors of the diners, while the female Services of Supply rushed the empty platters back for more. Even the aged, infirm and infantile were expected to take second helpings, while an able-bodied citizen who stopped short of three, four or five plates was likely to be reported to the Board of Health next day for suspected epizootic.

If there were any Proceedings in connection with these suppers, other than serving, stoking and stowing, I do not remember them. Possibly I was too far gone in repletion to notice.

At Sociables, Sunday School Picnics and Entertainments, on the other hand, organized Doings came first, in point of time, and feeding second.

A Sociable (prissily pronounced "Social" by the ministers in whooping up trade for such affairs) was an evening of parlor games for old and young. It was customarily an intra-congregation fracas, as distinct from a Church Supper which sought business from anybody in town with twenty-five cents to squander.

When I say that it featured parlor games I mean that only in the literal sense: the games were played in a room. But if you think that Musical Chairs, Up-Jenkins, Blind Man's Buff or Pin-the-Tail-on-the-Donkey were mild, safe games, or that church members in Bradford of that day were not contentious as Muggsy McGraw in his prime, or as full of mayhem, blood lust and skul-duggery as so many professional-league hockey players, you belong in the feeble-minded school. It was not merely the young who used to trip, slug, bite and gouge in these contests. Once I saw my own grandmother, thinking herself unobserved in the melee of Going-to-Jerusalem, take a swift uppercut at George Swan, the church treasurer, of whose views on liquor she disap-proved, though she liked him well enough otherwise.

On the other hand, the outdoor games at Sunday School Picnics though technically more strenuous, were safer to life and limb. In fact, except for a cauliflower ear or two, I do not think anyone in Bradford was ever the worse for competitive contests on those health-giving occasions.

A Sunday School Picnic always drew perfect June weather. The congregation (less those going separately in their own car-riages, or riding in herds on bicycles) assembled in the Square at nine o'clock of a Saturday morning, and piled aboard a convoy of special trolley cars, of the open variety. The first object of the young was to rush the front seats of these glamorous convey-ances. Failing success in this, you waited until all the seats of a car were full, and then, as it was just about to set off, leaped upon the running board of the car, where you rode, grandly insouciant, clutching a vertical handrail and letting the breezes of God's June day blow through your hair and up your coat-sleeves and pants-legs.

The chosen theater of operations of a Sunday School Picnic expedition was normally at one of the several ponds or lakes within half a dozen miles of Bradford. Here, in a passably level stretch of sward with a spectator slope overlooking it, would be laid out the courses for potato races, egg races, dashes, three-legged and sack races, tug-of-war, horse-shoe pitching and other sporting events, many of which were run in both junior and senior divisions, while some had girls' and ladies' classes as well.

These games were always elaborately reported in the following week's *Enterprise*, of which the editor and publisher was Bancroft Gill, a member of our congregation. Bancroft was society editor, feature writer and dramatic critic of this, the junior and sprightlier of the town's two papers. But most of all, Bancroft was the *Enterprise's* sports editor, for he loved to write in the lush argot of sports reporting in that age, and filled the *Enterprise* with accounts of even kids' sand-lot games. In consequence, the competitors in our picnic games were full of the old Rutgers Will-to-Win, for they felt the eyes of Bancroft upon them and knew that within a week their performances would be recounted for all the town to read, in terms reserved by bigger sheets for the final throes of a Harvard-Yale game.

On the side, Bancroft was a considerable baseball player himself, with a very dramatic manner in the pitcher's box, where he liked best to perform. So at our Sunday School Picnics he was always in charge of the ball game scheduled for after lunch.

Unfortunately, lunch always put a crimp in this exhibition of skill by laying out a large part of its intended audience and stupefying most of the players. By two-thirty or so we were all as stuffed as so many G.I. barrack-bags and in imminent danger of coming apart at the seams. The small fry, of course, started immediately to work off their surfeit by exploring in the woods and heaving rocks (or sometimes one another) into the lake. Young couples of the moon-calf age would go for walks. Bancroft would rouse his ball players and chivvy them off to the hayfield diamond near by. But nearly every other grownup stretched himself (or herself) out in the shade of some tree, propped his derby hat (or bonnet, as the case might be) across his eyes and sank into a coma, utterly undisturbed by an interesting collection of the insects of that region exploring the inside of his (or her, as the case might be) pants.

The other principal festivity of our church was Christmas, which offered not only carbohydrates without stint but a performance of Santa Claus unparalleled (I hope) in all the history of the human race.

The Christmas proceedings in our church took place on the night of the twenty-fifth. They centered upon a giant evergreen

tree which had been lugged in and set up at one side of the platform, where it dwarfed the towering organ pipes themselves.

I don't suppose the greater part of our Christmas night services
differed from those of most churches then or now. There were
the usual terrific blasts from a red-faced choir, with the organ
bellowing away wide open, the usual prayers and hymns, trom-
bone solos, sweet-girl duets, elocutionary readings by maiden
ladies, tableaux featuring angels with all-too-familiar faces, reci-
tations by little smarty pantses of both genders — all rendered
fortissimo . . . It was not until we came to the giving out of
presents that our church really became individual again.

Our gift system was this: A small number of specially ad-
dressed gifts were hung on the tree for individual distribution.
These were all in the nature of awards of merit for church performance. There was invariably a purse for the pastor, a token
for the superintendent of the Sunday School, gifts to specially
liked teachers from their classes, something for the janitor and a
carefully restricted few presents for such workers as the leaders
of the Christian Endeavor Society. In consequence, we could
make quite a ceremony of individual-gift distribution and still
have time for the handing out of an identical, unaddressed
Christmas stocking to everyone present, as a closing chord to the
evening.

In the distribution of gifts, our perennial Santa Claus was a
Texan named Collard. How this man, a ruddy, blond-moustached
giant with an utterly untamed accent, had ever landed in our
Old Colony community, or what he did there, I don't know. In
ordinary church affairs he was inconspicuous. For fifty-one weeks
in the year he was merely a big, healthy-looking ox in a Prince
Albert coat, who sat with his pretty little wife in a pew over at
the side, sang hymns rather more loudly than well, and otherwise
never opened his face. But on Christmas, Mr. Collard was transfigured. He *was* Christmas. Santa Claus belonged to him just the
way Rip Van Winkle belonged to Joseph Jefferson. He had
created the rôle.

Strictly speaking the rôle was not a new one, except as applied
to Santa Claus. In fact it was a very old one, not merely time-
honored, but chewed to hell by every moth in three hundred

years of the theater. Mr. Collard's interpretation of Santa Claus was that of a ham actor playing a Shakespearean Clown or Fool.

No; that is not putting it strongly enough. Mr. Collard's Santa was a bad copy of a decayed Thespian doing the kind of clown part no longer seen (thank God!) upon the stage. In Shakespeare's day, an idiot was considered funny, a spastic funnier and a combination of the two sidesplitting. Around the Shakespearean rôle of Fool there grew up, over the centuries, a traditional, stylized, actor's "business" of staggering, stuttering, starting, fumbling, palpitating, goggling, drooling and preceding every line with a staccato "Eh-eh-eh-eh!" supposed to indicate the most comical mental disorder ever discovered in Bedlam. Somewhere, in God knows what touring stock company, Mr. Collard had seen one of the worst of these performances, had found it excruciatingly funny and had brought his memories of it — such as they were — to the creation of the part of Santa Claus in the Congregationalist church in Bradford, Massachusetts.

When it came time for the giving out of gifts, there was an offstage jingle of sleighbells, and Mr. Collard, made up conventionally enough as Santa Claus, burst on to the stage walking backward and rubbing his rump in lively pantomime of having just been kicked or bitten by a reindeer. (Laughter.) Collard-Santa staggered around, faced the audience and — discovering himself heavily observed — went into a psychopathic dither, featured by palsy, rolling of the eyeballs, knocking of the knees and abortive flight in a dozen different directions. The laughter at this reached its height when, recovering from one tottering rush, he backed into a bough of the Tree, from which he recoiled with a wealth of eloquent gestures to indicate that it was prickly to the *derrière*. Ensued some business of trying to eat a glass ball off the Tree (more laughter) and then he discovered the presents to be given out.

Opening these one by one, he displayed their contents with a wealth of lively invention. He was expected to take — and did take — liberties with each gift, as by rapidly opening and closing an umbrella, or pretending to blow his nose on a lady's lace handkerchief. Not until he had wrung every drop of laughter from a present did he read the card on it (with much droll turning of the card upside-down) and bawl out the name of the blushing recipient, who thereupon came forward to claim his gift.

The presents on the lower limbs of the Tree were the lesser ones, for the lower-ranking operatives in the congregation. The gifts for the High Brass of the church were always on the top-most branches, with the pastor's highest of all and last for distribution.

To reach these, Collard-Santa had to fetch a stepladder. This he brought in from offstage with an infinity of comical difficulties — tripping over it, unfolding it wrong side up, getting his head caught between the steps, and the like. . . . Eventually he got it set up beside the Tree and mounting (with many a pretended slip), reached and distributed the major gifts of the evening. In the early days of Collard's rôle this was apt to be a slight let-down, for there were, at best, limited comic possibilities in open-ing up a wallet and exhibiting a much-needed check for the pastor.

Nevertheless, the majority of the audience were habitually reduced to sheer paralysis of the midriff by the time Collard-Santa had arrived at the end of the individual presents, and it was often necessary before the general distribution of stockings to revive some ancient biddy with smelling salts, or to rush in a glass of water for the purpose of hauling a buxom dame out of "the" hysterics.

It is true that about forty per cent of the congregation found Collard's Santa distressing in the extreme, but in a democratic community there was nothing they could do about it, short of staying away from the proceedings. And some of them, like George Swan, who were church officials, couldn't even stay away, no matter how acutely localized a pain Collard gave them.

One year George, standing in the wings and suffering violently while Collard continued on and on, was overcome by his emo-tions just as Collard was plucking the current dominie's wallet and check from the top of the Tree. It happened that the foot of Santa's stepladder was within the wings, right where George was standing. Moved by impulse, then, George bent down, seized the lowest step and lifted it some six inches off the floor. Nobody out front, of course, saw George do this. But everybody saw the effect at the top of the ladder. Collard was neatly pitched off into the green branches of the Tree, through which he went sliding and slithering down to earth like a side of beef in a chute at a packing house.

The effect was terrific. Such shouts and roars and screams and squeals of laughter had never been heard in our church. The pews creaked and the rafters shivered. Canes fell out into the aisles and ladies' hair came down in showers of hairpins. Two small girls in Miss Violet Upham's Infant Class lost control of their little sphincters, and Old Man Carpenter coughed his teeth clear out of the balcony. . . .

But if George Swan thought for an instant that this was his triumph, he soon found that he had, as the feller said, another think coming. Collard may have made a Fool of Santa Claus but he was nobody's fool himself. Even as he slid down from branch to prickly branch of the Tree, he took in the laughter of the crowd, accurately gauged its volume and quality, realized that it came from a belief that this was all part of the show, perceived the perfection of the climax that somebody's accident or design had presented to his Act, and resolved to make it his own. Crawling out, then, from the lower branches of the Tree, Collard simply rose, pulled off his crimson cap and made such a sweeping bow as Richard Mansfield himself never gave to the plaudits of the multitude. From then on, every year, as long as he played his Great Original Rôle of Santa Claus, Mr. Collard topped off the performance by taking a dive — all 250 pounds of him — from the top of the ladder into the yielding branches of the Tree. And George Swan had to watch it and like it, for it became our accepted signal that the end of the individual presents had been reached and the distribution of stockings for each and all was about to begin.

A Christmas Stocking, as known in that day and age, was a noble package. Made, like its effete descendants of today, from red mosquito-netting sewed into a stocking shape, it was in size very nearly what the hosiery trade used to call an Opera Length Outsize; it would have done nicely for any of the hefty burlesque beauties who used to carry spears in the famous Billy Watson's Beef Trust.

But even so, this gargantuan stocking was strained at the gussets to contain its freight of edibles. As minor items in this were oranges and apples; assorted nuts; candied popcorn; animal crackers; candied ginger-root; and about a derby hatful of horehound lozenges, candy peachstones, wild-cherry drops, peppermint wafers and butterscotch jawbreakers. The major items were three: (1) a candy cane of Paul Bunyan dimensions; (2) a coconut, complete in its shell; (3) a good honest cargo of Christmas Candy, as distinct from other candies such as those noted above.

Christmas Candy is — or was — hard candy in ribbon form, the ribbons (an inch to an inch and a half wide) being loopwise-folded in the manner of a ruffled collar in an Elizabethan or Rembrandt portrait. It came in a great variety of colors, either clear or translucent, plain or striped, and in every flavor, including many such as the natural checkerberry (a doughty, primordial form of the present-day wintergreen) which have since vanished from the art and science of confectioning. . . .

I read in the memoirs of other windbags how in the time of their youth, feast days were commonly followed by visits of the family doctor laden with gallon jugs of castor oil and sometimes armed with a stomach-pump. This was not so among the Congregationalist families of Bradford. I do not remember ever to have been dosed after any of our church feedings, or to have heard of a stomach-pump applied to one of our persuasion. Clearly, this immunity was not due to deficiency in quantity or quality of provender, or to any lack of application in surrounding it, or to any more efficient installations along our alimentary canals. I can only attribute it to the superior digestive virtues of Congregationalist dogma when well frappéed with sociability.

15.

A HANDFUL OF HANDMAIDENS

In those simple-minded days, a white-collar family like ours, though hopelessly unable to afford such luxuries as electric light, gas fuel or the telephone, could and did have domestic help.

It was "help," you understand, not "servants." Not in small-town or rural America, which were still resolutely democratic in word and deed. A wench-of-all-work, if unmarried, was a "hired girl," called by her first name; if married she was a "hired woman" and went by the formal handle of "Mrs." In either case she was a member *pro tem* of the family, expected to eat at the same table, sit in the same sitting room and contribute her two cents' worth — or two dollars' worth, if she felt like it — to the family *causerie*. For her ten dollars a month and keep, she might split kindling, chop the heads off chickens, shovel walks and wrestle ash-barrels in addition to routine cooking, pot-walloping, clothes-washing and housecleaning, but nobody regarded her as a servant, much less called her so.

In our family there were three strings or dynasties of hired females, Scotch, Irish and Native. These were in fact the only kinds that hired out in Bradford. Swedes had not yet been invented, Krauts were unknown in our part of the country, and the only colored gals ever seen in town were the burnt-cork Topsys in traveling Tom shows.

(There was, however, one colored citizen in Bradford — a man-of-all-work named Dumois. And even he was Afro-American only by elision, for his extraction in full was Afro-West-Indian-French Canadian, and he had come to Bradford straight from his native Quebec, where he had been in youth a lumberman. These and many other biographical details we boys gathered at considerable length during Dumois's professional engagements at our homes, for he was a lively raconteur and would much rather talk any day than beat carpets. Naturally enough, he spoke with a rich **Canuck** accent. Not recognizing this as such, we supposed it to be the true, authentic pronunciation of "darky talk," which we knew otherwise only in print, from a study of the Sunday comic sections and the works of Joel Chandler Harris. Oral and printed versions didn't seem to jibe very well, so one day I persuaded Dumois to read me a passage from *Uncle Remus* in order that I might get the hang of its accent. He wasn't very good at reading but he was willing and indubitably black, so I persisted and eventually mastered once and for all the colored dialect. By gar, I find she is prononce lak you say Braire RabBEE an' de Tarre Bébé. And half a century has failed to shake my conviction that all colored people who talk otherwise are palpable impostors.)

The Scotch line of our hired girls had been started by my mother, who had a considerable shot of Scotch in her own veins, and so felt a special kindness for lasses from north of the Border. It had been continued by my father through the accident of his meeting a Scottish clergyman at some church conference or other in Boston. This dominie ran, on the side, an employment agency devoted to importing guaranteed-innocent Scotch girls from his home city of Edinburgh, for placement with godly American families. A householder in the know would go to Mr. MacWhatshisname, present church credentials, contract to employ, sight unseen, any girl whom the reverend gent would summon, and advance her passage money. She would work out this advance on arrival. In consideration of his chance-taking, the frugal New England householder got a girl at notably under the local going price. The girl's parents got her to America free — or at least on a deal that involved no unbelting of cash, which is the same thing to a Scotchman. And the parson made a modest percentage out of the commision on the girl's passage money, from the steamship line. Everybody was happy.

The Scotch girls were all singers, and good ones. Maggie, last and best remembered of this line, used to troll a song of longing for her young man who was in South Africa, being chivvied from velt to *kopje* by the Boers. Its brave, bouncing tune and the lively lilt she gave to it contrasted oddly with the wistful refrain:

And it's Oh! in my hairt
That I wish him safe at hame.

Maggie's Jamie got to be a legend in our establishment — so brave in kilt and bearskin shako! — and when at last the South African campaign was over and word came that the battalion was landed at home, we had a grand parade of lead soldiers in Jamie's honor, with one of our Rough Riders, dressed for the occasion in a tiny kilt and bearskin of Maggie's making, at the head of the parade. A shawl-draped chair represented Edinburrrgh Castle, and Maggie played piper's airs on a paper-covered comb. But when next year Jamie appeared to fetch her away, he was a great disappointment. No kilt, no pipes, no scairlet tunic, no bearskin shako. Just a red-faced young man in a wrinkled everyday suit and a cloth cap, whose only word about war was, "It's no' so much."

With Maggie the Scotch succession came to an end, but happily my father's addiction to the clergy as reliable employment agents continued. The result was a series of Irish girls from the frequent batches that arrived in town, consigned by their families at home to the care of Father Reilly of St. Mary's Church. These the good Father placed with painstaking care among his friends in town, of whom my father was specially favored.

The Irish were country girls, with a fine, open-hillside informality about them and an engaging innocence in the mechanics of town life. Margaret, for instance, could never quite feel happy in shoes or coming down our steep backstairs face first. As for the combination, she flatly refused to attempt it. If she had to walk down these stairs in shoes she came backward, fearfully clutching the rail, as one descending a ladder. In the morning she never put on her shoes till she had managed the descent in safety — and even then she was fain to delay until warned by my grandmother's frosty glance at her stocking feet. Shoes, she swore to God, murdered her feet. She was a little scared of dishes, too, so that if sent from the dining table for more butter, she would return with a half-pound chunk balanced on the butter-knife, her left hand cupped protectively beneath it.

"Wouldn't it be safer," my grandmother asked on one such occasion, "if you took the butter plate?"

"It wouldn't be safer," said Margaret, "if I took a hundred plates" — an argument which set my mathematically minded grandmother, for once, flat against the back of her chair.

All the Irish were eloquent, but none more so than Nora, one of the last of the line, a big, strapping, black-haired girl with an infinite wealth of hyperbole and a gift for vivid narrative. On one occasion she went to church with her friend Mrs. Dorgan from across lots in back. It was a foul March day, but they braved the weather to hear a sermon by Father Reilly's assistant, an incisive, Savonarola-like young man whose passionate intensity they greatly esteemed. "He's wicked as a wasp," said Nora admiringly.

Well, the rain that was in it would dhrown a herring, and in consequence Mrs. Dorgan was that bad taken you wouldn't hear a sound in her house only the full of her coughing. But on the day after that my grandmother saw her hanging out the washing and inquired if she was better.

"Better?" snorted Nora, "she's perishing! But yesterday she was dead altogether."

Mrs. Dorgan used to come in sometimes to help with our washing — not so much, I think, for the money as for curiosity about our family. On one such day, while the two of them were beating the hell out of our linen in the woodshed ell of the house, I heard Nora extolling the merits of my elders.

"It's the docthor is the grand lepper," said she, praising my father's agility. "He'd jump over your head and him never knowing you were there. Sure, he's knacky as a hare."

And of my grandmother, whose seeming austerity awed Mrs. Dorgan, Nora reassured her friend, "Aah! . . . Herself is free and loose as an old goat."

We lost Nora, as we did all the other Irish girls, to Cupid, for they were buxom, high-colored colleens, who were snapped up by local or visiting bachelors practically as fast as they learned to cook. Nora was captured by one Ryan, who on Saturdays played third base on the Bradford ball team and during the rest of the week worked as a brim-curler in a Connecticut derby-hat factory.

Ryan was no Adonis. In fact, he looked rather like a platypus, and Nora was for long coyly derisive of his appearance. "You'd bake a cake on the end of his nose," said she. But brim-curlers made handsome money in those hard-hat days, in token of which Ryan wore a mouthful of gold teeth that would put your eye out clear across the infield. It was these, I think, that won Nora, for a couple of years later when she reappeared briefly for a visit from Danbury, she, too, gleamed like Tiffany's front window in the afternoon sunshine.

By that time we had entered upon the Down-East succession of hired girls and women. These were captured as needed by my grandmother and brought back alive from the wilds of Maine. It never took her more than three days for a successful safari to those parts, which is remarkable if you know the deliberateness of Down-East people in making up their minds.

Even more remarkable were the specimens she brought back. They were, to a wench, surpassingly unbeautiful. Indeed, you could have sawed off their heads, stuffed them and hung them on the walls of a gameroom with entire success.

May, for example, looked like an albino hippopotamus, even to the ears, which were small and round and stuck out from folds where her neck joined her skull. But she made such wonderful apple pies that in no time at all a widower who had sunk a tooth in one of them at a supper in the Methodist church which May attended, laid siege to her and carried her off to a farm just outside North Bradford.

Then there was Phyllis, who looked like a baboon and was built like one, squat, muscular and close to the ground. Yet she was one of the most earnest, thoughtful and intelligent anthropoids ever seen outside a cage. She became a leader in the Christian Endeavor at our church, and would have taken a Sunday School class except that she felt her first obligation was to keep my grandmother from ruining the Sunday dinner.

Phyllis's great interest, however, was athletics. She had been raised as a tomboy among many brothers in Maine and had reputedly been able to best them all at any sport they essayed. She was a great baseball player, with a special fondness for the catcher's position, from which she could peg a ball down to second (with the catcher's snap that starts just behind the head) so fast that few ten-year-old players in our neighborhood could hold it without wincing.

Phyllis took to going into Boston on her days off to see the Red Sox play, and in the evenings to attend any exhibition of scientific skill in fighting or foot racing that happened to be on the cards in that intellectual city. Failing these, she would go to a stock company melodrama to weep when innocence was abused, to tremble when virtue was imperiled and to applaud when love at the end was united with bravery. Afterward, she would come home, glowing, on the eleven-forty train.

One evening, however, she was attracted to the Old Howard, a burlesque house just off Scollay Square, by a poster advertising Cora Livingston, the Lady Wrestling Champion. The excellent Cora will be remembered affectionately by now-aging generations of Bostonians, native or temporary, and I do not doubt that the heart of many a silvery State Street trustee will quicken at this mere mention of her name.

Cora's act began with her wrestling one or another of variously billed professional opponents. At the triumphant conclusion of this, she would issue a challenge to throw any lady in the audience. This was rarely accepted. Even Phyllis, who watched the early part of the proceedings with barely suppressed snorts, didn't have the courage to go up onto the stage unsupported. But next day she took my grandmother into her confidence, demonstrating a weakness she had detected in Cora: a susceptibility to the simple chancery back heel.

Now my grandmother's husband, my late grandfather John Greenleaf Leavitt (whom I never saw), had been not only a clergyman but in his day a rurally famous amateur lightweight wrestler. So my grandmother perceived the cogency of Phyllis's reasoning, fell in with her plan and in fact helped her to run up on the sewing machine a set of over-all black tights with a fringed satin bloomer effect around the tropic latitudes.

And on the next Thursday night the two of them, with the tights in a brown paper parcel, entered the Old Howard just in time to catch Cora's act. (Phyllis wouldn't take my grandmother in earlier; she said she felt a responsibility for her employer's morals. Of course, the Old Howard would be practically a Chautauqua by today's polite theatrical standards, but at that time it was considered no fit place for ladies. Which, perhaps, is why so many of them went there.) When Cora's challenge came, they were out of their seats like two shots, to the delighted surprise of the audience. And quicker than it takes to tell, they were being ushered into a dressing room backstage.

Quicker even than that, Phyllis walked out onto the stage and threw Cora.

The audience's joy was exceeded only by that of Cora who, beneath her stage affectation of ferocity, was a fine and generous-hearted creature. Indeed, the curtain had hardly fallen when Cora made Phyllis a proposition for a return bout on the following Thursday. With my grandmother's consent this was quickly arranged, and announced to the audience.

The match, when it came off, proved so successful (the now-wary Cora taking two out of three falls) that Phyllis was engaged to perform weekly under the stage name of Pegeen O'Rourke. And so for some weeks my grandmother traveled to Scollay Square every Thursday evening with Phyllis, and from the wings of the Old Howard emitted shrill huzzas whenever Pegeen O'Rourke clamped a half nelson on Cora Livingston.

This, as it happened, was so nearly half the time that presently Phyllis Pegeen got an offer to star in her own right at an Opera House in Kansas City. My grandmother would not hear of her declining it, so the worthy girl left in a shower of affectionate tears and — it is heartening to record — made her fortune in the Great Wide Open Spaces. To be precise, she met and married an exemplary Texas cattleman. And since he in due course became an oil multi-millionaire, Phyllis was enabled to become not only one of Neiman-Marcus's smartest-dressed dowagers, but a power for good in Texas churchgoing and Sunday School circles and a splendid patron of the Christian Endeavor Society.

Glowing with her success as guardian and mentor to Phyllis, my grandmother went back to Maine and returned with another masterpiece. But this time of considerably different kind and vintage.

Mrs. Buzzell was a lady of such weird face, figure, dress and disposition that I hesitate to describe her, lest my credibility be suspected. She was fifty or thereabout, a native of York County, Maine, but the widow of a Kentucky evangelist. She was long, spare, bony and muscular, with a face in which a hawk nose, a jutting chin and steel-spectacled eyes under beetling brows were merely the supporting cast for a fine black, new-moon moustache. She wore her iron-gray hair in four snaky, waist-long braids, and the tips of these braids were tied together with string, No. 1 to No. 3, No. 2 to No. 4. Her visible couture was anything of a more-or-less calico nature, with skirts coming so close to the ground that she always seemed to be kicking them impatiently as she walked, with the toes of the men's heavy shoes she affected.

Mrs. Buzzell was promptly christened "Ze Vitch" by our playmates, who saw in her the very archetype of traditional New England witch, combined with something vaguely sinister and Central European. And in truth if she had lived in the Salem of 1692 she would certainly have been hanged or squashed for a witch. But not successfully; she was too tough. Now that I come to think of it, she may very well have been a hang-proof witch who survived those days and still does survive somewhere, kicking her calico skirts and swinging her braids as she walks. Her history, as far as I know it, gives ground for such a surmise. But at the time, her witchlike-ness rather wore off and we thought of her as "Zevitch" — merely an outlandish name for an outlandish person. But of course we always called her, politely enough, Mrs. Buzzell.

Mrs. Buzzell never smiled, and her laughter, when it came (usually in derision), was wild and hyena-like. She talked a good deal, but in spurts and largely as though debating with herself. While washing dishes she would apparently see religious visions at which she would groan or call upon God. On the other hand, her casual communications when out of my grandmother's hearing were apt as not to be punctuated with barnyard scatology — which of course gave my brother and me a good deal of prurient delight.

But she had her merits. She could cook anything that would go into a pot, a pan or an oven, and broil steaks over a hardwood

fire fit to demoralize a convention of vegetarians. Since my grandmother was spectacularly erratic in these respects — as I shall
relate presently — she valued Mrs. Buzzell highly. And the more
so because Mrs. Buzzell, while justifiably opinionated about cooking, would occasionally let her have her own way in the kitchen
and even abet her in the imaginative composition of dishes that
often as not turned out to be terrible and had to be hastily replaced by Mrs. Buzzell operating a skillet with one hand and a
kettle with the other.

She knew what to do for an ailing hen, and would tell my
father, when she got good and ready. She could handle a skit-
tish young horse on an icy pavement at the railway station when
the train came in. In fact, she knew a good deal more about
horseflesh than anybody suspected. And that knowledge, in the
end, was the cause of our losing Mrs. Buzzell, to the distress of
our gizzards if not of our eyes.

During our last spring in Bradford, Mrs. Buzzell was summoned by letter to a family conclave of her late husband's kin in
Kentucky. By some chance, this visit coincided with the date of
the Kentucky Derby.

It was Stone Street's year, and Mrs. Buzzell (as the story pieces
together) picked winners in the last six races, pyramiding, each
time, as much money as the bookies would take — a staggering
sum in the end.

This womanly virtue won her on the spot the pure love of a
visiting French Vicomte, impecunious but a member of the
Jockey Club of France. She never came back to Bradford. We
forwarded her haircloth trunk, in sincerest sorrow, to the French
Line pier in New York.

Down-East accounts disagree whether she put her hair up
about the time she bought that château in the upper Loire Valley, but they are unanimous that she kept her moustache, which
was such as a Duchesse, even, might have envied.

16.

CULTURE IS A GIDDY TROLLOP

Glancing, just now, at what I had written about Congregationalist Bradford I am afraid I gave the impression that our church was altogether abandoned to the delights of preaching, prancing and provender. This is incomplete. We had our rational hours, too. And if those hours weren't always strictly sober, the fault must be put down not to Religion (which in New England had hollow legs) but to Culture, a giddy trollop and herself a little weak in the upper story.

New England, of course, had always been a pushover for learning. From their earliest days, the otherwise close-fisted Pilgrims had been lavish with indulgence to education. They had shelled out not only for the College at New Towne (which afterward became Harvard in Cambridge) but for a regular courtesan's treasure of sparklers, clear out to the farthest reaches of the Aroostook where, as late as the turn of the century, forty-pupil rural academies earned their endowments by teaching Greek to embryo potato-farmers. Dairymen in Vermont were accustomed to exhort their cows in passages from Plato. I myself have heard a repairman in the Berkshires conspue a broken sawmill in terms freely borrowed from the Bard of Avon. The nearer you got to Boston, the stronger was the yen to cut Culture in for a slice of all operations, sacred and profane. And Bradford was all but within sight of the State House dome.

To be sure, Bradford, like the rest of Massachusetts, had calmed down from the Bay State's affair with Culture in the Golden Age when Men were Men, dashing off Classics at every breakfast table, old manse or lakeside hut, and when the very factory girls of Lowell spent their evenings writing a literary magazine. But the warmth lingered on. A man didn't have to be aged to remember rubbing elbows with Emerson, Holmes and James Lowell in the Old Corner Bookshop, or a woman passée to have been blessed by the laying-on of Longfellow's own hand.

In other sections of the country, it still took a heap o' livin' to make a house a home, but in the Old Colony all you needed was an attic full of back numbers of the *Atlantic Monthly*. West of the Hoosac Tunnel, people naïvely supposed the James Boys to be named Jesse and Frank; we on the Boston side knew they were called William and Henry and had their books to prove it. More, we even had William come to Bradford once and deliver a lecture in person under the auspices of the Congregational church itself.

We had a Ladies' Discussion Group that served up the same kind of fare, but in tearoom-sized portions, so to speak. My grandmother considered herself entitled to stay away from these feasts of reason whenever the menu didn't set her mental digestive juices aflow. She claimed her constitution had been undermined by a compulsory regimen of them in her earlier capacity as wife to a clergyman. Nevertheless, she went to all those that had to do with Art or Ancient History, for which her mouth watered naturally, and out of a sense of duty she attended any which dealt with Temperance. So, in one way or another, she was hooked for perhaps three Ladies' Discussion meetings out of five.

We boys were not, of course, compelled to attend the grownups' intellectual fiestas, though we were free to go and did so whenever they promised to be lively with lantern slides, feats of skill or strength, narratives of adventure or non-sissy music, which is to say, something on the order of Swiss Bell Ringers. These were relatively rare in adult entertainment. On the other hand, they were the regular bait in mental treats laid out for the young.

I am sorry to say that these juvenile entertainments were commonly frauds. I do not remember one which did not carry a concealed fishhook of morality or worse. There was a retired sea captain, billed as the hero of half a dozen shipwrecks, who barely tipped his hat to a life on the ocean wave, and spent the rest of the time telling us about the poor heathen children in the Marquesas who had no clothes to wear, nor Sunday Schools to go to, and urging us to pledge our pennies to provide them with those twin afflictions.

A reformed army officer, with a reformed bugler along to fur-

nish sound effects, was fine and gory, and we shivered with delight
to see the bullet hole in the New Testament which had saved his
life. (Clean through II Thessalonians it went, and was only
stopped by I Timothy.) But he sought to persuade us that soldiers never swore — which left us to conclude either that he was
a liar or that the G.A.R. in our town had mastered a great many
accomplishments since their soldiering days.

You may wonder why, after a series of such sells, we did not
have the wit to stay away. It was not that we were fooled. We
knew there would be a worm in the apple of entertainment, a
hangover attached to the jag of diversion. But so long as the
show was good, we did not mind paying the piper. And occasionally the show was excellent, the price extraordinarily low.
There was a prestidigitator once who gave us an honest hour of
flying cards, disappearing goldfish and ribbons hauled from his
open mouth by the fathom, rod, pole or perch — and asked in
return only that we sign the Pledge, never so long as we lived
to touch alcoholic liquor.

Sometimes we were able to work out the taste of being had, by
prompt post-meeting action. Once there was a chalk-talk man who
had us nearly rolling out of our seats for the better part of an
hour with a thousand pretty fancies and delightful surprises.
The hook, when it came, took this form: First he drew a series
of lines like this: / / / / / /. They were cigarettes. Each
one when lighted gave off smoke: ⌒⌒⌒⌒⌒. And the
smoke and cigarettes in time formed a rope, the enslaving cable
of Habit: ⟋⟋⟋⟋⟋. After that, we all adjourned to the
railroad roundhouse just back of the church, where the older boys
gave us younger ones each a drag at a real cigarette, so that
those of us still in the cornstalk or sweet-fern or Cubeb stage
could feel that our cable was started.

(Cubeb is an herb which when dried and smoked is supposedly helpful for catarrh. Cubeb cigarettes of that era had a
peculiar, undescribable pungence, piquant and without deleteri-
ous after-wallop, even to a six year old. On this account they
were considered by moralists worse than tobacco: They incar-
nated Sin without Retribution.)

The grownup entertainments were not frauds in the sense that ours were, though I am afraid one or two of the entertainers were even more so in the precise, legal sense. Or perhaps it was just that my father was an easy mark some of them could not resist. In his capacity as committeeman he frequently had to stoke up a celebrity for the fireworks by bringing him or her to the house for a pre-performance supper. So we got fairly well used to seeing minor authors, bird-call imitators and stereopticon-slide lecturers putting away roast beef by the slab and mashed potatoes by the hodful. My grandmother used to say she could always tell by their ears which ones would make off with a hand-towel.

Of course we had a great many Cultural Attractions who were on the up-and-up, and doubtless very improving to their hearers. Unfortunately, boys don't go to hear — unless the advertised noises are going to be loud and/or rhythmic — so I can't tell you anything about William James or Samuel McChord Crothers, or any of a profusion of budding authors, some no doubt long since risen to fame and subsided again to out-of-print.

Most of the Attractions that attracted me and my contemporaries were on the order of lady whistlers; ventriloquists, hypnotists, mock trials, debates, and lectures illustrated with stereopticon slides.

Few of these are worth describing as types, for they linger on to this day and may be experienced by any citizen with a hardy constitution, a quarter in his pants-pocket and a devil-may-care light in his eye. I remember particularly only two such entertainments that I should care to see again. One was a debate that nearly split our church asunder; the other was a historic, if abortive, lecture.

The great debate which shook our church to its very foundations arose out of a spelling bee.

For several weeks we had had a series of these mild affairs, contested by young people in the Christian Endeavor age group. In these, the arbiter had been the town's official school spelling books. But as competition became keener, the teams took on ringers from the adult membership of the church — people like Judge Dearden, Dr. Wales and Bancroft Gill, editor of the *Enter-*

prise. Simultaneously the officials began to heave in words from full-size dictionaries.

On one evening Bancroft, having spelled *metacenter* correctly, as he thought, was called out by Mazie Sleeper, the Sunday School superintendent, acting as referee, who held that it ended in *-re.* Bancroft, a baseball player at heart, made loud moan about this, and pointed angrily to the word spelled his way in Webster's Unabridged. Mazie dragged out from ambush Worcester's Standard, a volume of comparable size, in which he triumphantly showed the word as *metacentRE.* Instantly the spelling bee was forgotten in a hot, impromptu argument over which was the authoritative dictionary, Webster or Worcester. Major Capen, intervening, proposed what he thought was at once a neat armistice arrangement and a nice stroke of business for the Men's Forum, which had lately been suffering for want of lively topics: Let *Webster vs. Worcester* be put over and scheduled for the next Forum debate.

It was like proposing that tonight's barroom fisticuffs be settled by a race riot, to be held next Saturday evening in City Hall Square at eight-thirty sharp. Everyone instantly took sides, gathered reinforcements, joined the main body of his faction and started preparing for the ruckus.

To understand why this was so, you must know that New England — and in lesser degree the entire country — had once been split into two bitterly opposed camps by the "War of the Dictionaries."

In 1846 Webster's, which had been developing through successively improved editions since 1806, was challenged by Worcester's, a newcomer edited by Joseph E. Worcester, a former collaborator of Noah Webster himself. The great Noah had been an unabashed and contentious Yankee, carrying the torch for American, as opposed to British, pronunciation, and for simplified spelling — typified by *ax, plow, color, center.* . . . But Webster, and the learned editors who succeeded him, had, regrettably, been Yale men. Worcester, though not a Harvard man, was the darling of Boston and Cambridge. He favored *axe, plough, colour, centre,* and many other British usages, together with pronunciations that he thought mar'¬d off the Hub intellectual from the yokel of, say, Chicago or some other cow town.

These differences alone would have been enough to set off a blaze of controversy. But from 1860 through to the 90's the fire was piled up with ever-new fuel and blown ever-brighter with incessant bellows-work by the publishers of the rival dictionaries. For in those days it was considered just good, lusty fun for rivals in commerce to style each other in print, crooks, frauds, blackguards, liars, horsethieves, well-poisoners, betrayers of noble women and garroters of innocent babes. Missionaries and *agents provocateurs* from Webster's and Worcester's scurried around lining up prominent men behind one or the other book. Webster's got the statesmen, generals and politicians (right down to those who bought dictionaries for the schools). But Worcester's got the college presidents and most of the literary lights. Newspapers fulminated, societies boycotted, students argued, pastors frothed at the mouth, common citizens socked one another in the eye. . . .

By the 90's active hostilities had more or less died down, for Worcester's, outdistanced in competition, had no fat left to feed the conflagration. But in Massachusetts, feeling was still comparable to that in the Border States just after the Civil War; everyone was willing to forgive and forget — but only so long as the other fellow kept a decent rein on his tongue. Just let him open his face, though . . . And by the Nineteen-oughts, the scent of battle had begun to blow back on the breeze of nostalgia.

So the Major's proposal touched things off in our church. Bancroft rounded up the Webster faction, with the ardent support of my father, who though an uncertain speller himself and likely as not to follow Worcester without realizing it, was Websterian both by conviction and *ex officio* as a member of the School Committee. Dr. Wales, who didn't give a damn about spelling, joined them because he greatly admired the current Webster thoroughness in scientific fields. They had a considerable number of other allies, including an embarrassing one in Deacon Talbot, whose home Webster was of an ancient vintage, showing the pronunciation of *deaf* as "deef" — one of the original Noah fe-

tishes highly approved by the Deacon, but long since vanished
from later editions of Webster.

On the other side were Mazie Sleeper, a weak leader but
strongly supported by Judge Dearden, a tower of strength, and
George Swan, a fountain of invective, along with Mr. Curtis,
whose wife taught elocution. In fact, the Major had to subdue
a militant movement among the women, led by Mrs. Curtis, to
be let in on the men's hostilities, for many of the intellectual females of our congregation held strong views about pronunciation
— along Worcester lines.

The evening itself was a gaudy affair, with the biggest Men's
Forum audience in all Bradford history. And since practically
everyone present was a rabid, frothing supporter of one side or
the other, we soon had two spontaneously organized claques
going full blast. The mildest point made by Dr. Wales was good
for thunderclaps of applause, while the sallies of George Swan
drew roars of laughter and whoops of triumph.

This naturally spurred the other speakers on to prodigies. My
father, normally an uncontentious man, willing to allow anyone
his opinion, got worked up to an unnatural, hornet-like pitch, in
which he stung several of his best friends so painfully that they
didn't forget it (or allow him to) for weeks afterward. Judge
Dearden tore Bancroft Gill figuratively limb from limb and
rubbed salt into Bancroft's bleeding stumps by quoting Worcester
usage from the very pages of the *Enterprise*. Deacon Talbot,
incensed at this injustice, drew a lurid picture of the contrast
between the Judge's life (which he said was sybaritic) and that
of Noah Webster (1758-1843), a paradigm, as he described it, of
all the stern virtues that had made this Republic great.

What this had to do with the subject, nobody, by this time,
gave a damn. Those who weren't applauding every sentence of
the Deacon's, or booing every alternate one, were sizzling all
over with words to use when they could get the floor, or running
up to whisper in George Swan's ear things they knew George
could say about the Deacon better than they could. . . . It got so
that even the saintly and learned old Mr. Twitchell could not
cite the undoubted fact of George Washington's admiration for

Noah Webster without being greeted by cries of "Oh, no!," "Shame!," "Sit down!"

The Major, acting as Moderator, could no more moderate these and a thousand other outbursts of innocent fervor than he could have abated the great winter gale of 1898 by banging a gavel at it. All he could do was watch his chance and when (as was inevitable) Old Man Peabody took a poke at his G.A.R. companion, Ira Hardwick, for alleging that Webster's edition of 1859 had been pro-Rebel, the Major closed down the meeting and adjourned it *sine die*.

Thereafter, our church stuck to the safe and sane in intellectual matters. Or tried to, by scheduling only such harmless diversions as stereopticon lectures on foreign travel. But even one of these ran off the track one night, proving slightly insane and utterly unsafe.

We had in our town an amiable old charlatan named Elijah Stiles. He was always known as 'Lige, to distinguish him from his elder brother Abijah, with whom he shared a house and on whom he kept an eye. Abijah was a broken-down surgeon, commonly reputed to subsist on opium, and so regarded by most people as rather a scary character, in contrast to the harmless 'Lige. Both were Civil War veterans, with pensions.

'Lige eked out his stipend by lecturing around in near-by towns on Mesmerism, Calligraphy and Travels with the Camera in the Holy Land, Also If Desired, A Voyage in the Mediterranean and Life Among the Indians.

In accordance with Holy Writ, 'Lige was not without honor save in his own country. Bradford would have none of his lectures, on account of a dark suspicion — limited in extent but strong in quarters where it really mattered — that 'Lige could not hypnotize, knew nothing about handwriting and — as to the Holy Land and adjacent parts — that he had never been there. That he had, in fact, bought his entire stock of slides from Paddy Sheehan, janitor of the K.ofC., who kept them when some scoundrel ran off with the receipts without paying for the hire of the hall.

'Lige was a handsome subject, with hair worn rather long in the back, an elegant curly moustache, and large gray eyes that looked the more romantic for being extremely near-sighted. For this defect he owned a pair of old spectacles, but would never wear them in public, on which account he moved with a bland uncertainty that gave him an undeserved local reputation for being not quite all there in the head — less so, indeed, than his wreck of a brother. Nevertheless, he did fairly well with out-of-town lecture dates; it was his boast that he had given The Holy Land as far away as Ashuelot, New Hampshire, and Life Among the Indians twice in the town of Medford. And in Bradford itself many good people wondered openly why we had to go afield for lectures when 'Lige was right there waiting only to be asked.

So one day he was asked. Our church had scheduled a travelogue on the Scenic Beauties of the River Rhine. The lecturer was unavoidably detained in Boston — probably by the police — but got word to the Bradford authorities in the middle of a rainy afternoon. It was too late to call off the show — or get anybody but 'Lige to pinch-hit. So the deal was made. 'Lige would show Travels with the Camera in the Holy Land. And Four-Eyes Belcher, the overgrown boy who was not only organ-pumper but, on occasion, operator of the stereopticon machine, was instructed forthwith to pick up 'Lige's case of slides and oil up the projector for an evening of Improvement.

Now, Four-Eyes was, as it happened, a business man with many interests, and all his four eyes were out for what would today be called a fast penny. For a nickel he would let you come and pump the organ on Sundays while he read Old King Brady (yours to rent for a mere cent afterward, if you did a good job of organ-pumping and kept the air-pressure up to requirements). Another of his enterprises was allowing groups of his friends — at one cent per head — to examine all the slides of any forthcoming attraction at the church, in a private preview in the Sunday School washroom.

On this particular afternoon, Four-Eyes might have done very little business, so short was the notice he had, except for the chance of meeting our ball team coming home through the Square, all wet and dejected from having been rained out down on Morse Street. To us, Four-Eyes offered a bargain rate: all three sets of slides in 'Lige's carrying case for the price of one — and as added inducement (when he saw us wavering) two Hassans and one partly smoked Sweet Caporal to share among the nine of us afterward.

On first glance at the slides, we felt we had been had — and badly. The Holy Land in our judgment was worth nobody's cent. We pulled out slides here and there at random, but they were all the same: low, barren hills, Turkish mosques, rivers that didn't even look like good swimming. We laid these slides down and turned to the next batch. This was hardly better; diligent search showed only a few things worth looking at: ships, dancers doing the Tarantelle, a bullfight. . . . There was some muttering; the last set of slides had better be good. . . .

And they *were* good! Life Among the Indians! This was something like! Plain and colored, photographs and paintings, outdoor scenes, wigwam interiors, close-ups of tomahawks and head-dresses, ponies in action, Frederic Remington pictures of prairie fights, old prints of stabbings, torture, scalping of palefaces . . . Gosh! Forgetful even of our bonus cigarettes, we stayed until nearly dark, then left Four-Eyes sorting out the numbered slides and putting them back in their appointed slots.

That night I had to go to the show, to hold an umbrella over my grandmother en route. But I did so only after a good deal of squawking, which very nearly succeeded. When I think how near I came to missing that performance!

It started much like any lecture of its kind: with 'Lige droning along about the voyage, a picture of the ship, a group of passengers (including a vague shape 'Lige said was himself) — and so on. Soon we were in the Holy Land, stuck in it, mired in it and sinking ever deeper in 'Lige's rhetoric as he warmed to his familiar routine.

I stopped listening and devoted myself to a scrutiny of the rungs of Mrs. Sturgis's chair in front of me, looking up only when the CLICK-CLICK! of 'Lige's signaling-disk heralded the coming of a new picture.

From this apathy I was roused by the stiffening of my grandmother's figure in the seat next to mine. Echoing in my ears were 'Lige's last words:

". . . known — and justly so — (CLICK-CLICK!) as the Ship of the Desert. This remarkable animal . . ."

Looking up at the screen I found myself staring smack into the eyes, close up and resentful under a tousled forelock, of an indisputable American Bison or Buffalo.

". . . reputed to be able to subsist for forty days and forty nights without water . . ." 'Lige was continuing, oblivious, in his well-worn groove. Either, in reliance on the sequence he knew so well, he had not looked at the picture, or glancing at it obliquely and near-sightedly from his far corner of the platform, had been unable to detect any difference between the buffalo and the expected camel.

My view of the beast was cut off by Mrs. Sturgis turning around to my grandmother and tapping her forehead. My grandmother nodded in agreement. Fortunately for 'Lige, he was shut off by his myopia from sight of these and kindred rude gestures throughout the audience. He swam happily ahead. ". . . in long, picturesque caravans from the storied East." CLICK-CLICK! And the buffalo was pushed off the screen by the Pool of Siloam.

Twisting and craning around, I looked to see how Four-Eyes was taking it. Not very well. Certainly not in calmness. Sweating visibly, he was going through the forthcoming slides, hauling each one out, holding it up to the light and replacing it in feverish haste. Presently I saw him set one aside and start hunting in another section of the slide-carrying case, faster than ever . . . CLICK-CLICK! Four-Eyes jumped as though shot, fumbled for a second or two, then recovered and shoved into his machine what turned out to be a river — upside down but indubitably the rolling Jordan called for in the script. 'Lige rolled, too, unnoticing, tranquil and sonorous.

The audience was silent but increasingly alert. And none more than I. Yet for half a dozen frames we had only a succession of valleys, ruins, villages, cedars, mosques and picturesque characters, all very exactly fitting 'Lige's never-halting description.

Then, while the screen still showed a photograph of the Patriarch of Jerusalem in full robes of the Greek Orthodox Church, 'Lige started to build up for a slide that was going to be something pretty special. ". . . depicted in a beautiful painting which re-creates for our spiritual delight that ever-memorable scene (CLICK-CLICK!), The Sermon on the Mount."

Nothing happened. The Patriarch of Jerusalem stayed where he was.

CLICK-CLICK!

The Patriarch jiggled violently and was still.

CLICK-CLICK! Everybody looked around at Four-Eyes. He was holding a slide ready in one hand, but with the other frantically lifting out and discarding slide after slide from 'Lige's carrying case.

CLICK-CLICK! "Come, young man!" said 'Lige, and backed up for a fresh start. ". . . a beautiful painting re-creating for us The Sermon on the Mount."

On the screen, the Patriarch leapt like a startled faun and slid swiftly from view. There was an instant's flash of vacant white, followed by a blur of sliding color, and just as 'Lige repeated for the third time, "The Sermon on the Mount," there came to a halt before us, in perfect focus, vivid in every detail — Custer's Last Fight.

A gasp went up from the audience, as sharp and audible as though each one of them had been socked in the midriff with a sandbag. For this particular version of Custer's Last Fight was a lulu. Reproduced from a lurid chromo of the 70's, it was crowded to the margins with gun-flashes, powder-smoke, writhing wounded, galloping Indians, gory corpses, and in the midst of all this the long-haired Custer himself, sword in hand, firing his last pistol bullet into a press of howling savages. You may occasionally see a chromo of this picture today, in old-fashioned saloons. But the slide-maker had, if anything, improved on the chromo; the places where the corpses had been scalped were the bloodiest red ever seen by mortal eyes.

'Lige, of course, perceived the audience's gasp. He turned around, squinted at the picture and fumbled for his glasses.

At that moment, somebody up front whinnied and pandemonium burst loose. Half the audience collapsed in roars of laughter, while the other half was divided between squealing, gabbling and standing on its hind legs to utter choked sounds and gurgles fondly believed to be words expressing outrage.

By this time 'Lige had got his glasses on and had a quick eyeful. Instantly he leapt from the platform and strode through the mass for the stereopticon machine. But Four-Eyes Belcher was gone. 'Lige swiftly gathered his slides, crammed them any-which-way into the case, closed the case and carried it back to the platform clasped like a baby to his breast.

For a full minute he stood there, facing the uproar, his chest rising and falling, his eyes flashing very big behind the thick-lensed glasses, his moustache blowing out like a flag with every breath. Then silence descended upon the crowd, swiftly, expectantly. . . .

"Some son-of-a-bitch," said 'Lige, "has muggered up my lantern slides!" And turning, he strode from the stage and out the door and so forever from the purlieus of the Congregationalist church of Bradford in the Old Colony of Massachusetts.

17.

THERE WAS A MAN

A different kind of fish was 'Lige's brother, Abijah. He was the only hero I ever knew of in the town of Bradford. And that in a queer and dreadful way.

As I have warned you, most of the names in this book are out of thin air, and some of the people are changed, one way or another. This name is changed but the man was very real. I can still see, sharp in memory, the vacant-eyed old human wreck we boys used to avoid as he prowled the streets. And I have no reason to doubt the story of his last days as I got it from my father, who came as near knowing the ruined old medico as anybody in Bradford.

Back of this, the near-by city of Brockton was (and is) very real. And all too real was the violent boiler explosion which, with the fire that followed it, destroyed a shoe factory in that city on the morning of March 20, 1905, with a loss of fifty-eight lives and a toll of one hundred seventeen injuries, most of them agonizingly severe because they were burns. You can read about that catastrophe in the library files and in the records of insurance companies. It still stands out as a grim landmark in the history of industrial accidents.

On the other hand, you won't come across even the real name of Dr. Stiles, no matter how closely you scan the yellowing newspapers. There were too many heroes that day for anyone to notice them all, much less to get and print their names. And Dr. Stiles, for reasons of his own, wasn't courting mention. But my father put the fragments of the story together afterward, and I give it to you as he gave it to me.

Dr. Abijah Stiles, then, was a derelict of the drug habit. He had been a surgeon in the Civil War, and a spectacularly fearless one, men said. Old Man Peabody used to tell of him, walking right out into the hail of shot under Marye's Heights at Fredericksburg to pick up and carry back a boy who had been ripped open by shell fragments and was screaming in pain. "You won't believe it, but the Doc stopped first to give that kid a shot of opiate before he picked him up and lugged him back over his shoulder."

After the war, in private practice for a while, Dr. Stiles was brilliant but erratic. And presently there began to be rumors that he was up to other things than medicine. So he went to sea, and was for many years a ship's surgeon in the China trade. When he finally came ashore, he had a brush with the law — reputedly for drug-running and drug-selling. From this he escaped with the mild penalty of disbarment from medical practice. And — apparently — with a hidden cache of opiates for himself, just about sufficient to sustain him in his helpless addiction for the remaining year or two he might expect to live.

At any rate, he settled in Bradford on his Civil War pension, with rooms in a separate wing of his brother's house. Here, he kept very much to himself, emerging only now and then, to glide furtively through the streets, to sidle into a store for a purchase, and then to make his way quietly back again. A vague old wreck of a man with a limp, white moustache and unseeing blue eyes, wandering dreamily toward an end that could not be far off now.

Relics of the past were no novelty in that area. Our very factories were old. Many of them, in shoe manufacturing, or textiles, or rubber, were as old as steam power itself — rambling wooden buildings shaking as though with palsy under the vibration of their worn old machines, and soaked with the oil of many years' operation. They were firetraps, of course, and the more so because sometimes they collapsed first, trapping people in their ruins, and caught fire afterward.

The most dreaded cause of such a collapse was one you rarely hear of in these days of modern engineering: the explosion of a steam boiler. Of course, if you remember your Mark Twain (*Life on the Mississippi* and *The Gilded Age*) you know that in the early days of steam power, primitive boilers often blew up with frightful effect. What Mark Twain doesn't say, but what engineers will tell you, is that a boiler explosion can be a particularly violent and destructive kind of blast because of the terrific dynamics that build up in water and steam imprisoned under great heat and high pressure. And that certain types of boiler used right up to the beginning of the present century were all too likely to let go without warning, in one instantaneous concussion.

In the Old Colony, during the Theodore Roosevelt years, everybody knew of such things, at least by hearsay, and dreaded the possibility of such an accident in his own town.

Nobody was more aware of this than the doctors, who knew too well how short-handed in medical attention and medical supplies any town might find itself if caught by a really big explosion-and-fire catastrophe.

Doctors couldn't be mobilized quickly; the 'phone service was primitive and uncertain; even when located and summoned, doctors in the horse-and-buggy era couldn't get to an emergency fast. Moreover, almost no town at that time ever had enough reserve medical supplies to cope with a really big disaster — not enough bandages, antiseptics or emollients for burns — or anodynes for agony.

Even Dr. Stiles knew this. He used to keep track of science, as well as he could, by reading such publications as he could afford (and as would accept his subscription) and by borrowing other periodicals and books from the one or two professional men in Bradford who would still speak to him.

One of these was my father, who took in not only all the learned journals immediately concerned with cells, animal or vegetable, but those that dealt with bacteria vs. man and with other aspects of public health.

To him Dr. Stiles would come, usually in the dusk. I remember opening the front door to him, and how he would come in, timidly, as though more afraid of me than I of him. Under the swan-necked student lamp at my father's desk he would at first be merely a bent old semi-circle of a figure painfully following the lines of fine print in the accumulated scientific journals. But when something fired his special interest, and he would look up to question my father about it, he would be for a minute a different man, with a jaw startlingly decisive, a moustache no longer limp but very military, and eyes that blazed very blue in the lamplight. Yet when it was over, he would go away again, with a bundle of folded journals under his arm, sliding out into the night as though fearful somebody should see him.

By such means Dr. Stiles, whom no reputable doctor would speak to and who was boycotted by all medical societies, kept tenuous touch with what was going on in the war of mankind vs. disease and disaster.

Very well. At three or four minutes before eight o'clock on the morning of March 20, 1905, Dr. Abijah Stiles entered the store of James Behan, Esq., Hardware, Sporting Goods and Bicycles, also Bradford Agent for Ford's Horseless Carriages. He wanted to buy a lamp wick, and he knew that Jimmy Behan always opened early. As he came in, he felt a distant shock, like a quarryman's blast, that shook the floor beneath his feet and made Behan's windows rattle.

Behan, however, was talking over the wall-type telephone. Talking to somebody six whole miles away in the city of Brockton. Talking? Suddenly he was shouting.

"What!" he bellowed. "What are you trying to say? I can't hear you. I can't make you out. Say it slower!"

There was a brief interlude of squeaks from the telephone, and then Behan slammed the receiver on the hook.

"My God!" he cried. "The boiler in Grover's shoe factory has just let go and blown the whole place to hell!" And he lit out for the Town House, to warn the Fire Department to stand by. Afterward, he used to say he was so rattled he couldn't even be sure it was Dr. Stiles in his store, that morning.

The old man stood for an instant collecting himself. Then he walked out of Behan's and marched into Cassidy's, next door. Fruits, Nuts and Imported Delicacies. Here he flung a $5 gold piece on the counter and without delay or explanation scooped up every bottle of Italian olive oil off Cassidy's shelves.

Carrying these, he strode round the corner to Lambert's livery stable where, by great good fortune, he found a fast trotter already harnessed to a light rig, in case of a call from some drummer.

Heaving his olive oil into the buggy, Dr. Stiles followed with a bound. "I couldn't believe it was him," Lambert later told my father. "He jumped like a kid."

He stopped briefly at his lodging for an armload of freshly laundered sheets and pillowcases and for certain other supplies in a small, polished teakwood box with a brass handle.

Then he was off, bouncing over the dirt roads to Brockton as fast as Lambert's second-best trotter, fleeing the sting of an incessant buggy-whip, could leg it.

He reached the block in Main Street, in Brockton, while the dust and steam were still hanging in the air, and just as the real hell of the day was gathering speed. For a great fire was roaring into one edge of the jackstraw pile of timbers that had been Grover's main building — a frame structure in which, half an hour before, some two hundred people had been at work.

A few of these had got out. But comparatively few, and not more than twenty-five or so uninjured. Most of the people were still in there. Some, mercifully, had been killed in the collapse. Others, trapped in wreckage where the flames began, had already died, screaming. But the greater number were still alive and imprisoned — caught on the splinters of oil-soaked wreckage, trapped in oil-soaked corners, pinned beneath fallen machinery or oil-soaked beams, crushed — but still conscious, many of them — between oil-soaked floors. Toward these, the fire was raging, right in the teeth of all the water the Brockton Fire Department — with help arriving from two near-by towns — could throw at it. For oil and water don't mix. And the oil was there first.

Firemen and volunteers were swarming into the wreckage, wrenching at twisted boards, heaving and prying at sections of flooring, releasing by prodigies of frenzied strength all those who could be freed, tugging at others until the last instant in the face of the advancing flames, wherever they could grasp a shoulder or a leg or a hand reaching out through a gap in the debris. . . .

Of all the scores who wrought so desperately that morning, only a few were particularly noticed or remembered. People in the Old Colony still tell about the two priests from a near-by church, Fathers Kelleher and O'Rourke (and those, my friends, are real names), who were foremost in valor and energy among the ruins and in the very tongues of the flames. But there were others, no one knows how many, who rushed in to help as fast as they arrived. And among these was a frail old man with a bristling white moustache and blazing blue eyes. Abijah Stiles, M.D., sometime surgeon in the Army of the Potomac.

The wonder was that they got so many of the trapped and injured out before the fire reached and destroyed them. Some, indeed, they freed only at the last minute from already-blazing timbers, and brought out partly burned.

But the tragedy was that for so many there was no chance. When all had been done that mere human strength could do, there were still dozens of people pinned beneath weights nobody could move or cut through, with the few axes and saws they had at hand and in the ever-fewer minutes before the fire should arrive.

These people knew that the end was coming and what kind of end it would be. They could hear it reaching their friends, as they waited. Most of them asked for someone to help them make their peace with God. For that there were the priests. Afterward they called messages to their families. And for that there were friends who stayed near them as long as they could. And nearly all of them, when they began to feel the approach of fire, begged for something to make them not know — for anything to put them beyond pain.

And for that? Well, there are some things an old man can do if he goes and gets his teakwood box with its syringe and vials, and crawls with it into splintered holes and beneath fallen floors where the smoke is so thick (yet red with the flame just behind it) that you have to work by a sense of touch, and so hot that you can't stay for more than the needful second or two. Guided by the cries, feeling his way unnoticed through the smoke, and not staying long anywhere, an old man can reach quite a lot of people. And help them, in his way.

All too soon, though, the fire drove him out, and the friends, and, last of all, the priests.

There were, however, the hundred or more injured, most of whom were still lying where they had been dragged, waiting for first aid. Among these the doctors were busy. And though more doctors were coming up all the time, there were still for a while not enough medical men to attend to all the people who had been broken or crushed or burned, or all three. And certainly there were not at first enough bandages or oils or medicines — or sedatives for the worst sufferers.

And here again there were things that might be done by an old man who could pass in the confusion for a properly licensed doctor from somewhere-or-other. Dr. Stiles's sheets and pillow-cases, torn into strips, were soon gone, and his olive oil. So he went around with his hypodermic needle and his teakwood box — as long as there was anything left in it — doing what he could.

And then, just about the time when the authorities were get-ting things straightened out and organized — just about when somebody might come around asking a supposedly licensed prac-titioner questions he was in no position to answer — why, then Dr. Stiles heaved his teakwood box into the embers of the fire, sought out his hired buggy at the hitching post where he had tied the trotter, and getting in, drove back to Bradford, slowly and empty-handed.

And what, you ask, was the sequel? Did he get acclaimed by somebody who had recognized him, for the heroic part he played? And did he thus regain at the end a last moment in the esteem of his profession and his fellow men?

No. Nobody among the few who noticed an old man there, knew Dr. Stiles to recognize him. And though people like my father, putting two and two together, began to suspect the truth, the old man would neither admit nor deny it as long as he lived. It was only after he had gone that other twos-and-twos, falling into place, made the story seem certain to people who knew Abijah Stiles, M.D.

Did he, then, become transformed into a better man by the splendor of his redeeming deed, and having got rid of his hoard of enslaving narcotics, become a free man again, and so end his days in peace and calmness in the Old Colony of Massachusetts?

No. He didn't. He died, as a matter of fact, quite soon after that.

Soon, and — for want of the drug on which he had come to depend — in unbearable agony of body and mind.

As he knew he would.

18.

GRAB-BAG LEARNING

I should be gypping the Goddess of Education if I failed to acknowledge that part of her bounty which my brother and I picked up by staying out of school. For a total of more than two years between 1902 and 1905 we were kept out for supposed delicate health imagined by my father with our assistance. In certain later years we got hauled out for as long as a solid month at a time, in fear of epidemics, real or suspected by my jittery parent.

My father was able to get away with these outrages (which did indeed annoy our friends and presumably their parents) because he was on the School Committee, and because he had the courage of a cockeyed conviction: that the human grub will chew up more information faster, and digest it better, if exposed to properly coated wood-pulp and allowed to gnaw for itself, than if clutched by the gullet and force-fed. He was able to make this stick in the first two years he held us out, for we actually overhauled our coevals by a whole grade, in the judgment of a schoolmarm sent around to examine us. But after that it was a hazardous experiment that must often have given him the shivers, for while we picked up a deal of assorted information that qualified us as holy young prodigies in subjects that interested us, in other directions we were ignorant as a brace of apes and a good deal less plausible.

The stuff of our out-of-school education was in four parts: a lofty stack of back-number magazines, bound and loose; a large but haphazard collection of books, mostly old; an excellent battery of dictionaries, encyclopedias and atlases; and a pile of sample textbooks showered on my father by publishers, mostly dealing with subjects far beyond the grades we were supposed to be keeping up with.

In this mass we wormed at will. And our will lay along a very definite line. We had one simple standard for judging a book. If it had pictures we sampled it, and often read it; if it didn't, the hell with it.

Fortunately, pretty nearly everything that saw the light of print in those days was illustrated. The magazines, in particular, were superb — stack after stack of *The Century, Harper's* and *Scribner's* of the 1890's, the vintage years of American magazine publishing. We got to be experts in such widely divergent subjects as the Battle of Santiago; the sinking of the armored cruiser (*not* "battleship") Maine; the countries bicycled through by Joseph and Elizabeth Robins Pennell; Jack London's San Francisco Bay; big game hunting in Africa; and the Life and Times of Mrs. Wiggs of the Cabbage Patch — to mention only a few of hundreds of pieces we chewed up entire.

We took in as much as interested us of anything else that had illustrations. But we generally spat out fiction unless it promised humor or homicide. We spat it faster if it threatened any interminable tripe about Love among adults, and fastest of all if it was by Mrs. Humphry Ward or Mr. Henry James.

All this gave us an arabesque of useful and useless historical, geographical, social and economic information. It also gave us what might be called a barroom acquaintance with Grammar and Syntax. That is to say, we became loosely companionable with these two censors in their unbuttoned, off-duty hours, without the formality of an introduction and without, in fact, knowing their names. We did not realize that outside the swinging doors of good reading, Grammar and Syntax were formidable officials, to be feared, worshiped — and avoided — by all proper taxpayers.

Punctuation, alas, failed to attract our attention.

Of books, our house held great store. Many of them were generous-size tomes, probably unloaded on my grandparents during the Homeric age of subscription-agent publishing. These included a good deal of Mark Twain, from the *Innocents Abroad* to *Life on the Mississippi* period. There were also numerous enlightening works dealing with essential-to-understand events like the carving up of Dr. Parkman by Professor Webster, the execution of Gibbs the Pirate; and the shooting of the Hon. Philip Barton Key by Mrs. Sickles's jealous husband. From the illustrations alone in a multi-volume Guizot's *History of France,* it was possible to absorb a fairly well connected notion of that remarkable country, without troubling to read the monumentally dull text. On the other hand, our ideas of British history were pretty loose at the edges, being pegged down uncertainly by King Arthur, Richard the Lion Heart, Sir Walter Raleigh, Samuel Pickwick, Esq., a fine assortment of military and naval commanders who had surrendered to Americans, and Jack the Ripper. (We didn't discover G. A. Henty until later, in the Public Library.) Of Central Europe and the Near East our information was strictly from the works of Baron Münchausen. Asia, for us, consisted entirely of Kipling's Mowgli's Jungle. Africa we knew, on the authority of H. Rider Haggard, to be a sort of jewelcase in which lost white races with queens of unearthly beauty were hidden (like brooches in pink cotton) under layers of Masai warriors and lions. But of the Seas and the Ships on them and the Islands in them, we had a comprehensive knowledge out of every writer from Defoe to Jack London on whom we could lay hands.

Our knowledge of science was immense, detailed, and spectacularly inaccurate. Our natural history was mostly vintage-1812, out of the cheerfully mendacious *Swiss Family Robinson;* our science was hot off the 1863-73 pen of M. Jules Verne. However, we did pick up a good deal of later news from the many admirably illustrated textbooks sent to my father by publishers hopeful that he would get them adopted by the Bradford school system. These last, of course, didn't have any more to do with our grammar-school requirements than M. Jules Verne's Ruhmkorff Apparatus, but we took in and stowed away a treasure-trove of facts about volcanoes, mammoths, butterflies and the moons of Jupiter, in case anybody should drive up in a hack and ask us. So far, nobody has.

Our general information, too, owed much to a Webster's Unabridged (on an iron tripod stand), to a set of the then-new and still-admirable *Century Dictionary and Encyclopedia* — with its fascinating atlas — and to an 1884 edition of the *Encyclopaedia Britannica* in twenty-five huge volumes. The "Century" was especially good on drawings (out of Viollet-le-Duc) of mediaeval castles with moats, drawbridges, portcullises and the like. The

"Britannica" had an exhaustive treatise (with full-page plates) on the science of fortification according to Vauban (1633-1707). This elaborate geometry of redans, curtains, bonnets, bastions, hornworks and lunettes was still supposed to be hot stuff in the early Twentieth Century, for not until 1914 did the Germans blow it to hell at Liege. One day Major Capen, coming on us executing a creditable Coehorn system in a sandpile, was pleased to smile approvingly, as a nostalgic old soldier today might beam to see Boy Scouts contriving a flame thrower. But when we stuck a Viollet-le-Duc Eleventh Century *donjon* in the middle of it, the old gentleman stalked away muttering in his moustache.

In the last two years of our infestation of Bradford, my brother and I discovered the Public Library, and were soon among its most prominent lushes. The books we took out were mostly romances by such immortals as G. A. Henty, Horatio Alger, Harry Castlemon (*Frank on the Lower Mississippi, Frank on a Gunboat*) and Ralph Henry Barbour (*The Crimson Sweater*). Each of these spawned books by the dozen, built around a boy hero or heroes, who often defied and confounded grownups. So their works were heady stuff, full of wisecracks which, when practiced on our father roused a baleful glare in his eye and often enough a hairbrush in his hand. Still, that is one good way to learn how unwise it is to respond to the remarks of your elders and betters with "Interesting, if true."

On the other hand, the Library had a complete set of bound volumes of *St. Nicholas,* than which there never was a stronger enchantment or a richer treasure of information. *St. Nick,* of course, was still going strong as a magazine. Its regular arrival at our house made the beginning of every month official. There never were printed anywhere, in any book soever, pictures as glamorous as the Howard Pyle illustrations for his King Arthur series. There never was a thrill to equal that of seeing your own name in print in the "St. Nicholas League" department, as the winner of Honorable Mention for a picture of a train going like a bat out of hell and emitting perfect billows of scrawled smoke.

But if we soaked up general information by the bucket, we shed certain special knowledge that we were supposed to keep up with in our periods out of school. We were as un-fond of arithmetic books as a cat is of a bathtub full of water, and when pitched into one yowled as loudly and scrambled out as hastily.

It was my grandmother's job, however, to see that we got regular dousings in number work, and to do her justice, she went through the motions. Each day she would seat us with pencil and paper before our copies of Wentworth's Arithmetic and sternly bid us plunge in. But when, at the end of an hour, she found we had got no more down on the paper than half a dozen grubby digits and a picture of the U.S.S. *Connecticut,* she would give up compulsion and do one of two things: either she would sit down and seek to get us to reason out problems in words and diagrams, without putting a figure on paper save as a memorandum, or she would let us in on a quick and easy shortcut to the answers we were supposed to get.

Both these courses were based on a profound despising of set patterns, rules and formulae. Any fool, she said, could cook a chowder from a recipe, printed or memorized; on the other hand, anyone not a fool could figure out a chowder when and if he or she happened to acquire unexpected title to a mess of clams or a tombstone-size slab of swordfish. It was the same way with arithmetic problems in life, but more so, since few people kept arithmetic books around to consult, and nobody ever remembered the formulae that were in them.

This was admirable, but time-consuming when my grandmother would push aside the textbook and bid us get down and think a problem out. Over an example that would take any class-taught kid three minutes with pencil and paper, I was apt to get involved in an hour-long debate with my grandmother, defending myself right and left from: "What makes you think you can do it that way? Are you sure? . . . All right; at this point he has split at least three and seven-tenths cords of wood; can you prove he hasn't split thirty-seven? . . . How? . . . Mercy! Common sense in arithmetic? You surprise me! What do you mean by common sense? . . ." That way, you might not get very far in a page of Wentworth's examples, and at the end of a session Farmer Brown might be left still hacking away at his cordwood, but you got a brisk workout of the vocal cords and, without suspecting it, an occasional bang on the brain-pan.

Of course there were, my grandmother admitted, some problems that had to be solved with artificial aids like πr^2 or the rule of proportion. But these formulae were really no more than gadgets. And if you had to use a gadget, you might as well use an outright mechanical one that was quick, efficient and no more likely to be mislaid than a formula is likely to be forgotten. She had an old applewood Gunter Rule, hand-scribed by some nameless Yankee instrument-maker of the early 1800's. In effect it was a primitive form of slide rule. With it and a pair of dividers, you could do percentage or proportion like nobody's business and extract square roots faster than you could spit out cherrystones. I learned to do this after she had taken a look into Wentworth's explanation of the square root and correctly judged it beyond my retarded mental capacity. So at a tender age I came by a fond regard for the slide rule, not as an engineer's working tool but as a slick trick to beat the mathematicians at their own game.

In order to expose us to Art, my grandmother used to send us, unaccompanied, on expeditions to Boston. Strangely, my father made no objection to these. It was just one of his illogicalities that he, who took the most extreme precautions against unlikely accidents, was willing to turn us loose among the thunderous drays, streetcars, railways, subways, hansom cabs and hacks of Boston's crowded, confused and roaring streets. And if you think that city traffic in the horse-drawn age was a safe place for a couple of small boys to go gawking around, then you never stepped, as I did, blithely into the path of a four-horse brewery wagon, and heard the thunder of sixteen great hoofs trying to stop short on the slippery cobbles — or looked up to see the muzzles of the leading pair of Percherons right over your head. Needless to say, we omitted mention of this on our return, so we were allowed to keep on with our educational tours of Boston.

These normally started at the old Museum of Fine Arts, which stood where the Copley (now Sheraton) Plaza is today. It was a fine, intimate old place, in which you could wander for hours among cases of jeweled watches, Egyptian statuettes and mummies, cameos, seal rings, gold-inlaid daggers, helmets and armor. . . . We got to know the pictures, too, and reckoned their painters as old friends of grandmother's: Stuart, Whistler, Turner, Holbein, Grueze, Dürer. . . .

But for our money the great pictures were those catty-corner across Copley Square: Sargent's Prophets and the Holy Grail series by Edwin Austin Abbey in the Public Library, a place of high and glamorous gloom and of echoing shadows. A gander at these was our regular appetizer for a Child's Restaurant load of sausages and mashed potato. Fortified with this, we would explore for, and usually find, the Old State House or Faneuil Hall.

Once we found our way clear to Bunker Hill, riding on trolleys that went screeching through a subway as enchanted and otherworldly to our eyes and ears as a boat-ride tunnel at an amusement park. And from the top of that monument looked out over all the world, for it was a clear day. A brave world it was, with a harbor fringed with green headlands and dotted with ships, and a golden light on the hills as far as you could see to the north and west, and to the south, Boston, like a toy-block town capped with a golden dome. Descending, we made our way to the then-new elevated railway and rode past docks and warehouses along the waterfront to the South Station — surely, in the days of its great, glassed train shed, the most thrilling of all railway depots, with its throngs of hurrying people and the reek of coalsmoke and steam, and the clangor of bells and the black gleam of great locomotives.

19.

TRIBAL RITES

In the time of the First Roosevelt there were no Boy Scouts. Scouting had not been invented, and even boys existed only in an imperfect form. We were not manly little chaps; we were not very honest; we were clean only under orders and with loud protest; when we set fire to the woods it was not with educated sticks but with primitive matches; the only knots we knew were bow knots for shoes and hangman's knots for hanging girls' dolls; we had by heart plenty of oaths, but none of them learned out of manuals; and if any of our elders had ever seen us do a Good Turn he would have thought — with reason — that we were delirious.

In our games and sports we were bound by ancient rituals, customs and taboos that dictated when we should start or stop doing anything and pretty much how we should do it.

As soon as the snow was off the ground in March, and while the soft, bare earth was still chilly to the knuckles, we played marbles.

Marbles themselves were of three classes: common marbles, alleys and taws.

Common marbles were at once the implements and the currency with which you played For Keeps. They were at that time of three main types: the current commercial models were of earthenware with a baked glaze, often lumped with moon-crater excrescenses. Obsolescent but still for sale in older-fashion stores, were the brick or clay marbles, uncoated, impeccably round, but fragile. Antedating these by untold years were stone marbles inherited from fathers or grandfathers, or won in games through which they had been circulating, indestructible, for generations. These you never hazarded until you had been cleaned of all the other common marbles you owned.

There were also exposed to sale in town off-standard marbles of various sizes and of Chinese manufacture. These were made of unglazed clay, ringed with numerous narrow bands. People must have bought them, but they never appeared in games.

You carried your common marbles in a drawstring bag, contrived for you by your mother or grandmother. My brother and I rejoiced in bags of extraordinary capacity, color and material. For my grandmother, who could herself shoot a neat alley — though in the Down East fashion, with the back of the hand flat on the ground rather than the first joint of the knuckles — made us each a new bag every spring, out of remnants from whatever costume she happened to be running up for herself at the time. We were ever gay in scarlet or plaid, or somber in black velvet.

Alleys — the larger shooting marbles, the cue balls, so to speak — were commonly of glass, with twisted-ribbon spirals of varied colors inside, around their polar axes. Some alleys, descended through the ages, were of agate — and hence were known as "aggies" — but these were in my day and region considered to have less magic power than the glass ones.

Such alleys were used in the formal game of marbles which was, in its essentials, much as it had always been and, I presume, is now, wherever it may still be played: the ante-ing of a marble put in the center of a ring by each player; the pegging of alleys in turn from a base line at these marbles in the ring or at another player's alley.

Immemorial, too, were the formalized cries and claims that accompanied this shooting: If when it was your turn to shoot you cried, "H'istins" before an opponent yelled, "No h'istins," you were entitled to raise your knuckles off the ground before shooting. This and similar yelps for or against certain other liberties had been in use (with local variations) for generations. William Dean Howells' *A Boy's Town* describes them in the Ohio Valley of the early 1840's, from which one may infer that they were then ages old.

At this particular game I was never any good, being not only inept but, as all my life, slow witted. In a morning I could lose a whole nickel's worth of marbles — a ruinous margin of loss. However, I escaped bankruptcy by virtue of proficiency at the other and faster marbles game much played in Bradford: pegging at a taw.

A taw was an oversize alley, too big for thumb-and-finger shooting. It came in various forms: in spiral-ribboned glass like ordinary alleys, in clear glass with the semblance of a silver elephant or other romantic beast in the center, or like a vastly swollen common marble, in glazed earthenware. As in the case of common marbles, there were also in circulation in our town taws of an older day, beautifully turned out of stone or agate.

In peg-taw, the taw was half buried in firm earth, and standing contestants pegged common marbles at it from a more-or-less distant mark. He who hit the taw became its temporary proprietor and was entitled to keep all marbles pegged at it that failed to hit. When one hit, of course, he yielded possession and became a pegger until he could hit again.

At this game I was Hell with the Long Harpoon. In fact, during a lifetime of fumbling and foozling at sports all other people are good at, the only kind of thing I ever won any prizes for was flinging or hurling or shooting something at a mark. Just as some feeble-minded people can eat broken glass with every evidence of appetite and good digestion, so I can throw cards in a hat, bullets at a target or vegetables at a charity-bazaar pastor. It is a poor specialty, but my own. And in Bradford, at peg-taw, it made me so rich my grandmother had to contrive an oversize bag (of watered silk in startling fuchsia color) to hold my winnings.

A little later in the spring came the season for top-spinning — a sport which in the suburban East, anyway, has either become extinct like the Dodo or gone underground like the practice of witchcraft. You can't even find a top in the stores. But in Bradford's Aprils of that era, any variety store that failed to show a counter of wooden tops in assorted colors and sizes, was deliberately risking the knee-pants good will of the town.

Common tops sold for two or three cents; superior jobs for a nickel, but these were the Cadillacs of tops, bigger, shinier, beautifully sanded and disdaining bright colors for opulent black or natural wood. Between you and me, they were also harder to spin.

To spin a top you needed a special string — commonly of hard-twisted cotton cord well rosined to give it gripping power. At its upper end was a wooden button. You wound the lower end around your top in a careful cone, beginning at the iron point or spur and working well up toward the bulge. You then pinched the upper end of the string between the first two fingers of your right hand with the button on the outside. Clutching the top between these two fingers on its upper surface and your thumb on its spur, you flung it — with its axis vertical — on any hard surface such as a tar walk or (if you were unwatched) the kitchen floor. If you did it right, and gave an artful whip to your top string at the last instant, a good top would spin for a minute or so, depending on your skill and the smoothness of your surface. An adroit operator could scoop up a steadily spinning top into the palm of his outstretched hand. There it would continue spinning with a low hum and a pleasantly tickling sensation to the palm.

About the same time as tops — that is, about the time the ground dried out and got firm — came the season for stilts. These were simple to build, in any height your skill or daring warranted. All you needed was a pair of slats (bed-slats were preferred) on which you nailed foot blocks at your chosen elevation, leaving enough slat above them to go behind your arms and shoulders as you walked. Daring spirits nailed straps, stirrup-fashion, from block to slat, but most of us either knew better than that, or shortly discovered it by falling on our faces with feet still caught on the foot blocks.

In the same season, which is to say before baseball, came that for making and (you always hoped) flying kites. There was a considerable interest in kites at that time, for the Blue Hill Observatory was accustomed to sending aloft its weather instruments attached to box kites, and armies had experimented with the power of a string of box kites to lift a man. My 1940 edition of the *Britannica* still thinks (Vol. 13, pp. 421-422) that this is a novel and tarnation-clever way to get an artillery observer into the air, or to take air photos of the enemy's forts.

Our kites were always in the traditional form, with a framework as of a cross, its tips joined by a taut periphery of string.

Over this, once it had been laboriously assembled out of slivers of shingle, we stretched butcher's paper, cut with flaps that could be pasted down around the edges with flour paste cooked up on the kitchen stove.

Nobody ever thought to defer the building of a kite until he had in hand the price of a ball of boughten string. So our kite-strings were customarily assembled from lengths of common white store string, abstracted from top layers in our household string-drawers. (The lower strata in those capacious bins prob-ably consisted of sinews saved from the time of the Indians.) Once several of us persuaded Moonface Peaselee to borrow a reel of his father's fishline for a kite we were building as a com-munal project. Of course, kite and string promptly got hung up in the tops of a row of maple trees, whereby those of us whose allowances were stopped learned the difference between tapered salmon line and grocery-store string.

You got a kite into the air — maybe — by running with it against the wind and letting out string as the kite gained altitude and the air currents took hold. More often, your kite nose-dived and hit the ground before it was fully air-borne. Once in a while we would get a kite in the air and sit holding it and watching it for hours as it rode, far and tiny in the sky — a something which, incredibly, we had put there.

We made numerous attempts to put up a kite in a thunder-storm, with a key attached in imitation of Benjamin Franklin. But if it was hard to get up a kite in fair, breezy weather, it was next to impossible to get one aloft in the face of an impending shower, with hell's own hurly-burly of violent and contrary winds. Invariably the rain-sodden kite would swoop around and crash into Mrs. Beazley's henhouse, trailing its line across A. Hamilton Cutler's grape arbor and over the top of the Twitchells' catalpa.

There were also, in one of the Bradford stores, Japanese kites of gaudy tissue paper stretched on light bamboo frames, in shape like a hybrid between a bird and a monstrous bee. Nobody I knew ever bought one.

In fact, this store (which was the one that used to carry the Chinese clay marbles) rarely sold anything. It specialized in low-price toys and confections, mostly of oriental origin. It was owned by a pair of maiden-lady sisters named Campbell, one of whom glowered threateningly out of its windows all day long, as though daring customers to come in, while the other tickled its innumerable counters and trays with a feather duster. Her dust, mingled with the scent of lichee nuts, candied ginger, incense cones, Sen-Sen pastilles and general fustiness, gave the premises a fragrance of antiquity unforgettable after all these years. In my nonage we avoided the place except when impelled to go there for a type of lead-barrel water pistol carried nowhere else in town, but I would give a great deal today to lay thumb upon the cast-iron latch of the Campbell sisters' door, to hear the bong of the bell its opening set off (and the tinkle of glass chimes set swaying in the unaccustomed air) and to sniff once again that incomparable aroma.

Many of our sporting implements didn't come from stores; they were self-made, and of these most were seasonal by their very nature. For instance, early spring when the sap was running was the time to make whistles out of cylindrical twigs of willow from which the bark could then be loosened easily.

The jackknife for this and other manufactures was as inevitable a part of our equipment as our pants, in the right-hand pocket of which it invariably rode.

Invariably, that is, except when it got lost, which was tragic: the reaching for that familiar shape and weight in your pocket; the inability, at first, to realize it was not there; the frantic search of your other pockets; the clawing through grass and leaves around you; the retracing, over and over again, of your recent steps; the despairing search as darkness gathered, of all the places you had been. . . . You can have your lost ladies; give me back the knife with the cocobolo handle . . . or the one with pliers on the end . . . or that incomparable one with the ivory sides and the innumerable blades and attachments that Charlie Porter brought back as a present from Birmingham itself, after his trip to England.

Grievous as these losses were, they were soon enough made good in our family. For my grandmother, who had been raised with a jackknife in her pocket, knew very well that a civilized weekday could no more be got through without one than a civilized Sunday without a Bible. In doles for ordinary purposes she was necessarily frugal with her small change, but when a jackknife had to be replaced she was generosity itself, and often accompanied us to Behan's to give us the benefit of her experience in selecting a new knife. For this purpose she usually carried along a pocket whetstone, to try and see whether Behan's offerings really would take and hold the edge he claimed for them.

The jackknife was the only tool we could use with any skill. Our projects with saws, hatchets, hammers and other tools unobtrusively borrowed from our fathers' woodsheds were rarely more ambitious than a pair of stilts or of barrel-stave skis. And even in such cases we usually put deeper gashes in ourselves and in the tools than in our materials. True, we would occasionally be fired by Dan Beard's *American Boys' Handy Book* to start a tree house or a board hut with a secret entrance, but these heady plans cracked ominously with the first split board and they exploded entirely with the first whacked thumb. Dan Beard was — and still is — a fascinating author for the young, but much more so to read than to follow.

With the jackknife, however, we were slick operators and endlessly patient. There was plenty of good, clear white pine for carving; it was known as "common wood" and so valueless that much of it was split up for kindling. (Try to buy clear white pine today; it is literally as expensive as some kinds of mahogany.) Out of pine we fashioned with our jackknives such things as very elaborate pistols, contrived to shoot small squares of cardboard by rubber-band propulsion. On these, in imitation of the early Colt craftsmen, we carved Buffaloes, Indians and Confederates. And we notched their handles to commemorate successful, i.e., both accurate and undetected, shots at one another in school.

We got, in fact, to be very adroit sculptors with the small blade of the jackknife. I had a favorite slingshot, made of a fortuitously perfect crotch of ash, with a knob at the base of the handle. This knob I carved in the likeness of my father's head. And even allowing for the fact that he was easy to caricature, with a monumental beak, a balding head and a bush of hair behind, I thought it a very superior job. My grandmother herself said with a straight face that it compared favorably with the better-known works of Phidias and Michelangelo.

Slingshots were, properly speaking, items for late spring and early summer when the songbirds were abundant and incautious. You spent considerable time searching out a good, well-balanced fork of wood, and when you had cut and peeled it, took care to let it season. Meanwhile, you were saving up a nickel to buy an oversized rubber band at Meekins's. This you cut in two exactly equal pieces, making sure one cut was through the joined place. An oblong of leather combining strength and pliability in exactly the right proportions was your next care, and many a Bradford father loudly wondered where in tunket one of his dogskin gloves had gone to.

When the whole was assembled, you visited Fisher's gravel pit and there collected a pocketful of pebbles of uniform size — for preference about five-eighths of an inch in diameter. Now let the savage eagles masquerading as thrushes and tanagers beware! And if it be argued that we were bloodthirsty wretches, why then it can be alleged — and with no more justice — so are the hundred thousand or so stout citizens who annually sally forth to defend themselves with high-powered rifles against the attacks of deer, moose, antelope and bighorn sheep.

Our real bloodthirstiness was directed at one another, but not with slingshots, though stones were our missiles. In that area, stones of convenient size for throwing were always known as "bricks"—though whether this term was a prudish euphemism or a tribute to the Irish among us, I do not know. At any rate, we were forever embroiled in brick-duels with one another, or in pitched battles with brick bombardments from as many as twenty boys on a side. Why anybody survived boyhood in the Old Colony with two eyes I am unable to explain. To this day barbers frequently admire the handsome constellation of dents, pits and bare specks I bear on my scalp as a sweet souvenir of innocent childhood.

But I am getting ahead of myself. Brick-throwing was an all-year amenity, and I have not yet cleaned up the sports of spring.

Baseball, of course, was the chief of these. It was very like small-fry baseball anywhere today in volume of noise and intensity of passion. The only differences were those of antiquity. Notably, all fielder's gloves, known in that age as "pads," were constructed with a raised, C-shaped mound running from thumb around the base of the palm. The most highly regarded ones were made of very hard leather — in one case I remember, of alligator hide.

The coming of May compelled us to the observance of a rite of which I can find no trace, in the latitude of New York and the age of television: the hanging of May Baskets. A May Basket was a fringed-paper-decorated cardboard box, fitted amidships with a fringed-paper-decorated loop handle and filled with confections of one kind or another — normally from the one-cent candy counters of the town. You contrived this fancy piece by scissoring out, snip by snip, fringes of tissue paper, which you then pasted around the sides of your box, overlapping, shingle fashion. Having filled the box, you chose an evening when you knew its intended recipient would be at home, deposited it at his door, rang the bell and ran. You ran with a certain coyness, for the friend on whom the May Basket was hung was obliged by Moral Law to come out, chase you and, catching you, to bring you back into his house, where you shared the contents of the basket. (The correct terminology was hanging a May Basket "*on*" another, not "for.")

According to strict anthropology, I suppose, May Baskets should have been hung on members of the other sex. But at our age we would never have considered so overt a gesture of affection. Boys hung them on their bosom friends among boys; girls on their best friends among girls. It was perfectly understood that if you hung a May Basket on a friend, he had to hang one on you. Or Else.

The exception to this rule was the May Basket hung each year on any reasonably popular, i.e., surviving, teacher, by the members of her class. This was promoted by the girls who, among them, built a basket about the size of a suitcase, and extorted from their parents most of the price of filling it. Boys were expected to contribute if they wanted to participate in the hanging and the subsequent gorging. Many of the boys were too sternly dignified for such foolishness. The more fools they! A two-cent kick-in to the class Basket would get you into Flossie's or Bella's or Granny's house where, while the girls were playing the piano and singing with Teacher, you could wolf down as much as ten or fifteen cents' worth of assorted sugar, gelatine and coloring matter.

Shortly after the May Basket season began that for tree-climbing, a ritual so thoroughly observed that there were days when the entire boy population of the town was aloft, chattering in the trees like Kipling's Bandar-Log but falling out perhaps more frequently.

May and June were, of course, the months for birds' nesting, when practically every boy started a collection of eggs. For your information, in case you intend to begin robbing our feathered friends, the difficulty lies not in laying hands on eggs, but in getting them down the tree safely. The serious collector will not, if he is well advised, stick them in his pants-pockets, much less in the slack of his blouse. The approved technique among junior oölogists in Bradford was to lay the eggs in your cap, gather the ends of the cap purse-fashion in your mouth and descend with all caution.

A further word to the intending collector: do not, on arrival at home with your treasures, stow them unblown at the back of the second-from-the-top drawer of the sitting-room writing desk. Absent-mindedness in this regard, if persisted in, may well expose you to the merited shaking of a reproving finger, if not, indeed, to the palm of your father's hand applied to the seat of your pants till the dust flies like smoke.

Of course we climbed trees not for eggs alone, or in mere obedience to custom, but for the pure pleasure of it. There are few delights quite comparable to that of moving upward deep inside the quivering greenery of a tree, shut off from seeing and being seen by the everyday world, worming your way aloft in intimate embrace with rough, brusque bark and coming at length to the slender young branches at the top that the wind sways. Here the tossing boughs open and close windows through which you can see now down upon the rooftops below, now up to the white clouds sailing by almost, it seems, within your reach.

20.

THE WORLD SO NEW AND ALL

May and June were the months when you took fire to see the world.

A bicycle, of course, was the magic carpet to all far enchantments — if you could only get one. But that was not easy; few Bradford families lightly purchased a new wheel for a boy; fewer still of us short-pants indigents had either the industry or the persistence to save up for one. So getting a bike was for most of us a campaign of attrition to talk our fathers into turning over to us the bicycles of their Gay Nineties youth.

In my own case, this was a long war indeed, for my father's wheel was a Columbia Chainless which he hesitated to put into my hands, first because it had originally cost him more than he could afford, second because he didn't altogether understand its mysteries, and being a little afraid of it himself feared lest it should somehow open up and take a bite out of me.

For some years, then, I and other wishful beggars in the same case had to go afoot, or in such public transportation as could be ridden in spasms of sudden affluence.

Four miles or so north of Bradford lay a wild, wooded area from the middle of which a rocky hill arose, still defying generations of quarrymen that had been pecking at it intermittently since colonial times. Around its base their deep, square-cut pits had filled with water of a strange, other-worldly green color, in which watersnakes lived. Higher up, in the still-untouched sides of the hill, were caves of split or tumbled rock in which the Lewis and Clark Expedition (incarnate in ourselves) customarily ate the last of its pemmican (dried beef sandwiches to you) before pressing on to the summit for a view of the unexplored world beyond. Spoilsports will contend that the far-off tepees of the Snake Indians that we saw pricking the horizon were only church steeples, and that the smoke signals of hostile Blackfeet, curling up from beyond the hills, were really made by factories. But no one will ever convince me that the distant line of blue I saw one clear day, through my hollowed fists for a telescope, was not the Pacific.

In warm weather, too, we would sometimes walk to the nearest points for swimming. Within the town itself there was no water more than about knee deep. So the Ol' Swimmin' Hole, so dear to eulogists of American Life, was entirely lacking in Bradford. You had to walk three miles to the nearest deep-water pond, which was mortal cold when you got there, and mortal hot to walk back from. Or you could buy a trolley ride to Glen Burnie Pond. This was not only expensive, but the pond itself was phenomenally frigid. Even youths and grown men were frequently taken with cramps while swimming in it, and had to be fished out and rolled over a barrel.

Glen Burnie, though, had a side attraction. In the woods near it was a sawmill which specialized in shingles. Its proprietor, a red-faced man with a stutter, liked boys and was glad to have them visit his remote station. He not only let us go mountaineering at will up the enormous alps of his sawdust, but on our departure always invited us to take along such clean, fragrant cedar shingles as we needed for our various jackknife manufactures.

His shingles, being of fine, straight grain, made admirable darts for casting with a sling. You whittled a narrow shingle into an arrow-shaped projectile — the thick end of the shingle being sharpened for the point, the thin end shaped as the feather. Midway along one side of the flat shaft you cut a slanting notch, its point facing forward. Into this notch you inserted the knotted end of a whip, contrived from a limber sapling and a length of string. Then, holding the feather end of your arrow in your left hand and the butt of the whip in your right, you took aim at a suitable distant object (such as a friend mowing his father's lawn) and with a sort of discus thrower's turn of the body and flinging-out of the whip, launched your arrow in the air. It almost always missed your friend and fell to earth you knew not where. Unless, of course, you heard the tinkle of falling glass or the hearty mention of sacred characters from some adjoining property.

If we had a nickel apiece, or better still two nickels, we could ride on a trolley as far as that wealth would take us, and walk back again. This was always at least half a day's trudge, and in one direction it put us within striking distance of Great Blue Hill, the Pike's Peak of those regions — a nubile enough eminence both in appearance and matter-of-record elevation (635 feet), but a noble peak to us. For from its top you could see the tiny, far-off, golden globule of the State House dome, and then look down at the world beneath your feet where ladybug-size hay wagons crawled on slender white twigs of road, and toy trains puppy-growled along their threads of track. These waved at you, now and then, microscopic signal flags of white steam that came to your ears, long after, as that most enchanting of sounds, the faint, hollow whistle of a far-heard locomotive. Not even the deep-chested midnight rumble of a great ship announcing its departure from New York can touch that brave and wistful cry.

Sometimes, indeed, we got to make longer voyages entirely by trolley, changing from line to line as I have mentioned in describing how the Old Colony looked. But usually — in my brother's case and mine, at least — these were subsidized journeys. Our elders, recognizing in themselves the symptoms of incipient screaming meemies, packed us off for visits to relatives in one or another of several Old Colony towns. At the time, I often used to wonder at the liberality with which my grandmother poured out of her reticule and into our cupped hands perfect torrents of nickels for such journeys. Now, I wouldn't be surprised to learn that in order to get a respite from us, for however brief a period, she had also bribed various cousins and her sister-in-law, Arrie, with her choicest possessions. Certainly I remember recognizing in Aunt Arrie's house a whole stack of stereopticon pictures of the Chicago Fair which had inexplicably disappeared from Bradford.

Aunt Arrie and Uncle George spent their summers in a rambling old mansion in Cohasset. It was set in a negligently attended and bee-loud acreage of run-down gardens, non-operational fountains and rusting cast-iron summerhouses, and was within easy walking distance of the beach at Nantasket and of the rocky, wave-washed coves along the coast south of that beach.

To reach this happy place of exile, you could go across the Old Colony, zigzagging from town to town by trolley. Or you could go by way of Boston and the Nantasket boat from Rowe's Wharf. Perhaps it was my grandmother's conscience that so often moved her to give us the really big money (seventy cents apiece after we outgrew half-fare age) for this more roundabout journey. For which a special blessing on her soul. And another for that she used to pack us off on the milk train, so that we got the first boat down Boston Harbor, past its islands green-gold in the level morning sunshine and its dun-and-blue headlands beyond, and the wonders of ships coming in, salt-encrusted, from all the oceans of the earth, and the gulls riding easy in the air alongside, with the sun shining through their wings as they wheeled.

This enchanted voyage had a climactic wonder: the boat on its way touched first at Allerton, on the tip of the peninsula of which Nantasket lies at the base. And your ticket stub entitled you, if you chose, to debark here and ride the rest of the way on an electric train made up of cars like open trolleys, but bigger and grander than any mortal trolley. And faster, too, as they roared (with a fine br-r-rang of giant electric gongs) along the sandy shore beside the sea, into a wind blowing straight and sea-scent laden from the Spanish Main.

For the ocean as a place to swim, we did not care much. I think this was the aftermath of one awful afternoon my father had put us through when we were quite small. Thriftily figuring that no six year old's modesty was worth anybody's dime for a bathhouse, he undressed and dressed us in the barely shadowed space underneath the boardwalk. Later-life dreams of running up Fifth Avenue in the altogether have nothing on the recollection of being stripped in full view of the passing promenade of fashion along Nantasket Beach.

Nevertheless, Nantasket was sheer glamour to us. The beach was a boundless sandpile for building neat estates. There was the sea to look at, with its tiny, far-off triangles of white sail, sunlit on the horizon. From the amusement park across the way came strange, exciting sounds: the thunder of the roller coaster, the oddly mingled music of a beer-hall band competing with a merry-go-round calliope. . . . And always there was in our nostrils the romantic odor of the sea — for so we considered an aroma composed in equal parts of hot dogs, hamburger-and-onions and the wet brown kelp that came in on the surf.

Toward the end of our time in Bradford, my father's bicycle suddenly and unexpectedly became mine. It was not so much that I wore my parent down; he had developed the ability to draft, in a sound-proof compartment of his mind, whole monographs on plant cell structure as observed through a microscope, while seeming to listen to my endless declamation of reasons why I should use his Columbia Chainless. Rather, it was the fact that the rim of the front wheel of this machine had developed a kink that brushed against the fork once every revolution and so seemed to guarantee that the monster could never be pushed to dangerous speed. So he gave in.

My grandmother promptly fixed the kink. With a lever and fulcrum rigged out of builder's two-by-fours she bent the fork bow-legged. This gave my Columbia a raffish appearance when seen from bow on, but enabled me to risk my neck unimpeded, on the steepest hills. All my father could do at this late stage was to forbid me to buy and attach toe-clips, the marks of a real scorcher, which he held to be dangerous. This grieved me, but only temporarily. It was a real distinction in our town to ride a Columbia Chainless.

Unfortunately, the front tire had been rubbed down to the fabric at the kinked place, so it didn't hold air very well, even though wrapped at that point with many layers of black friction tape. I had to stop every few miles and pump it up again, and on a day-long trip could count on the tape wearing through at least once and having to be stripped off and replaced. However, practically every juvenile tire in town was in the same case from ancient punctures and cuts, so we never started anywhere without making sure that our tool kits had plenty of tape and rubber cement and that our pumps were in good working order. And what were a few flats in the course of a day of such enchantment as the artless roads of that era offered?

Outside the town there was next-to-no other traffic. You had the whole road to yourself, mile after mile of it, winding fair away. If there were hot and dusty stretches, there were to offset them long tunnels of shade beneath old trees. If there were hills to pump up, red-faced and panting, there was always the promise of a new world to be seen from the top. And if at the end of a long, glorious, No-Hands swoop down a smooth, firm hillside, there were ruts in the hollow to fling you on your ear, why so it is in life.

We always started for some definite goal, like Great Blue Hill or the seashore, but rarely got there, for the roads were sketchily marked. Yet always we would come upon some wonder, if it was only a crew of bill-posters putting up signs of incredible brilliance and splendor for Barnum & Bailey's Circus, or Forepaugh's. And always, somehow, we got home again, which does not happen infallibly in life.

Until about the end of our stay in Bradford we had never ridden in an automobile. No ordinary family in those days owned a car; the handful of people in town who did own them never thought of inviting small boys to ride. We would have given our entire cigarette-card collections to go for even a short spin; to make such an Over-the-Hills-and-Far-Away journey as today's young hopeful can endure only with the solace of a store of comic books in the back of the car, any one of us would have submitted without even a groan — much less a shriek — to having his ears washed.

But eventually Charlie Porter, the richest man in town, and a great sportsman whether aboard a horse or behind one, bought a motor car. And as soon as he had got it broken to bit he invited eight of the boys who lived near by to go for a ride with him. For Mr. Porter — I still think of him as Charlie — was a friend to all his knee-pants neighbors. He not only didn't mind if we raced across his terraced acres and through his well-clipped hedges, but often as not joined the Indian War Councils we held in the Medicine Lodge that pretended to be the toolshed under one end of his bowling alley.

It was at the conclusion of one such pow-wow, on the morning of Labor Day, 1907, that Charlie invited us to go that very afternoon for a ride in his new Rambler.

For most — perhaps all — of us it was life's first adventure in a horseless buggy. I am moved to set it down here, not only for the information of future generations who can never know what Motoring was like in its Athenian age, but for the nostalgia of other creaking Pantaloons and plump Pierrettes who remember such gaudy occasions in their pre-salad days.

We assembled at Charlie's house right after dinner, which would put it at 12:30 P.M. Charlie's Rambler was waiting there, the doors on either side of its tonneau swung open invitingly. It had earlier been driven over by Mike Tyrrell, Charlie's coachman, who had mastered its terrors sufficiently to get it across the three hundred yards or so of side street from Charlie's barn if given half an hour's notice, but who was not expected to hold it from rearing, out on the open roads. For that, Charlie himself, a Daredevil and a Mechanical Genius combined, took the responsibility.

Our tribe piled in, ordinary braves in the tonneau, chiefs and medicine men in the front seat where Charlie would presently join us. Right now he was busy checking the essentials that you had to be sure of before the take-off. Among the things Charlie had to check — for it was going to be a whole afternoon's run — were the two spare tires, the tire pump, tire iron and blowout patches, the extra oil (in a kerosene can with a potato on the spout), the engine tools, two or three dozen critical bolts and (in case we should not make our twenty-five-miles-and-back before dark) the acetylene in the brass generator that stood on the running board.

Charlie then checked his passengers, locked both the doors of the tonneau, buttoned up his duster, carefully adjusted gas, spark lever and switches, pumped up the air pressure on the gas supply and (before that pressure could fade) ran to the crank. This was already unleashed from its leather retaining sheath. Charlie cautiously maneuvered it to catch compression on the up-stroke, gave the crank a heave and was rewarded by hell's own racket from the engine. He scooted nimbly around, sprang into the driver's seat, pushed in the choke, advanced the spark and retarded the throttle, and switched from battery to magneto.

Then he wiped his forehead and waited for her to warm up.

During this interval one of the Porters' hired girls came out, all dressed up like a maid in a magazine picture, and dusted off the car with a feather duster. This was a piece of swank Charlie had learned stopping at fancy hotels on a two weeks' tour to the White Mountains and back; at such caravanserais chambermaids always came out and dusted off a tourist's car before he started on a stiff hundred-mile day's grind.

When all was ready, Charlie adjusted his goggles, tightened his gauntlets, wrestled mightily with two cast-brass levers, tooted the bulb horn and let in the clutch. We were off!

On the way to the Square Charlie briefed me on my part in the navigation of the voyage. He had to desist, of course, whenever we approached a side street, for these had to be taken with caution. But the gist of it was this: Our navigating instrument was the speedometer, which we should set on the Square at exactly our statute mileage from Boston. Our Navigation Guide would be the Automobile Blue Book in my lap. I was to check the one against the other, so as to let Charlie know whenever it came time for a change of course. At these times I was to read him (if I could, bouncing along at twenty miles an hour) the directions for our change. These went something like this:

28.4 Sign MASON'S LUMBER WORKS. Turn sharp right, passing white church. 1¼ m. beyond, cross bridge over river at old sawmill. Turn left at once and follow river, keeping left at forks. At 31.7 turn *right* across bridge and keep left of river, along left bank to small bridge, which cross. Immediately turn left (sign, WHIPPLE'S TAVERN). Continue on left side of river, crossing another bridge to left bank. At 34.5 take left fork.

39.8 Approaching HINGHAM. Do NOT go into center of village, but at edge of town turn *sharp* left around white house. . . .

Those were the days when the boughs of the trees hung low, even over the main highways, so that now and then Charlie had to slow down and weave around them, lest we should all be raked by twigs. For his Rambler was guiltless of windshield and our heads stuck right up into the air, like those of so many fledgling sparrows out of a nest. But on one glorious straightaway we hit forty miles an hour, with the air blurring our eyes and thundering in our ears, and the rattle of flying pebbles on the underside of our plunging chariot's mudguards. Each of us hung on to some handy piece of ironwork with a clutch of delighted terror, half expecting at any moment to be hurled into eternity, and even Charlie himself bent low over his wheel and gripped it so hard the leather of his gauntlets stretched taut from knuckle to knuckle.

We made a great circuit to the shore and inland again, and so back to Bradford from the west. And came upon that town as all fair towns should be come upon — at sunset, with the golden light from behind us gilding the spires and the houses and lying long across the lawns. And everywhere friendly people were going home to supper in friendly homes.

21.

WINTER IS ICUMEN IN

In lower latitudes, people's vital juices accelerate in spring, but when fall comes and the days grow shorter, their blood thickens and their humors begin to congeal.

In New England it is quite the other way. There, the passing overhead of the autumnal equinox is a promise of zing-to-come, and the pace of life picks up. Imperceptibly, at first, but more and more, with every shortening day and every fall of a scarlet leaf, until with winter it is at its liveliest and heartiest.

Among the male young of Bradford the first manifestation of this quickening came when the game of Chase began to flourish.

Chase was our form of Cops and Robbers, Cowboys and Indians, Space Cadets and Atomic Hijackers . . . or what have you. It was like these, but it scorned their nomenclature and pretense.

It was simple, direct and excruciatingly satisfactory. The fugitives ran; the chasers pursued them with whips. If a chaser caught up with a fugitive he was entitled to take as many and wicked larrups at him as he could get with his whip.

This imposed a natural equalizing system: if as a chaser you cut yourself a good, long, limber and punishing whip, then you sacrificed some of your speed; if as a fugitive you were overhauled easily, it was likely to be by someone who carried a light and not very painful whip of some such stuff as forsythia. Speaking as one with much experience at both ends of a whip, I can tell you that the most efficient ones were made of birch — a secret discovered centuries before my time by the pedagogues of England.

The minute school was out there would be a choosing-up of sides, and the first chooser had to give the second his option of being chaser or chased. Most of us, being natural savages, preferred chasing. Once this was decided, the pursued were off. The amount of start they got was precisely the time needed for the

chasers to find and cut the necessary whips. The pursued could
run in a body or disperse according to taste. There were no rules
or bounds except that you couldn't go indoors. And so we ran,
in the long autumn afternoons, through orchards rosy with
apples, under maples orange and blazing yellow, down hillsides
green with hemlock and blue-and-purple with asters. And the sky
turned violet in the west and the sun went down beyond Bradford. Then, as never since, it was really the chase, and not the
quarry that mattered.

Strictly for quarry, though, was chestnutting, which opened
with the first frost that split the burrs and weakened the stems
that bore them, so that they could easily be shaken down. The
blight has since killed all New England's once-common chestnut
trees, and with them the sport of going after chestnuts. For this,
a long, crisp Saturday was indicated. You took a small flour bag
and a stout hardwood club or two apiece — the big end of a
broken baseball bat would do nicely. The club was for throwing
into trees or beating on branches to jar loose the burrs that were
ready to fall. You started while the hoarfrost was still white on
the ground, so as to get to the choicest and heaviest-laden trees
before some tribe of fellow foragers. At this hour you might often
see, in the fields you passed on the way, a fox gliding along sinu-
ous as a snake — a moving brilliance of orange on a field of silver-
green.

The American chestnut, when extracted from its burr which
you cracked with a stone, was considerably smaller than the
Italian chestnut of commerce, and neither so sweet nor so soft
in texture. On the other hand, it had a sharper, nuttier flavor,
and made fine roasting at home. If you were cagey enough to
put aside some of your take, and hoard it till Thanksgiving time,
you could exact a fancy penny for it from your grandmother. A
mercenary thing to do, considering who ate most of the chestnut
stuffing out of the turkey, but we had neither morals nor ethics
about such things.

Nor had we any morals about Halloween in its outdoor phase.
The modern, efficient ethics of that festival had yet to be invented by whatever nameless but immortal pubescent invented
the powerful slogan "Trick or Treat!" Where the modern tot

honorably withholds the vandal hand in exchange for a handout, we knew no better than to distribute our attentions without threat or hope of profit.

The best that could be said for our outdoor Halloween operations was that we sought to visit the more drastic of them on crabs who during the balance of the year abused us by keeping baseballs batted through their windows, or strewing grit on their sidewalks during the coasting season. But even on these we rarely inflicted more than the reminder of an unhinged gate or the opening of a henyard door.

Otherwise our pranks were deplorably mild, and were played upon the just and unjust alike. The bean blower — a small tin tube with a wooden mouthpiece through which you could shoot common white beans with fair accuracy — was directed at any lighted window, but the tick-tack was an attention reserved for friends; it was too laborious a contrivance to waste on enemies. This consisted of a small metal weight, such as a nut, suspended from a string in near-contact with a windowpane. By an extension of the string, the weight could be remote-control operated from near-by bushes. Your chosen victim was supposed to affect a becoming degree of exasperation, else you wouldn't do it to him again next year.

On the other hand, Halloween parties, with bobbing for apples floating in a washtub of water, were conducted with the strictest observance of accepted morality. Which is to say that any unwary bobber was subject to having his head held under water by his friends until he had inhaled about a teacupful of this health-giving beverage.

Naturally, fall was the time for football. This, like baseball, was similar to the small-boy game of today, allowing for the differences in rules and allowing even more for pronounced differences in equipment — or absence thereof. In that neolithic age you played in your everyday, or school, suit, though if you owned a turtle-neck sweater you put that on in place of your jacket. Occasionally one of us would own a pair of bamboo-reinforced shinguards inherited from a high-school brother, and once in a while somebody would be the proud possessor of a molded rubber nose-guard. (The top strapped around your head with elastic; the lower end was secured by a mouthpiece you bit on. Through holes pierced in this mouthpiece you breathed, if at all.)

For helmets we wore our hair, allowed to grow long for the season, as was the custom of the time. This custom — which originated in collegiate circles — was founded on the fond but mistaken belief that a good shock of hair would deaden the impact of a hostile toe or (in small-town football) of an outcropping of honest New England granite.

Winter arrived officially with the first freezing-over of a skatable surface anywhere in town, and vanished with the last trace of snow that could be coasted on.

Skates were of four principal kinds, none visible to the bifocal eye today. They were all designed to be attached to your ordinary shoes; skates with built-in shoes must have existed, but they were never seen in our parts.

Common steel skates, with slightly rockered runners, were contrived to bite on to your shoes by the operation of a lever somewhat like that which you now swear at when wrestling with tire chains. Two clamps gripped each sole forward, and three clutched your leather heel. A strap from aft, tightened over your instep, helped keep your heel from pulling off — you hoped. Girls' skates were similar but had no heel clamps; they were furnished with a leather harness astern for strapping around the ankle.

In common skates there were two makes; Barney & Berry, trademarked with a die-stamped hole in the shape of the ace of spades, and Winslow, trademarked with the ace of clubs. I was a stout Winslow man, myself, particularly after I got a pair of Winslow's skates in what was popularly known as the hockey type. This had a flat runner with a longer-than-ordinary tail aft. Its clamps fastened individually with key-operated screws. It was, moreover, nickel plated. These features combined to give the owner a feeling of smug superiority akin to that now conferred by the possession of the newest and shiniest car on the road. The Winslow Hockey's flatness of runner also contributed to the delusion that you were Hell on the Ice.

The third variety of skate popular in Bradford was also

straight-bladed, and even longer. This kind had a wooden top, shaped like a long, narrow boat. A conical screw, twisted into the leather of your shoe heel, anchored it astern; a complex lacing of stout straps did the rest. But the straps had to be drawn tight and kept tight, else you were likely to find yourself going in one direction while your skates went in another, with damage to the ice if not to your head. So, your feet soon acquired a complete insensibility, and you were able to walk home again only after warming them and wriggling them for a long time before a fire on the shore.

There were also in circulation at that time wooden-topped skates with curled-up prows arching over your toes in the Currier & Ives style. These, which had descended from fathers and grandfathers, had a mere pyramidal spike to ram into your heel, and were even more untrustworthy than the screw-heel kind. Nevertheless, they were proudly flaunted by their owners, including not a few of the older generation such as George Swan, who used to offer to referee our hockey games.

Nobody paid any attention to him, however. Our hockey was merely a half-tamed variety of shinny, invariably played with a stone for a puck. A five-cent bentwood stick was an affectation; many of the best players used naturally curved sticks they had sought out in the woods, cut and shaped with their own jack-knives.

I omit from classification as skates a double-runner variety sometimes inflicted by parents on children considered too wobbly in the ankle to stand up on proper skates. Such infants as wore these were the kind who, in summer, wore kneecaps in black kid leather (fastened in place with elastic) to protect not their epidermises but their stockings.

The principal skating places in Bradford were shallow ponds that occurred here or there on the bosoms of cranberry bogs. These were hardly big enough to hold a hockey game and a snap-the-whip operation at the same time. But they froze early and hard. And off from them led passages and lagoons wandering through the bogs in a labyrinth, on which you could skate for an hour at a time, alone or in single file, without once covering the same track.

Some three miles out of town was a deep-water pond belonging to Charlie Porter. It was set among tree-clad hills which, in retrospect, seem to have had the height and steepness of headlands enclosing a Norwegian fjord, though probably they were very modest rises. On this pond, when it was newly frozen with a couple of inches of black, transparent ice, skating was sheer enchantment. You usually had the whole virgin surface to yourself, for few other people troubled to come out so far. The ice rang to the sound of your skates, and when at the end of a fast half-mile you went into a long backward glide, you could see the marks of your skates feather-white on the unspoiled black of the ice, and hear the hills giving back to you the echoes of your own strokes, as of some other fellow far away.

When the ice was snowed under, we went coasting or sliding. The terms are interchangeable with one another, but under no circumstances with "sleigh-riding."

Sleigh-riding is what you do in a one-horse open sleigh such as you may see in Currier & Ives prints, or on Page 2,363 of Webster's New International Dictionary, Second Edition. Standard accessories are one (1) knowledgeable horse, complete with jingle bells, one (1) buffalo robe and one (1) fun-loving girl. If she doesn't love fun or if you are bashful you had better take along 2 and no/100 hot soapstones.

You can also go sleigh-riding in a two-seated sleigh, or in a hay-filled teaming sleigh hired for the occasion, as I have described in discussing the education of the young in Bradford. When you ride in a grocer's sleigh, accompanying him on his delivery rounds in winter, you are sleigh-riding. Unless, of course, your grocer is driving a pung, which is a type of cargo sleigh with one long, low runner on each side, as distinct from the high runner or the double runner of a sleigh proper. In that case you are punging. In a more special and delightful sense you are punging if you hitch a ride on a pung in motion by hopping on the narrow framework ledge along either side of the pung body and successfully staying there, either by the good nature or the absent-mindedness of the driver, until you see another pung going in another direction and change to it. Punging is a form of sleigh-riding.

But never — repeat *never* — are you sleigh-riding when you go downhill on a sled or variety thereof such as a bobsled or double-runner, whether you do so belly-whopper, sitting up, standing up, backward, sardines or two-deep.

Give me that, and I will give you the right to apply the word "sled" to the mid-century version of that article. In fact, I will make you a present of this heretic vehicle itself, flexible open-work steel runners, steering bar and all. The authentic, old-time-religion sled has merely gone into a deep sleep, like Frederick Barbarossa, and will some day come back to restore coasting to its one-time glory. I know because my Webster, an authority on such things, pictures it in the above-named edition and on the page opposite "sleigh." Quite correctly, Webster's illustrates the sled in the two forms sanctified by divine revelation: a girl's sled and a boy's sled.

A girl's sled was of wood, except for the strap-iron surfaces of its runners. These runners were open frames, and high enough to carry the girl rider ten or twelve inches off the ground. This altitude had been established by a commission from The Smithsonian Institution by direction of President Franklin Pierce, as a suitable height to keep the fringes of pantalettes out of the snow. Girls in the early 1900's were still supposed to ride these vehicles sitting up, like little ladies, and some of them did.

A boy's sled was four or five inches high, and built of the best oak, shod with round steel rod, shaped to its runners. The runners were solid wood, pierced on either side with handholes. The top of the sled was gaudily enameled, and lettered in gold with a name, in the manner of a ship or an old-time locomotive. New England sleds, at least, bore the names of famous trotting horses. Mine was "Prince Alert."

You steered such a sled either by momentarily dragging a toe, rudder-fashion, in the snow on one side or the other, or by giving the whole works a heave to flop it in a new direction, or by a combination of the two maneuvers.

When my brother and I outgrew our first sleds and got longer ones, my father took the old sleds down to Ira Hardwick, the blacksmith-wagonmaker, and had him build them into a double-runner. This was the regional name for a bobsled. It was a primitive version of the kind you see on TV and newsreels, kiting along at a mile a minute, down some winter-resort chute. Primitive especially in that it had no steering wheel (an automotive idea only later applied to bobsleds) but was steered by hand or foot directly applied to the leading sled.

There were plenty of double-runners in town, for Ira Hardwick was one who would rather build a double-runner for love than repair Kelly's lumber-pung for money. Some double-runners in Bradford were very fancy jobs indeed, with footrests along the sides, and long enough to carry eight or ten close-packed kids. Ours could take six at a pinch, but was better with four. The steersman lay prone to guide the forward sled by hand; you could steer a double-runner sitting up, with your feet on a crossbar of the leading sled, but that was a chancy procedure on a fast hill. Wedged behind the steersman sat the passengers, with a pusher-offer clinging on at the rear end.

Sleds were best on the short, steep hills, but double-runners were best on the long ones, especially when a street like Maple was well packed down and glazed over, so that you could get the last inch of its half-mile slope.

It was the custom of that time for towns to roll the snow on their streets with a six-foot-diameter horse-drawn road-roller, rather than to plow it. This packed down the snow for sleighing and more or less insured that it would last, with renewed laminations of snow rolled as it came, until people could safely put away their sleighs and bring out wheeled vehicles again. This process turned every hilly street into a coasting run, onto which horse-drawn traffic ventured at its peril. There was little enough of such traffic, anyway.

If for any reason the streets wouldn't serve, the sidewalks would. These were plowed, but never down to bare pavement, and any citizen mean enough to shovel his patch of walk or (worse) to sprinkle it with ashes was reminded of his thoughtlessness on the following Halloween. Fortunately, most citizens of Bradford had a fine Christian sense of values; they were willing to risk their own necks from a slip in the hope that the small-fry would break theirs in a collision.

Best of all for double-runner sliding were the gutters, which were plowed with a narrower plow and which, when the slush in them froze solid, made ideal runs — narrow, safely walled with snow on either side, and hard-slippery as a new-frozen pond itself.

And the best of times for these was a moonlight night so cold that your feet squeaked on the snow as you toiled to your appointed hilltop, and when you got there so still that you could hear from the far-off foot of the hill the shrill cheers that marked the end of your predecessor's run and signaled the moment you could begin your own. You lay down in the steersman's position, grasping the points of the steering sled and feeling your wet mittens freeze instantly to its runners. Your crew loaded up behind you, each holding the legs of the one behind him, and your brother shoved off. Once away, you picked up speed, so that by the time you were opposite our house you were slamming along so fast the air sang in your ears and your heavy-laden craft made a hollow clatter like incessant thunder. Your arms shook to the tremor of the sled and Lily Merrill, riding just behind you, squeaked like the slim little filly that she was.

Three rituals in Bradford lasted the year around. Appropriately enough, they were all connected with warfare. One was brick-throwing, which I have already mentioned. One was fights. And one was the organization, drilling and marching of short-pants companies of soldiers.

Fights were bound by the traditions of boys' books — many of which stemmed from *Tom Brown's Schooldays* — and of our elders, who never tired of mendacity about their own prowess and endurance as youthful Heenans and Sayers. That is to say, any fracas that started as a flare-up of temper, or just as a boasting contest, was quickly organized into a set match by friends who came running from all sides yelling the glad tidings, "Fight! Fight!" Before you knew it, you found yourself in a ring of partisans, faced with an opponent against whom you had no particular grudge. (I do not remember what the *casus belli*, if any, was in at least a dozen fights I remember otherwise all too well.) The only thing to do was to haul off your coat and go to it, mauling and being mauled.

We were none of us boxers; we always intended to get older

boys to teach us, but never had time. So the usual result was gore by the bucket, diluted at the end with the tears of the loser. In both of these I contributed a share that increased toward the end of my stay in Bradford, for everybody else started growing faster than I, and friends whom I had been able to whale, two in an afternoon one year, pasted the living daylights out of me the next.

In consequence, my face, which infant photographs show to have been repulsive enough in a baby's bonnet, became so much more so that not even the primly proper life which I led until 1920 could improve it (as sweet thoughts transformed the visage of Lord George Hell in Max Beerbohm's *The Happy Hypocrite*). In that year a sympathetic telephone operator in the office of my first employment kindly told me, "Yer really a nice guy; it's just ya puss." So I abandoned my face to be an autograph album for low thoughts and worse habits.

From these I now get annual returns on a compound-interest basis. The current year's installment was delivered at a convention of newspaper circulation department goons which I was attending in the capacity of an employee-relations writer. Milling among the throng, I was hailed by a perfect stranger.

"For God's sake!" he said. "Have you been in an accident?"

I gulped for words, but found none.

"Your *face!*" he cried. "What's happened to it?"

"Nothing but heredity and an evil life," I said.

His mouth opened and his face crimsoned. "Forgive me," he said, "until you spoke I thought you were Smith. A very dear friend of mine."

Later I got them to point Smith out to me. He was easily the most villainous-looking character in a congregation not noted for sanctity of life.

It was not my numerous wounds, however, that got me to be Captain of the Bradford Boy Cadets. It was just that I had decorations to bestow. There were around town a dozen assorted companies of Junior Zouaves, Volunteer Minuteboys and Young Rough Riders. None of them had more than a dozen members. I figured I could get at least eight by offering the privilege of wearing my father's pole-vault and high-jump medals. Or more if I could interest anyone in an "Oh You Kid" badge from Revere

Beach and a Best in Home Preserves ribbon that Mrs. Buzzell had won at a fair in Maine, but scorned as frippery. Eight was all I got, though.

We had no uniforms, but we made up for lack of them by grimness of armament and splendor of rank. We bristled with air rifles, cap pistols and wooden sabres. Three-eighths of us were officers, four-eighths either non-coms, color-bearers or musicians. And since we had to have at least one private, Hiper Hasty consented to fill that honorable grade in consideration of being allowed to bear one of every kind of weapon we had, and to wear the gaudiest of my father's pole-vaulting medals on a Knight Templar's sash belonging to Newton Ballou's Uncle Jonathan. Not infrequently we marched in step.

On lesser holidays of the year, such as Washington's Birthday, we held solemn parades of our own, marching through the snow to the beat of Boxer Parton's drum as brave as Washington's Continentals at Valley Forge and, I should judge, looking damn near as cold. At least Mrs. Charlie Porter always used to invite us in off the frozen streets and feed us hot chocolate when we passed her house, so we always took care to do so, exhorting Boxer to whale that drum hard as we approached.

22.

IDOL WORSHIP

The town of Bradford had numerous glories when I lived there. But in the eyes of its large, active and lyrical boy population, none was more splendid than the Bradford Fire Department. Often, as we sat smoking sweet-fern cigarettes behind Crocker's greenhouse, we used to offer to bet one another a million dollars to one that there was no fire department so good (for its size) in all the world. And I still glow with pride in Bradford to remember that even at these attractive odds there were no takers.

The shining signs and symbols of the Bradford Fire Department were its five pieces of apparatus. In fact, these *were* the Fire Department in our eyes, as statues were the Gods to simple eyes in ancient Greece. Men were only high priests to them and horses their servants. Their rites were heralded with hoarse whistles and clangor and the galloping of hoofs. Their altars were the houses, the business blocks and (oh, if only . . .) the schools we hoped would burn down for them. The Fire Department, as we conceived it, did not exist to put fires out. Rather, fires existed to call forth and show off the might of the Fire Department. By these standards, the bigger the fire, the more it was to be praised.

The five pieces of apparatus of the Bradford Fire Department constituted a kind of heavenly hierarchy. They were secluded in the lower rear of the Town House, behind doors that were not only kept closed and locked, but were so constructed that their glassed panels were far above even adult eye-level. Ordinarily, it took two boys, boosting one another in turn, to get a series of brief looks apiece at our apparatus. Yet in the spring season for building and walking on stilts, it was possible to look long, and to get as satisfactory a view as the head-on position of the equipment allowed. From this angle, we knew every bolt, bar and gadget of our town's apparatus. So when they appeared in public, it was as though the moon were obligingly to turn around and allow astronomers a chance to study its hidden side. This occurred formally during Fourth of July parades, at which we were present by definition, and informally whenever there was an alarm of fire, to which we always responded unless imprisoned at school or in the nighttime restrained by fathers emerging in their nightshirts to shoo us back to bed.

Bradford's apparatus were, in order of divinity, The Steamer, The Best Ladder Truck, The Hook, The Patrol and The Reel.

The Steamer was Jove and Pluto combined: majestic, barrel-chested, gleaming, borne on chariot-wheels of scarlet, adorned with instruments, hung with lanterns and crowned with ringéd silver. When it started for a fire behind its pair of plunging dapple-grays, with Nick Banton on the driver's box flaunting a whip and whanging away at the dashboard gong, while Jim Hickey and John Ogilvie clung to the rear step and heaved pitch-pine into the flaming furnace and the stack emitted billows of black smoke, The Steamer was such a spectacle as drew men and boys racing breathless from all directions to watch it tear past and to follow panting in its wake.

But even this was only a foretaste. By the time you had arrived at the fire — and if the fire was a good one — The Steamer was in action, with a shuttering roar, loud and vibrant as that of a steam locomotive in full cry — except that it was right there in one place, thunderous, deafening, earth-shaking, setting up an ecstatic, thrumming quiver in the very gizzard of every by-stander within a quarter mile. Compared to this, the fire itself, if an ordinary or abortive one, was pale and faint. To a real fire The Steamer's roar was a background as divinely ordained as blackness to a thunderstorm.

There were some parts of town below the hilltop standpipe where the water pressure was so good that The Steamer was not needed at all. Fires in these localities were, in our eyes, only half-fires.

There were two ladder trucks in Bradford, one for everyday, like a Mother Hubbard, and the other for dress-up, like a best bombazine.

The Best one was hardly ever used; it was too big and too beautiful. An elegant, white-and-gold equipage, it was fitted with

a prodigious assortment of highly varnished wall-, roof-, pompier-
and extension-ladders, pike poles, axes, lanterns and patent door
openers. Few of these were necessary; there wasn't a structure
in town (if you excepted the church steeples) that couldn't have
been overtopped by half the ladders on The Best. Furthermore,
The Best required two horses.

How such a monument to civic extravagance had ever been
purchased under Town Meeting procedure in the Old Colony
used to puzzle strangers. But George Swan, the town's Voltaire,
used regularly to point out at Town Meeting that The Best had
been authorized at a session which happened by chance to be
held on the day that Lizzie Borden was acquitted. Thereupon
George would move to sell The Best. The cost of its retention,
he argued, was the price stiff-necked ninnies paid for their belief
in frustrated females, most any one of whom was likely to carry
an ax concealed beneath her petticoats, strapped to her leg. That
did it. Between the people outraged by the indecency of the
word "leg," and those who believed in Lizzie Borden, and those
who cherished old maids in their families, and those who wanted
to spite George, and those who had a New England reluctance
to take a capital loss, George's motion was snowed under like a
rose-petal in the blizzard of '88.

Yet the town could neither afford to maintain two horses for
The Best nor to get along without ladders at its fires. So it bought
and used for all practical working purposes, a one-horse ladder-
truck.

This was known as The Hook. It was light, fast, and painted a
workaday red. It carried just enough of ladders, poles, axes and
such to deal with any ordinary fire in town. And at the heels of a
fast, powerful trotter named Bessie, it could streak through the
streets of Bradford like a sulky behind Dan Patch moving up
through a crowded field. In a town where trotting-horse lore was
part of the operating life-knowledge of every boy old enough to
toddle to a livery stable, this was a merit that placed Bradford
far above any mere city which had only ladder trucks that barely
approximated our Best.

Well down in the hierarchy for divinity, though actually second
only to The Steamer in working importance during most of my

years in Bradford, was the hose truck, or Patrol, a red wagon which carried a respectable thousand feet of two-and-a-half-inch hose, together with extinguishers, axes, shovels, brooms (for brush fires), pike poles and two short ladders intended for quick work and equipped with hooks for catching over a window-sill or ridge pole.

Least of all our pieces — in size if not in importance — was the jumper hose reel — known as The Reel. It was essentially a larger-size, professional version of the two-wheel hose carts you see in industrial plants today. It could be attached like a trailer to the after end of The Steamer, and for laying additional hose when The Steamer was hooked up to a hydrant, it could be snatched around by a crew of men afoot, hauling it by means of a T-shaped pole which was fitted with chain extensions.

During the last two years I lived in Bradford, The Reel came to take a kind of precedence over The Patrol, as the result of a regrettable incident involving the latter's horses.

To describe this happening, it is necessary to explain the arrangements which prevailed in Bradford for uniting horses to apparatus quickly when an alarm hit, without the town's having to maintain a stable and staff of its own. For our Fire Department, like that of most towns of our size, had no full-time employees.

The horses were kept in Heber Lambert's livery stable, which was up an alley just across Pratt Street from the Town House. Livery stables, in that civilized age, were not only twenty-four-hour-service establishments but social centers as well.

Every day, from about noon on, the operations of a stable's paid hands were watched over by a corps of citizens who sat in back-tilted chairs, the better to pursue their vocation of whittling. At night these same citizens, with reinforcements from the underprivileged, or employed, class, played cards, yarned and did a moderate amount of drinking in privacy appropriate to a no-license town in a local option state. By the small hours when these volunteers left, the early-morning carriage-washers had begun to arrive, to make the buggies used by last night's sparking couples ready for this morning's drummers. From six o'clock on, these, with the hostlers and casual droppers-in kept the place well populated until the whittlers began to drift back for another tour of duty.

So there were always plenty of people at places like Heber Lambert's to slap harness on horses, to drive them at a trot across to the Town House and to hitch them swiftly to the apparatus. At Heber's, many of these people, including Heber himself, were volunteer members of the Department. Heber drove The Hook.

Though all the horses for our fire apparatus resided at Lambert's, only two of them belonged to the town: the pair of big dapple-grays that pulled The Steamer.

Bessie, speedster of The Hook, was Heber Lambert's own property, his personal buggy-horse, or rather his personal fire horse. He never rented her to even the most persuasive and opulent drummer, or took her on his own occasions farther than a short dash from the Town House.

In fact, Heber himself went rarely very far from the Square. On days when other livery-stable proprietors went off to the Readville Races or the Brockton Fair, Heber hung close to the center of town, in the sure knowledge that not he — nor anyone else — could ever hope to see a finer piece of horseflesh than Bessie between the sharves (shafts to you) of The Hook.

His ownership of Bessie and his zeal in keeping her at his own expense ever ready for the town's service, insured for Heber two prerogatives: driving Bessie in The Hook, at which he was superb, and being Captain of the Ladder Company, at which his merits were debatable — and debated, for reasons which I shall explain. But while many citizens would have preferred to see our ladders more expertly handled, the Selectmen knew a good thing when they had it, and Heber's interests were safely vested.

During most of my years in Bradford, The Patrol was drawn by a pair of blacks whose services were paid for as used. These were owned by Heber in partnership with Bratton, the undertaker. At an ordinary funeral, one of them would haul the hearse, the other the leading hack, in which the chief mourners rode. But for high-toned, or two-horse-hearse funerals, they did pair duty very handsomely in a patent-leather harness with black plumes. Since such ostentation was rare in our town, the two blacks, who were nobody's fools, began to associate being paired together with the pleasure of galloping to fires. This was not realized for a long time, since the blacks, when separate, showed no more than an ear-pricking interest in the distant uproar of a fire.

But there came a day when the mortal remains of old Pelatiah Newell, a citizen of years, piety and substance, were to be planted in Greenwood Cemetery with pomp befitting one of Bradford's pioneer millowners. It was, of course, a two-horse-hearse job and the blacks were at their nobbiest, with plumes fluttering in the breeze.

The preaching at the house was over, and the procession, headed by the hearse, was starting sedately down Elm Street when the alarm blew for a fire at Standish and Hancock. To reach this location, the Fire Department would have to go tearing across the head of the funeral procession like Togo crossing the T of the Russian fleet at Tsushima.

This maneuver was executed with spirit just as the procession neared the foot of Elm Street. First appeared a stream of running men and boys. The blacks looked expectantly. Then The Hook went by, with Heber holding a nice pair of lines on the speeding Bessie. The blacks stretched their necks and went into a fast walk. Now, heralded by the clangor of its gong, came The Steamer, belching sparks and leaving in its wake a trail of pine-smelling smoke. The blacks snorted, bridled and were with difficulty restrained by the venerable Asa Codman, our town's invariable hearse-driver.

But when, after an interval longer than usual, The Patrol appeared, bouncing along behind a pair of sorry, mismatched nags that would have looked better in a hayrack, the blacks reared, plunged and took off.

From their start to the foot of Elm Street, the distance was a good hundred yards and slightly downgrade. So by the time the blacks reached the Library corner they were doing an estimated 2:15, which was nice going for a pair to pole. Coming to the turn, they leaned expertly inward to hold their speed and plunged around at a dead gallop, for all the world like a team in Barnum & Bailey's Great Chariot Race — hoofs drumming, harness creaking, plumes aflutter. The hearse swept after them, skid-

ding over the roadway in a shower of gravel while Asa Codman
hung on for his life. After the turn he managed to get braced
again, but by this time the blacks were in the stretch and knew
it. Asa couldn't have stopped them if he had been Ben Hur himself. There were, indeed, witnesses who claimed afterward that
in the last furlong, as they were overhauling The Patrol, Asa hit
'em a larrup with the end of the reins. However that may be, the
equipage — blacks, plumes, Asa, hearse, Pelatiah and all — finished in the money, and not even sweating.

Perhaps if the fire had been a really big one, this outrage
might have been overshadowed and overlooked. But it was only
Mrs. Harney's henhouse, and was so quickly battered out by a
single stream that it left the blacks' performance standing out
like Sheridan's ride from Winchester. Their reputation as hearse-
horses was gone; Heber and Bratton had to sell them. The Selectmen, though powerfully attracted, couldn't see buying the
pair just for The Patrol. So the blacks went to Boston, where
they found their true vocation hauling a light, fast Chemical.

Heber might have been willing to put their successors at the
town's service, but Bratton wasn't. This left the town dependent
upon pickup teams for The Patrol, and these, even when readily
available, were apt to be slow. So during the last two years of
my stay in Bradford, the problem of immediate hose at a fire
was handled by attaching The Reel, trailer-fashion, to the rear
of The Steamer, which thus got a first installment of hose to the
scene without appreciable delay, leaving The Patrol to arrive
with the rest when, as and if a haphazard pair of horses could
get it there.

Now The Patrol's only remaining vestige of its old glory was
the second-rate one of covering brush fires, for which purpose it
was granted the use of The Steamer's dapple-grays.

For this species of fire, which was very common in April and
fairly common in October, there was little hurry. The alarm whistle didn't even signify what part of town the fire was in — just
ten blasts for what we called "Fire in the Woods." A dozen or so
firemen then assembled leisurely at the Town House, piled onto
The Patrol with their brooms and shovels and trotted off decorously to attend to whatever bonfire had got away from its pro-

prietor. Even kids could usually keep within sight of The Patrol on such missions, though why we did so, I don't know. Indeed, I remember only one brush fire in all my years in Bradford that turned into anything worth attending.

Young Mr. Williston, trial preacher at the Congregationalist church, zealous to make a good impression, set out to clear up the parsonage grounds and concoct a powerful sermon at one and the same time. He would rake a little, thinking up good, hot blasts as he went, then drop his rake and duck into the house to get the telling passages down on paper while they were fresh and sizzling in his mind.

This was all right until he started the bonfire part of the proceedings. Unfortunately, at that stage he was getting hotter than a firecracker with powerful thoughts. One of these drove him in on the run, to write; it het itself into incandescence; he got involved in wrestling with it — and by the time he emerged from ecstasy, the fire was in among the Concord grape vines.

As it happened, the parsonage had a telephone — a rare enough convenience for a Man of God in those days. So Mr. Williston was able to get word quickly down to Heber Lambert's that the bonfire had got away. Heber strolled over to the Town House, pulled number 10 on the Gamewell alarm system, and the leisurely process of getting under way for a brush fire began.

By ill chance, however, the parsonage grape vines ran right up the side of Old Mr. Dunbar's privy next door — one of the few backhouses in our town that were still operational. So by the time The Patrol got there, they had a nice little blaze to deal with.

There was sufficient hydrant pressure to knock this over both metaphorically and literally, without sending for The Steamer. But restraining Old Mr. Dunbar from his announced intention of heaving the parson into the newly opened pit took the united efforts of everybody who wasn't on the hose-pipe, for Old Mr. Dunbar was a peppery old party who had fought as a cavalryman under Buford at Gettysburg and cared neither for numbers nor divinity. "Hell's crupper!" he bawled, as they held him back, "what if he *is* a minister? Leonidas Polk was a god-damn *bishop!*"

By this time several of Mr. Williston's putative parishioners had arrived. Among them was Major Capen, who had been at Gettysburg also, as one of Warren's Engineers, and who, like most engineers, hated the cavalry for going around blowing up bridges that the engineers had to build all over again. He, too, had certain ideas derived from a quick survey of the terrain, and one of them was about what ought to be done right now with an unsanitary old fool too pigheaded to put in modern plumbing. It was not until Nick Banton fished his police helmet out from under the seat of The Patrol and did a quick change from fireman to Chief of Police, that Mr. Williston's runaway bonfire was finally got under what firemen call Control.

23.

TOCSINS, TACTICS
AND TECHNIQUES

A Fire — that is, the whole proceeding as distinct from the fire which occasioned it — began in Bradford with the sounding of the alarm. We had a box system that sketchily covered the built-up part of town. Pulling any box set off automatic machinery that blew the alarm whistle in a sequence of blasts, the number of which indicated the location of the box.

I say whistle, but actually ours was a combination of whistle and bell. I don't know whether this was intended as a sort of two-strings-to-your-bow insurance against mechanical failure, or whether it was designed to make our alarm distinguishable from those of near-by towns. But the combined effect was superb, for both whistle and bell were magnificent examples of their kind. The whistle was on the Gas House. It was deep, powerful and vibrant, hoarse and hollow, like the bellow of some Bull of Bashan, and when it let go in the middle of a still winter's night, it was enough to lift you right out of bed. The bell, though actuated by the same electrical system, was that of our Congregational church. It was a whopper of a bell that went "Bar-rum-m-m!" with innard-jarring overtones, at the end of each blast of the whistle.

A Fire, then, started with the measured "WHOOO-BAR-UM-M-M! WHOO-BARUM-M-M!" of the alarm which, being counted by every resident, indicated upon reference to a printed card the location of the blaze. Such cards were given out by merchants as more interesting and less expensive than calendars, and it was an improvident boy or man who ever went anywhere without such a card in his hip pocket.

So, immediately upon completion of the first round of the alarm, people lit out, streaking through the streets, across lots and through each other's yards for the scene of the hoped-for conflagration. When I say "people" I mean, of course, all people who counted. That is, boys, volunteer firemen, gentlemen of independent spirit and old men who could still leg it at a lively hiper. Women, girls, and men who thought more of their work than of going to fires were not, for such occasions, people.

Meanwhile, Heber Lambert's livery stable would have sprung into action, and the horses, with traces looped up in overhand knots, and driven by running men afoot, would be clattering over to the Town House.

Now the chief funtionaries would arrive on the run. These were, in order of importance and usually of appearance:

Nick Banton, Chief of the town's two-man police force, arriving in his *alter ego* capacity of Assistant Fire Chief. To see Nick — one of the world's handsomest cops (even in an age when cops were all majestic in bell-crowned helmets and belted frock coats) — leave his post as chief ornament of the Square, and go streaking like the wind for the Town House — all two hundred pounds of him — at the first bellow of the whistle, was to realize once again what every Bradfordian knew in his heart: that our town was safe from all manner of harm so long as Nick Banton watched over it.

Jim Hickey, Chief of the Fire Department and the other half of the police force, arrived next. How he managed this, no one ever knew, for Jim was the night-duty cop, and supposed to sleep during the daylight hours. But while Jim was in appearance only a sepia-print of Nick (being red-headed, red-moustached and built on a smaller scale), he was an awful smart operator. In fact, in his capacity of cop he laid more malefactors by the heels than Nick did — partly because in the nighttime he had more opportunity, partly because, lacking Nick's forbidding exterior, he had to rely on guile. In dealing with fire, which is rarely cowed by a level look and a grim jaw, Jim was Nick's superior, for he was a quick man at sizing up a blaze and a wily one in dealing with it.

Third to arrive — but only by reason of distance — was John Ogilvie, Engineer of The Steamer. John was maintenance engineer at Porter's factory. Gaunt, red-moustached and serious, father (by a good-natured, buxom wife) of an endless brood of kids, John Ogilvie was a Scottish steamship engineer come ashore. And like a good marine engineer, he was endlessly industrious, resourceful, methodical and careful. Porter's boiler and engine rooms were marvels of immaculateness and readiness. He had things, moreover, so well organized that no matter how critical the stage of a repair or adjustment at the factory, he could leave it in charge of an assistant and be off at the first sound of the alarm, on the run for the Town House, a quarter-mile away.

By the time John got there, Nick would have thrown open the doors to the apparatus, lighted the fire under The Steamer and seen to the hitching up of the horses. Other firemen whose employment was on or near the Square would have arrived. So Nick would spring to the driver's seat, horse-holders would let go the heads of the dapple-grays, and the Bradford Fire Department would emerge from seclusion, piece after piece, clanging and yammering and clattering away in full cry.

First off was always The Hook, behind the powerful Bessie and with Heber at the reins. Often they would be clear through the Square before The Steamer got out into Pratt Street, and like as not would have arrived at the scene of the Fire before The Patrol had even got under way with its load of late-coming volunteers.

It was now that Heber really Went into Action. Everybody agreed that it *was* action; in fact, that was what spoilsport property-owners complained of. He would drive Bessie and The Hook right up on the lawn, if there was one, or get them otherwise as near to the building as possible, then leap to the ground and single-handed set about decking the house with ladders.

Heber was a slight, spare, intensely nervous man, with long black hair parted in the middle and plastered down, in the fashion of a Charles Dana Gibson drawing, on either side of his face. When he got going, the hair would come unstuck and hang in a fringe right down across his blazing eyes, like a bead portiere half revealing a room lit by twin Rochester burners. As in the case of so many excitable small men, Heber could heave prodigious weights when the fit was on him.

And at a Fire it was on. He would snatch the topmost ladder from The Hook, stagger with it across intervening flower-beds, raise it in the manner of a huge war club and slam it against the building. If the eaves of the house were low, this would mean merely that Heber banged twin dents with the upper end of the ladder in the projecting shingles and roof gutters; if the eaves were high, so that the ladder could get under them, the chances were excellent that Heber would fetch a window so squarely that glass, muntins, sashes and all would fly like chaffy grain beneath the thresher's flail. But even before the showering fragments hit the ground, Heber would be off like an antelope, to get another ladder from The Hook. It did not matter what part of the building showed signs of fire, or whether it was actually afire at all; Heber covered it with ladders like a hamburger buried in potatoes *alumette*. Alone and unaided he gave it everything The Hook had except the last, or forty-five-foot extension ladder, to erect which he had to wait for help.

By now, of course, The Steamer would have arrived and hooked up to the nearest hydrant. Jim would have plunged inside the building to investigate while Nick got a tentative line of two-and-one-half-inch hose laid to the scene. John Ogilvie would be standing by the gauges, feeding just enough steam to the pumps to give them standby pressure, and ready at the cry of "Water" to turn The Steamer loose in full thunder.

Then The Patrol would draw up, its volunteers jumping off it and running with extinguishers, axes, pike poles and other impedimenta to be ready for orders from Nick. Other volunteers, driving up in buggies or grocery wagons, or panting after on foot, would be asking the fireman's perennial question, "Whatta we got?" — unless, of course, it was evident that they had got a real fire to deal with. But if it was only a chimney fire or a roast of beef ablaze in an over-het oven, or a housewife's imagination, most of them would go around, climbing various of Heber's ladders and rubbering into their fellow townsman's second-story windows.

At this point, Heber would come galumphing up at the head of a crew bearing the extension ladder off The Hook. Usually it was an impromptu crew, commandeered by Heber from arrivals as they came.

Now, the raising of an extension ladder can be a pretty piece of work when done by well-trained firemen. Such a crew snakes it out of its bed on the ladder truck, marches it to its appointed place and lays it down parallel to the wall of the building and a sufficient distance away. It is not yet extended. Their object is first to raise it to the vertical; then, steadying it there with attached poles known as "tormentors," to hoist its extension into the air; then to pivot the ladder, still vertical, so that it faces the building; and finally to lower it gently against the structure.

I describe this highly particular procedure partly because I shall have occasion to refer to it again, but mostly to make clear that it is an operation which must either be performed by a well-trained crew or, if attempted by haphazard well-wishers, can be effected only with one hell of a lot of bawling, pointing, running-around, sweating and shoving-into-position of bewildered assistants. This was usually the case when Heber got to the extension-ladder finale of his operations; unless there was real need for a ladder of such dimensions, the skilled men were otherwise occupied, so Heber had to make shift with such guerrillas or partisans as were itching for action. Normally, then, the extension ladder would get up only well along in the proceedings.

But when it was up, it was up for all the world to see, for Heber's crew invariably hoisted the fly, like Old Glory in the ribald song old Mr. Dunbar used to sing, "to the top of the pole." And since there were no houses in our town with more than two stories and an attic, and many were only a story and a half in height, Heber's ladder stuck up above them like Jacob's reaching clear to Heaven itself. Adjourning, then, to The Hook, Heber would exhume from beneath the seat certain carefully folded cloths, with which he would give Bessie an expert rub-down, pausing now and then to raise a fond eye to the pinnacle of his extension ladder.

In all these techniques, of course, we boys were knowledgeable as so many railbirds at a race track. We believed there was not in the entire universe a fire department as smart as ours. "Smart," that is, in the colloquial sense of clever, ingenious, resourceful — the only meaning ever given that word in small-town usage of the Old Colony. Fortunately for us, there was no one to raise questions by using "smart" in its modern, advertising sense of snappily turned out.

For this was our secret sorrow, never acknowledged even to one another: the Bradford Fire Department had no firemen's hats or rubber coats, or, indeed, boots, except such as its individual members owned and happened to wear. These glamorous trappings we knew only from pictures of city firemen. Our town would not provide them. The Selectmen considered it enough to have bought (some time in the 80's) a couple of dozen surplus Civil War overcoats — the long blue kind with capes. But even these were never worn except in dead of winter. Our firemen did their fire fighting (as merchant sailormen do their seafaring) in whatever old clothes they chose.

Many years later I was to learn at first hand that the fireman's helmet of traditional form is a clumsy, uncomfortable thing to wear — worse still to work in — and that the pleasure of taking it off when a fire is over is comparable with the proverbial delight of ceasing to hit yourself over the head with a brick. But at ten or twelve I would rather have had one than a halo — and, liefer than that, have seen our firemen outfitted with them to the last man. Often, studying in secret the subtle abruptness of curve and flare in firemen's helmets as shown in the pages of *St. Nicholas* or *The Youth's Companion,* I used to pray (with a devotion I wish I could muster today) that the Bradford Fire Department might one day be made perfect with this last sign of grace. But only in secret! To have betrayed, even to my brother, a doubt of the Fire Department's perfection would have been like admitting that our father could not, if he wanted to, lick John L. Sullivan.

24

VERSUS THE KITCHEN STOVE

The way my grandmother looked at it, the kitchen range was a sparring partner. Her workouts with it were spirited but friendly, and if the range occasionally won, why that didn't matter much, because everybody had a good time. This was in contradistinction to her slugfests against the Demon Rum and his surporters, which were grudge fights with a horseshoe in every glove. In these, she took it hard whenever the Demon got the decision, as he sometimes did in the town of Bradford.

At cooking my grandmother was like a boxer with a dependable left, an utterly unpredictable right, a passion for the roundhouse swing and a weakness for figuring out trick punches that often as not landed on her own jaw.

She was adept at certain everyday concoctions. Her doughnuts were small, decisive, crusty and so flavorsome it was hard to say whether they were better crisp and hot out of the kettle or aged to firmness by a week or so in the big stoneware jar she never allowed to get empty. Needless to say, they were never fried in anything but the choicest chicken fat. Her codfish balls were likewise above criticism, even in the Codfish State. Her brown-bread was a masterpiece, of which the components were assembled on Friday, so that there would be ample time for the loaf to steam on Saturday in a special dish with a hollow tube through the center to insure even cooking. Her baked beans were also impeccably built, and I use the term "built" advisedly, for she laid them down in the pot layer by layer, with due attention to the precise amount and position of pork and onion bits, and to the timing and proportion of molasses. In the construction of a chowder she was a master hand, whether the basis of the chowder was clams, lobster or fish. And her high point of accomplishment was, perhaps, that form of very thick swordfish chowder,

180 proof in seafood content and only sluggishly liquid, known
Down East as a "smother."

On the other hand, she was lamentable at most breadstuffs,
which she put together by eye, like a painter mixing colors on a
palette. Her johnnycake, to be sure, would have been considered
fine in other sections of the country, but it fell far short of New
England standards. And her blueberry muffins were often passable, since she had a nice eye for the blues and purples. Her flap-
jacks may or may not have been good; they were in my time only
thin blotters for the absorption of maple syrup by the quart.

But by common, ordinary bread (then invariably baked in the
home) my grandmother was regularly and utterly defeated. Part
of this failure was traceable to the fact that she had not the
patience to knead it by hand, but relied on a mechanical bread-
kneader which was supposed to be turned by one of us boys.
This consisted of a heavily tinned pail clamped to a table, and
with a clamped-on metal top. A crank on this top revolved a
snake-spiral of rod inside. Between the natural indolence of my
brother and myself and the impatience of my grandmother, our
bread, when she made it, never got stirred enough, so that even
if it had had the proper proportion of ingredients (which I
doubt) it was foredoomed to failure.

Fortunately, our hired girls and hired women were all good at
bread. And a great inducement to treat them courteously was the
prospect of getting them to cut off for you on Wednesdays the
end-slice of a loaf so hot from the oven that butter instantly
melted into it and permeated it as thoroughly and sublimely as
culture permeates the town of Boston, adding to its natural
fragrance a richness alike delightful in taste and somnolent in
aftereffect.

Most of our hired females were good, too, at soda-biscuits, but
the superior of them all, and for my money the uncrowned lady-
champion of the soda-biscuit, was an elderly relative — a courtesy
great-aunt — who used to visit us once a year. Aunt Vestie had
the divine gift of being able to produce about a quarter-acre of
biscuits, light yet substantial, fluffy but not dry, and to get them
onto the table in piping-hot relays, together with such a flow of

utterly admirable chicken gravy as would fill a small-size swimming pool.

Aunt Vestie was also the Vermeer of apple turnovers and the Rembrandt of pies, whether apple, blueberry, cherry, rhubarb, mince, pumpkin or lemon meringue.

The hired girls in our New England succession were uniformly good at apple pie, as you might expect in a section of the country where that dish was the breakfast-food *par excellence,* and though none of them could touch Aunt Vestie, any one of them could have given my grandmother cards and spades on apple or any other kind of pie, and won hands down.

Of my grandmother's pies, the less said the better. Or, perhaps, the more. The interiors of them were good enough — and in the case of her mince pies occasionally superb, for she was an imaginative composer. But the crusts would better have been taken down town and sold to Mr. Burrell, the cobbler.

Sometimes you hear it said by exaggerators that such-and-such a woman can't even boil an egg. Well, my grandmother really couldn't. Not reliably.

The reason for this was that she refused to have any truck with a clock or sandglass or other mechanical device for timing the boiling of an egg. She had her own measure, which was akin to the Down-East fisherman's way of counting off seconds by chanting, "One chimpanzee, two champanzee," and so on. Her timer was a song.

This song she had learned from her grandmother, who in turn had learned it in George Washington's day from *her* grandmother. This made it old and presumably reliable. It went like this:

> Old Mother Widdle-Waddle jumped out of bed
> And out of the window she stuck her old head,
> Crying, "John, John, John! The gray goose is gone
> And the fox has left this town-O."
>
> Then John went out on yonder hill
> And blew his horn both loud and shrill.
> "Zooks!" says the fox. "We've music still
> As we go through this town-O."

When sung deliberately, but not too much so, this song will take exactly thirty seconds. So the required number of rounds will make up to any measure of minutes. But if you are feeling brisk, as my grandmother usually was in the morning, then a supposed three-minute egg is likely to leer up at the expectant eater like the watery eye of a lush from a barroom floor. Or if, intending to do an egg to that precise, four-and-one-half-minute borderline between firmness and hardness, you get to planning out a battle with your sewing machine and so lose count of the stanzas and sing one or two more to make sure, why then that egg will be like one of Uncle George's billiard balls, only not quite so round.

To offset these failings, my grandmother had a creative artist's imagination in the concoction of multi-ingredient dishes such as soups, stews, sauces and poultry-stuffings. She would, for example, cheerfully combine the oysters-and-juice component of oyster stew with beef broth in place of milk. On one memorable occasion, indeed, she stepped up the horsepower of this with a quart or two of some rare variety of mushrooms which my father had collected in his capacity of botanist, producing thereby a brew of Olympian merit, however dreadful you may think it sounds. Ever afterward she itched to repeat this dish, with fungi of her own choice, and was only restrained from poisoning us all by the warnings of my father, who knew the vegetable growths of that region as a dick in the river-front section of New York knows his gunmen.

But she was not dependent on rare ingredients. She had a high opinion of the common peanut. If peanuts were as hard to get and as expensive as truffles, she maintained, chefs would lie awake of nights dreaming up ways to use them. So she ground up fresh-roasted peanuts in the meat chopper and heaved a handful of them into sauces, or a double handful into chicken or turkey stuffing, in place of chestnuts. Results: excellent. On the other hand, she became possessed of the idea that since peanuts were legumes, a gob of peanut butter would improve any lentil soup, and finding one gob reasonably palatable, went on trying more and more gobs with each new batch of soup, until even my father (who rarely noticed what he was eating) complained that if this was black bean soup he was Booker T. Washington.

Her weakness for peanuts was balanced by a dark suspicion of certain other common vegetables. Tomatoes had been regarded in her grandparents' day as poisonous (they were then known as "love apples"), and she was always wary of them. It was to her a triumphant confirmation of this caution when a big kettleful of sealed Mason jars, in which she had been persuaded by Mrs. Buzzell to attempt the canning of tomatoes, came to a boil and exploded, one after the other, like so many time bombs, plastering the ceiling and walls of the kitchen with gory red. She held that a man who ate parsnips was a homicidal maniac lying in wait for victims under the camouflage of sanity, and warned us that we would rue the day we ever trusted anyone who could stomach tapioca.

Sometimes she would start to compose a dish with Mrs. Buzzell acting in a consultant capacity. Mrs. Buzzell was, as I have said, an expert. But like most experts who have survived with their sanity, she was used to having her counsel disregarded or taken in reverse. To protect the best interests of her clients in such situations, she had adopted the experts' tried-and-proved stratagem of offsetting every inept move on the part of the client with an over-ept move of her own. And so there was an even chance that after a long succession of move and counter-move, the collaboration might turn out on the right side of acceptability.

This happened, one day, in a way that produced what was probably the worst dish we ever had in our house — possibly the worst in any house in Bradford, if not in the world. This was their devil-inspired version of Terrapin à la Maryland.

One day an enormous snapping turtle wandered into our yard and I, discovering him there, engaged him with a long stick. Now, you may think the order of *Chelonia* are sluggish, but if so you have had no combat experience with *Chelydra serpentina,* the common snapping turtle. He is as agile a defensive footworker as you want to see; you circle around him and he turns with you, keeping that formidable head stuck out at you with jaws open, making a hissing noise and snapping viciously at anything you put within his reach. If, remembering what it says in *The Swiss*

Family Robinson, you flop him over on his back with your stick, he flops right back again and makes a dash for you like a bull after a cautious, and by this time rather scared, matador.

My grandmother, hearing my yelps, came out, saw the situation, and bidding me hold the monster in play with my stick, worked around to his rear. There, watching her chance, she grabbed him by his big pyramidal tail and hoisted him, wriggling and snapping, right off the ground. I would sooner have hefted a wildcat. My grandmother carried him swiftly to the chopping-block near by, and with one sure, clean stroke of the hatchet we kept there for decapitating chickens, lopped off his big, wicked head.

My grandmother then took the body of the snapper, plus head, into the house, where she entered into consultation with Mrs. Buzzell about the proper use and disposition of the carcass. Snapping turtles, as everybody knew, made good eating; their meat, when properly prepared, was not unlike beef in flavor, with the small-scale, gristly texture of some parts of leg of lamb.

Mrs. Buzzell, who in her time had visited a place called Pimlico near Baltimore, and afterward invested the proceeds of a business venture there in a dinner of Terrapin Maryland, advised that this was the way of all ways to transfigure a late chelonian. She didn't know precisely how it was done, but she described the end-result. That was all my grandmother needed. She would no more have consulted a cookbook about the intervening steps than Willie Hoppe would have used a bridge on the billiard table.

Now, it may be that my grandmother, in preparing the cadaver, neglected to remove the gall bladder and other glandular sources of the snapper's viciousness.

Or it may be that the sauce was the trouble. My grandmother originally concocted it out of what she judged from Mrs. Buzzell's description to be the approximately correct ingredients. But in place of sherry she used some cider out of a jug we had on hand. It was going hard, which of course would mean it would normally have to be thrown away. So she put a generous dollop into the sauce.

To Mrs. Buzzell's experienced palate, the result of this was pallid. She estimated, however, that the only trouble was that the sauce was a little short of sherry in alcoholic content. So she went and got a big bottle of Lydia E. Pinkham's Vegetable Compound, which at that time included (for medicinal and preservative purposes only) a respectable percentage of C_2H_6O. She poured a cupful of this into the sauce.

To the strength of this, my grandmother took exception. She diluted it with an equal quantity of cider. Mrs. Buzzell snorted at the result, and added an offsetting slug of Lydia Pinkham. And so they worked alternately toward a compromise, except that on what should have been the very last balancing smidgin of cider, my grandmother's hand slipped by about a cupful, and this required balancing with Lydia Pinkham all over again.

All this time, the snapping-turtle-alias-terrapin had been stewing away, complete with glands, both ordinary and ductless.

So what do you expect? That night, not only the family but Mrs. Buzzell refused a second mouthful of the concoction and my grandmother herself gagged on the third. On the next day our hens wouldn't touch it, and three days later Mr. Leach, the milkman, who on his return trips collected swill for his livestock, took occasion to remark darkly to my grandmother that *somebody* along his route had been trying to poison his pigs.

My grandmother's battles with the stove were not limited to the terrain of food. Sometimes the stove defied her by smoking. When this happened — as when a sparring partner forgets himself and pastes the champ on the nose — you could expect fireworks. And on one such occasion we got them — quite literally.

One morning an owl or something had got stuck in the kitchen chimney. So when my grandmother touched off a carefully laid structure of paper, kindling wood and coal in the stove, the kitchen filled at once with choking blue smoke. Diagnosing the trouble from long experience with country chimneys, my grandmother's first impulse was to adopt the old-fashioned remedy of pouring a hod or two of coal into the top of the chimney. We did, in fact, bring a couple of hods upstairs to the window that gave out on to the gable over the kitchen end of the house. But my grandmother judged this too risky an operation if the obstruction could be dislodged by other means.

Descending, she went over to Mrs. Tenney's and there borrowed an enormous antique fireplace-bellows. She next laid a new fire in the stove — this one entirely of fine pine kindling. Lighting this, she blew it with the bellows into a roar that went right through the piping and up into the chimney, where in no time it incinerated and burned into nothingness the owl or whatever it was.

Unfortunately, the flame also set fire to the soot in the chimney, which immediately started roaring like an overgrown and angry stove, and belching flames and showers of sparks from its top.

In such a situation householders customarily turned in a fire alarm, and my brother and I were dying to run and pull Box 41, at the corner of Oak and Hollis. But my grandmother, who had been raised in country districts where fire departments were unheard of, forbade us. She would deal with the conflagration herself.

First she tossed onto the stove end of the fire a couple of handfuls of salt and shut all the drafts. When this didn't greatly reduce the roar, she got out all our old blankets, instructing my brother and me meanwhile to run both spigots of water into the bathtub. Into this she threw the blankets. Then we helped her out the back window and astride of the ridgepole of the kitchen ell, and handed her the blankets, one by one. These she spread out over the shingles on either side of the roof nearest the chimney, where the sparks were falling. As she did so, she calmly explained that this was the device by which her mother had kept the big house down in Maine from catching fire, the night the barn burned down.

This done, she called for the two hods of coal that were standing by, and dumped them one after the other into the open top of the chimney. The falling coal dislodged what was left of the soot, the fire stopped as abruptly as it had begun, and my grandmother crawled back along the ridgepole remarking that that was the end of *that* owl. Or whatever it was.

25.

THE NIGHT THAT
BEALS'S BLOCK BURNED UP

To hear me tell it, you would think the town of Bradford was continually breaking out into flames like some musicomedienne bursting into song.

In point of sober fact, most fires in Bradford were abortive ones. This seems strange in retrospect, considering that the town in the years of 1900-1908 was mostly kerosene-lighted and coal-range fed, that its buildings were chiefly of wood, ancient and built without benefit of fire laws, that few homes had telephones, that the town's scant two dozen alarm boxes were very widely spaced, and that the Fire Department was on a strictly volunteer basis. Yet there it is: We had relatively few fires that were any good. Now and then a house would give us a respectable show of flame, smoke and the smell of burning paint-covered wood on one corner, and would call forth The Steamer's real powers before it was cooled off. But most fires in Bradford were either practically fireless or were otherwise bitterly disappointing.

For instance, there was Chase's barn, way out on the open plains south of town. It went up one night in a fine blaze that lit up the countryside for miles around, but as a Fire it was a disappointment because there was no water after the well ran dry in the first minute, and the Fire Department couldn't perform. There was the shoddy-mill in the West End that burned one day when the snow was so deep nobody (nobody in our sense, that is) could get out there to attend it. And perhaps the sourest flop of them all was the Parochial School.

Not that this wasn't a good Fire in every respect but one. It happened on a free Saturday morning; the whole shebang burned with great, soaring, whirling gusts of flame and showers of sparks when floors fell; The Steamer roared and thundered for hours, whistling frequently for more coal; The Patrol laid a perfect spaghetti-plate of hose all over the lot; even Heber Lambert's extension ladder was needed — was, in fact, swiftly raised by trained hands under the command of Jim Hickey himself. . . . But all this was as gall and wormwood to us. A school burning up — and it wasn't our school! Sharper than a serpent's tooth is the unmerited good fortune of a friend, and those who felt its bite most deeply were the Catholic boys themselves, most of whom went to the town schools along with the rest of us. They had to stand helpless with rage while their happier co-religionists circulated among the crowd, calling for organized cheers at the collapse of every well-hated classroom. . . .

Such other real fires as the town had during most of the years of my residence took place, exasperatingly enough, during the summer absences of my brother and myself, who were annually rusticated to a farm in Maine. So we were almost reduced to the pusillanimous extreme of basing our rationale of the Bradford Fire Department's might upon the pale contention that it put out fires.

Almost, that is, until the night that Beals's Block burned up.

Beals's Block was the principal building on the Square. The only brick building on the Square, and one of the few brick structures in town, it stood right across Pratt Street from the Town House, directly in front of the trolley junction, catty-corner from the horse trough. It housed on its lower floor Beals's Cash Store, an emporium about the size of two side-street city stores thrown into one by knocking a hole in their separating partition. In fact, there was such a separating partition, and of brick, and its existence probably saved, in the event, all the rest of the buildings on the Square.

On the second floor, reached by an entrance alongside Beals's Christmas-toy, hardware and rubber-boot window, were various offices, occupied by business and professional people. I remember these in detail, because the largest of them was the dental establishment of Boxer Parton's father, in the back-room workshop of which Boxer and his friends were allowed to play among the semi-finished store teeth, plaster-of-Paris and other out-of-sight impedimenta of the dentist's art. When these lost interest we would explore the central hallway of the second floor and make friends with the occupants of the other offices.

These included: Judge Dearden, the town's most respected lawyer; Willie Ridgeway, Bradford's gifted piano teacher; Zephaniah Hobbs, watch, clock and doorbell repairing, spectacles fitted, also insurance and local representative of Strout's Farm Agency; Edward Everett Hale ("Bottlenose") Butterworth, photographer, children a specialty, a grouch if ever there was one, who hated his business and especially his squalling subjects, and who spent most of his time messing with inventions, none of which ever quite came off; Sadie Schnitzler, millinery and bonnets, a blonde with an hour-glass figure who was a great favorite of ours, but even more so of visiting drummers who used to hang around trying to get her to go buggy-riding.

Above the second floor, and reached by a ladder through a trapdoor, was a half-attic, used by Mr. Beals for the storage of a preposterous accumulation of late-Nineteenth Century unsalables, as who should know if not my brother and I who, with Boxer Parton, used to ascend that ladder on rainy Saturdays and explore among dress-dummies with Grecian Bend figures generously built out as to their *derrières*; stacks of Peters' Patent Collapsible Opera Hats; bales of Clemson's Cleanable Cuffs, Collars and Dickies; gross after gross of Meyers's Magic Comb for Hair or Beard; broken cases of Hoskins's Hemlock Oil Blacking for Boots and Shoes; odd lots of Emerson's Electro-Voltaic Kidney Belts, and many another unappreciated novelty of the 70's, 80's and 90's which might yet, as Mr. Beals saw it, come back into public favor.

In one side of the cellar of Beals's Block there was a great store of merchandise waiting to make its appearance, for Mr. Beals bought only twice a year, on trips to Boston and New York; he paid cash to get low prices and he had his purchases shipped in bulk to save freight. On the other side was the heating plant, and beyond it a great number of old barrels tight-packed with slightly used excelsior and other second-hand packing material which Mr. Beals, though not exactly a string-saver, kept around because you never knew when you might need it.

It was somewhere among this hoard of inflammables that fire

started early on a Thursday evening in May of 1908. I know it was a Thursday, because my father had just left for prayer meeting when the alarm hit 5-8, the instantly recognized number of the Square. My brother and I, lighting out down Maple Street, overtook our parent at the corner of Maple and Dutton where he stood hesitating, Bible under arm, obviously torn between Dutton-for-the-Square-and-Pleasure, and Maple-for-the-Church-and-Duty. I like to think that we saved his soul from hell, for he was evidently on the point of yielding to the Devil when we appeared and left him no alternative but exemplary rectitude — right down Maple for the church.

Others were not so virtuous; in Dutton Street we found ourselves among a dozen running men and boys; by the time we turned into Elm it was a crowd. Now you could hear The Steamer thundering in the Square. Everybody put on speed. Even Major Capen, who scorned to run, strode along at a brisk walk holding his cane like a drawn sabre. Swerving to avoid him, I ran smack into George Swan and went down on my breadbasket. My brother ran on, but George picked me up by the coat-collar. " 'Celerity,' " said he, as he dusted me off, " 'is never more admired than by the negligent.' " Years later I learned that that was only Shakespeare, but at the time I thought it was sheer George Swan and repeated it to myself admiringly as I ran on, blowing on my stinging palms.

Once around the corner, however, I forgot palms, George and punditry alike, for there was the Fire — right in Beals's Store, and a regular old Baster of a fire, too. One front show-window had already gone, and where it had been, a great flame was darting in and out like a snake's tongue. Right in front of this, and reflecting its angry light, stood The Steamer, roaring away and adding its own smoke and sparks to the ascending torrent. Heber's ladders were all over the front of the building. One hose line was playing straight into the fiery window, another had disappeared into the smoke-belching doorway.

The Square was rapidly filling up, but a boy can worm through any crowd. I remember that once, deep in a press of grownups, I stumbled and fell over a hose, and that it was iron-hard with pressure and quivering with life. I remember getting down in front, and the sight of the roaring interior of one side of the store, with a whorl of flame shooting up from a stairway somewhere in back and licking along the side-wall shelves and against the pressed-steel-sheathed ceiling. I remember how the hose, playing back and forth, would hit the stacks of shoe boxes or piece-goods ranged on the shelves and send them flying every which way in a shellburst of water, and how the very smoke inside was all orange and shot with whirling, detached wafts of flame. . . .

Then they began throwing things out the second-story windows.

At first these were light things: a volley of Doc Parton's semi-finished store teeth, a dozen flowered and feathered bonnets sailing gaily through the air, a swirl of legal papers, a flight of photographs, a shower of spectacle-lenses. . . . Between salvos the throwers upstairs would hang out the smoking windows, weeping and gasping for breath. Then they would duck back for another armload.

Presently they began heaving the heftier and harder articles. A succession of glass photographic plates scaling through the air drove the crowd (with me pushing energetically among them) back halfway across the Square. From there we watched the cascade: cartons of plaster-of-Paris, alarm clocks, framed pictures and diplomas, legal tomes, looking glasses, developer trays, machinist's vises, hatracks, swivel chairs, a magnificent pier-glass, trays of dental instruments, bookcases, glass-front cabinets, a massive cast-iron copying press, typewriters, carboys of acid, Judge Dearden's roll-top desk, Doc Parton's dental chair, Edward Everett Hale Butterworth's enormous bellows camera. . . .

Somebody shouted, "Come on around back! The goddamn fools are trying to get Willie Ridgeway's grand piano down a ladder," and the crowd was off.

This time, those of us who had been in front ended up in the rear, but we could see the piano, all right, balanced across the sill of a smoking window on the second floor, and held there by gasping men waiting for the ladder.

The ground level here was a story lower than in front, which, in that high-ceilinged building, put the piano beyond the reach of ordinary ladders. But now we saw that the resourceful Heber had got his heavy extension ladder and with the usual pick-up crew was in the act of superintending its raising. They had got it straight up and down, steadied a bit uncertainly by the tormentor-poles, but not yet extended.

Heber's voice rose from the middle of the crowd. "Watch her now, you on the poles, she's going up. . . . All right on the ropes. . . . Heave! Again, heave!" At each heave the top of the ladder rose three or four feet. "Heave! Heave! Heave! . . . . All right, lock her!" The top of the ladder was now forty-five feet in the air, way up among the clouds of smoke that poured from the windows.

Facing it, the piano still hung balanced on its window-sill. A hush fell on the crowd. In the midst of it came Willie Ridgeway's tearful voice: "My STEINway! Oh, my STEINway!"

"Chrissake shut up!" cried a hoarse voice from the window, and Chief Jim Hickey's head appeared. "Heber," he bawled, "you *hurry!* Fire'll be through this floor any minute!"

"We're in the stretch," shouted Heber, "we're just going to swing her." But his overeager crew had already started to pivot the big ladder. And as it turned it leaned — ever so slightly at first — just barely beyond the center of gravity. Not so far but what experienced men — if there had been any on the tormentor-poles — could have caught and brought it back.

"Watch it!" screamed Heber. "Catch it! Hold it, can't you! Grab it, somebody! Grab it! . . . Look out! She's going. . . . Everybody GIT!"

And she went. Slowly at first, at the beginning of her arc, then faster . . . and faster and faster . . . The crowd scattered like dust before a bicycle pump. . . . Fasterandfaster . . . WHAM! ! !

And as the echoes of the ladder reverberated there came an antiphonal sound. . . . CRASH! ! !

It was Willie Ridgeway's Steinway hitting the cement walk at the base of Beals's Block.

Half a minute later Jim Hickey, the last man out, came scrambling down a ladder at the front of the building. He was just in time, for as he set foot on the ground, the fire burst through into the second floor, mushroomed out and roared on up into the half-attic where, among the papier-mâché dress dummies, the celluloid collars, the imitation-amber combs, the hemlock-oil boot dressing and the various patent medicines of high alcoholic content, it really had a time for itself.

Now it was a question of saving not Beals's Block, but the whole rest of the south side of the Square, for the adjoining buildings were all of frame construction and would go like tinder if the fire got through to them. Jim's ultimately successful strategy was based (as I learn from my yellowed copy of the following week's Bradford *Monitor*) on the fact that Beals's Block was divided (however imperfectly) by a central brick partition. West of this, the building was gone. The other half would go, too, but if its going could be slowed, maybe the heat wouldn't get through the brick wall on the east, and touch off Meekins's drugstore.

But the populace didn't know this. And even if they had, there were always, in our town, plenty of stout-hearted souls who believed in Independent Action.

One group of these consisted of the Veteran Firemen whose Association owned and operated (normally for sport) the town's obsolete hand-pump engine, "Kentucky Babe." These enthusiasts conceived the idea of getting out their tub, hooking up to a hydrant at the other end of the Square, and wetting down some of the wooden buildings to the east of Beals's, outside *and* in.

No sooner said than done. One party set off for the Babe's quarters on Commerce Street; another laid hands (without asking) on the Fire Department's Reel, and started to lay a line of hose from the corner down Chase Street, then around the back of the buildings to the east of Beals's.

The Reel was heavy; the going was rough; the first veterans were tuckered out before they ever reached the corner. They were relieved by a score of willing admirers, but these, too, were winded by the time they got The Reel down behind the buildings, laying a ribbon of hose behind. Here they were succeeded by others, and these by others still with such frequency that by the time they reached the mid-block alley in back, no one pulling The Reel had any idea where they were supposed to go. All they knew was that they were heroically laying hose. A new relief, taking hold at this point, snatched The Reel up the alley toward the Square again, and emerging there, gave way to replacements who headed The Reel (still spilling its hose behind) east again, toward the Chase Street corner. Arriving there, exhausted, they were glad to come upon an unattached end of hose to which (so common sense seemed to indicate) their line ought to be coupled. So they coupled up the two ends, and went back mopping their foreheads and full of virtue, to watch the Fire.

Actually, of course, what they had hitched up to was the original end of the hose, where it had been dropped at the start of The Reel's journey. So now there was a complete circuit of utterly empty hose, without beginning or end, running all around half the buildings on the Square.

Nor was there any one of the original planners present to give a damn, for the veterans had all gone up to their Commerce Street quarters, where they were holding an indignation meeting: Jim Hickey, getting wind of their plan, had sent a man with stern orders for them to stay away from any hydrants, lest the water pressure, badly needed at The Steamer, should fail entirely.

The other group of direct-actionists consisted of G.A.R. veterans, gathered around Major Capen on the horse-trough end of the Square. It was characteristic of them that with a clear recollection of what a nuisance non-combatants on a battlefield can be, they kept carefully out of the way of the fighting forces. Characteristically, too, they refrained all through the early part of the proceedings from criticizing the operations of men who presumably knew the technique of a trade as they had known theirs. But at the high point of the conflagration, when the fire burst through Beals's roof and went skyward in a great whoosh of flame and sparks, it dawned upon them that there might be a stage when the town would need the skill and resourcefulness of people who knew how to use gunpowder.

Bear in mind that this was only four years after the great Baltimore fire and barely two years after San Francisco. Everyone knew that when a fire got really beyond control, the only way to stop it was by blowing up the buildings in its path.

After the episode of Willie Ridgeway's piano, I had drifted by chance over to the horse trough and now sat perched upon its edge, where the voices of the G.A.R. men came from right behind my ear.

"Too bad," said one, "they'll have to blow Meekins's. But if they got to blow anybody's it might's well be his. I never did trust a man that shaves all his face."

"Stuff!" said another. "How about McKinley? How about Davy Farragut? All the same, they better blow that building while they can get in there to place their charges."

A minute later Old Mr. Dunbar said, ruminatively, "I don't s'pose there's a man in this town 'cepting us, knows how to *blow* a structure."

Major Capen's cane scraped on the sidewalk. "Dunbar," he said, "you may be an old fool, but you used to be a yellowlegs and I bet you still know how to blow a bridge. Hey?"

"Buildings ain't no different," said Old Mr. Dunbar, "if you know how they're put together."

There was a silence.

"I'd oughta know," said Ira Hardwick, the wagonmaker. "Father, he built it, and I helped him. Mortise-and-tenon, pegged. Framed six by six."

"Ayah," said another voice. "But the beams are all dry-rotted by now, specially on this side."

"You sure, Henry?" demanded the Major.

"I was down there with Meekins last month, lookin' for some old-time stomach-bitters. Didn't find 'em, either. You could put a putty-knife through those beams, anywhere."

"Dunbar," said the Major, "I think we could do it."

"Easy!" snorted Old Mr. Dunbar, and spat in the horse trough. "Fifteen pounds on a corner, ten on the other jinings."

"Two kegs," said the Major dreamily, and tapped for a second with his cane on the pavement . . .

"By God!" he shouted. "We'll do it! . . . Mike, sandbags! Fifteen or twenty of 'em, loose-packed . . . Ira, all your biggest augers and some adzes . . . Dennis, a bucket of that blue clay from down the brook . . . Ruel, rope and heavy cord, lots of it . . . Dunbar, you and Henry and Peabody get over to Meekins's as fast as you can hiper; get in and start marking the places. . . . Joe, crowbars . . ." A few more crisp, crackling directions, then:

"Rest of you follow me. We'll go over to Behan's and requisition a couple of kegs of black powder and some fuses." And drawing his cane through his left fist, as a sabre from its sheath, he pointed across the Square. . . .

Well, Meekins's is still standing, as I noticed last summer, though it is under another name and doubtless has new under-pinning. But it wouldn't be if Behan's Sporting Goods, Gun and Bicycle Store, also Ford Automobile Agency, in May, 1908, had got in its annual supply of Fourth-of-July gunpowder. By a mere ten days on the calendar the town of Bradford was robbed of a fitting climax to the fire in Beals's Block.

26.

BREAD AND CIRCUSES

In that primitive age, relatively few of the spectacles provided for the ecstasy of citizens were furnished at a price-per-head and a profit-per-capita, by companies, co-partnerships, corporations, networks, chains or syndicates. Mass production of beguilement was a long way from its present perfection. Civic entertainment — in Bradford, anyway — was nearly all homemade.

This was of two varieties: bread-and-butter, or recurrent without special occasion; and circus, or holiday, entertainment, akin in regularity and ritual to the feasts of the Druids.

Halfway between the two were Playouts, a form of sport and spectacle unique, so far as I know, to that portion of Massachusetts and New Hampshire bordering the Gulf of Maine. These were contests between obsolete hand-pump fire engines (and their ostensibly superannuated crews) to see which could squirt a stream of water farthest. They were major features of the calendar holidays but they were also run off on a league basis, on various Saturday afternoons during the spring.

Playouts had started when the original hand-pump fire engines of the towns were retired, one by one, upon the acquisition of steam fire engines. The oldest old hand machines had been known as "tubs," since they were essentially oblong wooden water tanks which had to be filled before water could be pumped from them. These original tubs were filled by bucket-brigade relays of citizens. Later hand engines had suction hoses, to be immersed in wells or ponds. And still later ones drew their water from hydrants. But in New England they were still called tubs.

Steam fire engines had, of course, replaced the tubs in the 1870's and 1880's. But in frugal New England, towns like Bradford didn't junk their obsolete tubs. They kept them, first as auxiliaries in case the need should arise, then as relics in the care of Veteran Firemen's Associations. These bodies used them in sporting competition with other Veteran Firemen from towns near by.

This competition settled down into the form of a trial for distance. Competing tubs would take station, successively, at an oblong tank of water supplied from a hydrant. Into this tank their suction hoses were plunged. Their crews would man the pump handles ("brakes," they were called) and start pumping, slowly at first, then madder and madder till they were going like all get out. Meanwhile, two of the stoutest veterans would be holding a wooden peg in the nozzle of the outlet hose. When the pressure exceeded their holding power, or when the foreman (perched atop the tub) judged the wind came right, the peg was released and the stream shot out, its leading cloud of spray arching through the air like a congregation of avenging angels in full pursuit of their erring brother, Lucifer. The distance to the farthest drops of water, as registered on an unrolled strip of pink builder's paper, established a tub's performance. There was a money prize for the winner, and side bets often ran into fancy figures.

By the end of the Nineteenth Century this rivalry, in eastern Massachusetts, at least, had reached such a point that towns were selling their legitimate antique tubs for junk and buying later models, released by distant cities. Thus it was that Bradford, about 1901, acquired, purely as a sporting item, a tub of a late and efficient hand type. It came from the city of Louisville, Kentucky. This machine had been named the "Nathan Bedford Forrest," but on arrival in Bradford was promptly rechristened and relettered in characters of gold, "Kentucky Babe."

The Babe looked like on oversized rosewood coffin, or a longish square piano, borne on four elegantly polished, silver-hub-capped wheels. Her chassis had a crane-neck arch to allow the forward wheels to be swung, if necessary, at right angles, for a sharp turn.

Atop the piano-like body and parallel to its long axis were hinged the Babe's brakes or pump handles. This arrangement constituted her a side-stroke machine, as distinct from the Philadelphia, or end-stroke type.

When not in use, the brakes were carried folded together vertically, like the wings of a butterfly at rest. For action, they were unfolded as you might spread flat the covers of this book, and locked one to the other. Rock the book, walking beam fashion, on the pivot of its back, and you will see how the brakes of one side rose as those on the other side were pulled down.

The brakes-proper (which corresponded to rods along the outer edges of your book cover) could be fitted with extensions fore and aft, so that sixteen men in two facing ranks might man each brake, on each side of the machine. This would put thirty-two men, each capable of throwing one-half horsepower for brief stretches, into the pressure building up in the Babe's innards — no mean force to put behind a single spurt of water.

The Babe had a silver-plated pressure dome just forward of amidships, topped by a screaming eagle, commonly reported to be solid silver. Her tongue was a forged iron rod with loop handles for four trusty men, but these were steersmen and holders-backers on the hills; power for the Babe's forward motion was supplied by men hauling on two drag-ropes that could be unreeled from under the forward end of the carriage.

The Babe's suction hose came out from under her after end. For carrying purposes, this hose was curled up, and its tip run forward into a silver-plated tube above and parallel to the Babe's backbone. For this reason the Babe, and others that carried their hose in the same manner, were known as Squirrel-tail tubs.

So, if you must be precise, the Babe was a piano, crane-neck, squirrel-tail, side-stroke machine with two 8¼-inch by 9-inch cylinders, built by the Button Fire Engine Works of Watertown, N. Y. For brief spurts she could hit close to 250 gallons a minute.

Once Bradford had acquired the Babe and recruited a crew of strong-backed factory hands (by courtesy supposed to be Veteran Firemen at the age of twenty or so), our town went right up front in Playout competition, not only among tubs from the Old Colony but among those which on occasion traveled all the way down from Boston suburbs and even North Shore towns, to try their might against such as the Babe.

These occasions always began with a parade to the scene of action, which was usually the town ball field. Behind the Brad-

ford Military Band came the visiting tub or tubs, and last of all
the Babe. Each tub was drawn by its company in full uniform:
double-breasted flannel shirt in vermilion, blue, green, orange or
purple; enameled leather belt with the name of the tub in
sewed-on letters; jaunty visored cap and tight-fitting black
trousers. And any tub with real style had a small-boy mascot
dressed in a miniature uniform. No bat-boy for a world-series
team was ever more envied and hated for his eminence than
Hobart Faxon, the son of the Babe's foreman, who was mascot
of our machine.

Mr. Faxon himself was chief engineer at Charlie Porter's factory — a clever man, so they said, at doctoring up valves and
pumps to get the last pound of pressure, the last foot-second of
water at the nozzle. And certainly an inspiring leader as he called
the stroke, and an agile one as he perched with one foot on each
brake and alternately threw his weight from right to left, faster
and faster as the beat stepped up, buckety, buckety-buckety,
bucktybucketyBUCKETY . . . toward the final unloosing of the
Babe's torrent.

This flying mass of water usually carried far enough to outdis-
tance those of ordinary competitors such as the "Neptune," "Niagara" or "Ocean." And the Babe stood a fifty-fifty chance even
against Brockton's redoubtable "Hancock," given a fair break in
wind conditions and no undue disadvantage from skulduggery.

It was the self-imposed duty of all right-thinking Bradford
citizens to keep a sharp eye out for evidence of cheating by the
Babe's competitors. Strangers standing anywhere within a dozen
feet of the paper strip at a point where the farthest drop could
be expected were watched by a hundred Bradford eyes to make
sure they did not happen to spit at exactly the moment their tub
was shooting for distance. And it was the responsibility of everyone in that area to keep an eye peeled for telltale pellets of BB
shot. For a favorite dodge among competing tubs was to fill the
nozzle of the hose with shot. The shot, being denser, would carry
farther than mere drops of water, and being wet would leave a
supposed water-spot before rolling away, hopefully undetected.

In this connection, my grandmother, one day, rendered a signal
service to the town of her adoption. In the course of a dual meet

with the "Hancock," she was standing with Mrs. Tenney out by the end of the paper strip when the Babe let go. A truly phenomenal spatter of water landed right in front of them. As everybody else rushed up to see it, Mrs. Tenney, who didn't understand such things very well, happened to look down and see a tiny, bright sphere rolling to a stop at her feet.

"Why, Susan," she exclaimed, "what's this?" and began to stoop down for the globule.

"Look out!" cried my grandmother, grabbing her. "Your placket has come undone." And she turned Mrs. Tenney briskly around, fumbling with the hooks and eyes at the bustle of her skirt. "There," she said, finally, "you all but made a spectacle of yourself. But that hook doesn't look very firm. Perhaps we'd better be going before it gives way for good." Meanwhile, she had expertly ground the shot into the turf with her foot. My grandmother was one of the first women in town to wear O'Sullivan's Rubber Heels.

The ball field was the home grounds of the Bradford Baseball Team of the Old Colony League, an aggregation fondly believed by all Bradford small fry to be inferior in might only to the Red Sox themselves. And if it more often lost than won, why that only went to prove the known fact that all umpires were not only blind, but deaf, dumb, afflicted with trypanosomiasis or sleeping sickness, and crooked as a hentrack in the snow. Besides, our team always got bad breaks when a grounder hit a rock in the infield, or a fly ball dropped into a mudhole in the outfield.

The field, indeed, was happily informal — an open lot on the westerly outskirts near where the trolley crossed the railroad tracks. It had single ranks of benches along first and third base lines. I suppose fees must have been collected from adults who occupied places on these, but nobody ever thought of asking a boy for money. On the contrary, grownups would frequently offer you as much as ten cents for your place, so it paid to get there early. Of course you would have done so anyway, to get every minute's possible thrill from watching Bradford's great stars.

Of these there were many: Ryan, the gold-toothed hatter who later married our hired girl Nora; Mackley, a sardonic pitcher who, it was said, would have been in the big leagues except that his fast ball was too dangerous; Anderson, a nimble shortstop who did indeed later play Big Time ball . . . and others. . . . But above and beyond all the rest was Tommy Carney.

Tommy combined all the best features of all the great stars with several of his very own. He could bat like Napoleon Lajoie, field like Honus Wagner, scamper the bases like Ty Cobb and sass an umpire like Johnny Evers on his greatest day. He had an opulent mop of curly black hair which he never abashed with a cap and which he combed while on the bench, with a mother-of-pearl comb. But his perfections were not limited to the ball field; his talents went into only the briefest eclipse when the game was over.

After a mere couple of hours' rest at the K. of C. rooms, Tommy appeared as tenor at the Town Hall Saturday night cinemato-graphic exhibitions, singing solos of terrific volume and intensity, against a background of colored slides showing girls of unearthly pinkness simpering at young men in turtle-neck sweaters through archways of such roses as bloom only in the dreams of Messrs. Burpee and Peter Henderson. It was like having Babe Ruth and Enrico Caruso in one, with the Metropolitan Gallery of Art thrown in at no extra cost.

A motion picture exhibition, in those days, was a novel scientific affair. The dramatic possibilities of the flicker-camera had not yet been perceived by gifted pantsmakers. Consequently the only subjects available for cinematographic demonstrations were educational: a boat-ride down some fair French river, past turreted châteaux, under ancient carven stone bridges and between broad meadows lined with pollard poplars; shots of London, with the clouds behind the dome of St. Paul's and the toiling traffic in the Thames; animals in zoos and trains in motion. . . . Simple-minded burghers that we were, we accepted these as wonders and sat on the edges of our seats, old and young alike, gazing raptly into the maws of yawning lions and wincing in fright as a train went right by over our heads. The waits between reels, or the delays to repair broken films, were all but unendurable, even though they were beguiled with colored slides and with the songs of such as Tommy Carney.

Tommy's favorite numbers were those with a fond Irish tinge, such as "Top o' the Morning, Bridget McCue," but his most suc-

cessful ones were those of humorous intent. His Bradford pre-
mière of "Everybody Works but Father" was a sensation, but it
was nothing to that of a ballad Tommy introduced, one time,
at a K. of C. entertainment.

This was a dramatic pantomime piece called "The Gold-Plated
Yacht." Its many verses related in detail the distresses of a great
number of national characters supposedly guests on a million-
aire's yachting party. And if the lines of the one verse I remember
seem in print to have a certain monotony, then you must try to
imagine the dramatic variations flung into each line by the eyes
and facial expression and gestures and howls of the great Tommy
Carney. But you cannot possibly imagine the tremolo expression
Tommy threw into the opening line of the chorus, and especially
the word "pale."

> "Mary Garden 'mp-aha!'
> Jennings Bryan 'Mph-Ahah!'
> Carry Nation 'OOMPH-AHAH!'
> Pierpont Morgan 'WHOOMPH-AHAAAH!!'

> "All the people turned pale and rushed for the rail
> When that gold-plated yacht went out for a sail."

This terrific piece was encored to a frazzle, and everybody left
the hall singing it. Next morning half the boys in town — who
had been there — were teaching it to the other half, who had not.
And by nightfall parents everywhere were beginning to go crazy.
The worst of it was (for them) that even when they had clouted
their young into silence, the maniac insistence of "oomph-ahah!"
kept running through their heads and provoking the whinnying,
donkey-bray refrain, "All the people turned Pa-a-ale. . . ."

A few nights later the Choral Society threw its annual concert.
At this, one of the habitual star performers was Wesley Mather,
editor of the *Monitor,* who greatly fancied himself as a baritone
soloist. He was of the school which, while it would not give a
nickel to a widow with five freezing children, would Give a Man
a Horse He Can Ride at the drop of anybody's hat. At Choral
Society concerts his horse commonly got a boost from a string
quartette of which the leading spirit was George Swan, a lusty
performer on the bass viol.

George didn't like Mr. Mather; Mr. Mather didn't like George, and a feud had been smoldering between them for some time, marked by oral sparks from George and whiffs of smoke in the *Monitor's* columns whenever Wesley Mather had occasion to mention anything George had to do with.

On this night Mr. Mather was due to sing, as his final number, a brave thing called "Yo Heave Ho! Let the Tempest Blow." Between verse and chorus of this there was a transitional passage of six notes from the orchestra, designed to let the soloist catch his breath and latch on to the first note of the refrain. Mr. Mather, in his opening stanza, got the watch below and the hatches fast, 'gainst the hail and snow and the tempest's blast, and paused for the transition.

At this point George Swan, letting the rest of the quartette go softly down the right track, swerved his bull fiddle into the opening notes of "All the people turned pale," and gave her the gas.

"The really fine point, though," he later complained to my father, "was the one everybody missed in the uproar; I swung her a whole tone off key so the bastrich *couldn't* get back if he tried."

Generally speaking, however, the Choral Society's concerts were rated low as entertainment by the young. Our dish was the Bradford Military Band, which we held to be without peer for sweetness, volume and sock among all instrumental organizations of the world, bar none. Admittedly, the Boston Symphony Orchestra (which once gave a concert in our Town Hall) had more people and made a respectable amount of noise, but they had no uniforms and we bet a million dollars they couldn't march. Admittedly, too, circus bands were more gaudily tricked out than ours, but we bet a million *trillion* dollars none of them could play "Poet and Peasant" as sweet as our Band, sitting under an arc light on the Church Green, while the Japanese lanterns made fairyland of the outlying dusk, and the air was fragrant with cigar smoke, and all Bradford, old and young, sat on the still-warm sward, heedless of grass stains, listening, entranced.

But of course the Band was transcendent in its highest function of leading parades, with such a vibrant barrum-pum-pum of brass and shrilling of fifes and clash of cymbals and gut-quivering boom of the big bass drum as moved every foot in town to step to the beat of the "Washington Post March" or "The Stars and Stripes Forever."

This miracle was unleashed at occasional minor parades such as those preceding Playouts, but overwhelmingly at the two big military observances of the year, Decoration Day and The Fourth.

Decoration Day was, in a sense, only a half holiday, for school kept in the morning. Yet even school on this day was a thing apart from school, as the day was apart from all other days. For it was then that the Grand Army came in groups of eight or ten to each class, to sit with us in rooms we had filled with wild flowers, and be sung to, and spoken pieces at, and to say a few embarrassed words, perhaps, and then to sing with us again, and so file out blowing their noses and maybe dropping a cane because there are some times when a man, remembering things, doesn't see very well for a minute.

But in the afternoon, when the parade formed in the Square, they would be all right again, these old men in their blue coats with brass buttons and their gold-wreathed, gold-corded black hats, some of them bent and some of them gnarled and some of them upright and free-striding, but all of them quick to fall in, dress to the right and step out with a soldier's ground-covering pace and a nice guide-right-in-marching. Old men we knew as everyday familiars, tobacco-chewing, gravy-spotted, irreverent, full of strange oaths and wild tales, and a look in their eyes as who should say, "The hell with you, Johnny Reb, take That!"

We knew well enough they had been soldiers, and were used enough to their stories of sleeping on rail fences and living off cold water and hardtack in the mud, but seeing them this way was a reminder that they had done, too, that which they never talked about — marched into fire in line and in step (as was the custom in their war) with a hep! hep! and a *one,* two, three, four, the-guide-is-right-and-close-ranks-there, when the man beside you went down with a Minié ball in his stomach. Bradford sent 540 men to that war, of whom seventy-eight never came back from spots like the Sunken Lane and Marye's Heights and the Peach Orchard and the Bloody Angle at Spottsylvania.

After the G.A.R. came a militia company from Brockton as guard of honor, very business-like in blue with white gloves at the butts of their Krags, and bayonets slapping at their hips as they swung by with a crisp crunch-crunch of foot on gravel. And after them, the Spanish War Veterans, in blue coats with gray trousers, and the Sons of Veterans trying to look like soldiers, but succeeding a good deal less than the Boys' Brigade of the Congregationalist Church which followed, and the St. Alphonsus Cadets who brought up the rear. The rear of the formal parade, that is, but not of the procession, for everybody in town who wasn't marching abreast of the military organizations fell into rank and step behind, footing it to the music of the Bradford Military Band.

The parade visited all three of the cemeteries, at each of which Judge Dearden would recite the Gettysburg Address; and there would be a prayer. Then the veterans would fall out to lay flowers on the graves of those who had Fallen Out before and weren't marching in the flesh any more, while the other organizations stood at a respectful, low-voiced Rest. Then the parade would fall in again and finally return to the Square to halt and be dismissed. And the old soldiers would walk home with their families. Iron old men in the sunlight of late afternoon.

27.

DAY OF DAYS

The Fourth was a different kind of day. It was one of the two great high-voltage points of the year — perhaps by a shade the higher. Halfway round the calendar from Christmas, it matched that holiday for sizzle, though exactly opposite to it in the direction of current: Christmas was a time for getting. The Fourth a day for giving the works.

The works took a lot of saving-up for. True, fifty cents or so would buy as much noise, flash and violence as an active sprat could touch off in the intervals of a day full of spectacles and observances. But still, the accumulation of half a dollar at one time entailed furies of lawn-mowing and prodigies of good behavior all through June. When sufficient cash was in hand you took it down to Behan's and invested it in explosives, with all the care and calculation of a lifetime saver diversifying his hoard — and with no lack of loud counsel from your friends.

The ruling consideration was concussion. Not for us the sissy fireworks that emitted only light, however bright and sparkling. We might condescend to a few pence for a rocket or a Roman candle or a stick of sputtering red fire, but only after firecrackers had been stocked in sufficient numbers and kinds, together with fulminate and dynamite in various satisfactory forms. The Safe and Sane Fourth was still only a hand-size cloud unnoticed on the horizon of youth. Now that safety and sanity have completely overcast the July sky, it may be forgivable to record the principal ingredients of a proper Fourth for the information of young patriots who in some areas know no firework more lethal than a magnesium sparkler.

Firecrackers came in red-tissue-wrapped packs with gorgeous Chinese labels in gold. They were available in all sizes from inch-long and matchstick-diameter pipsqueaks strung together by the thousand, up to cannoncrackers about the size of a modern beer

can and warranted to deafen an elephant. You always laid in
some of these extreme sizes, but your staple was the common
firecracker, about two inches long and the thickness of a slim
pencil. Half a dozen packs of these, with punk to touch them
off, would set you back a quarter. On the other hand, if set off
singly they would last you a whole day. They did very well,
either by themselves or as charges for toy cast-iron cannon, from
which they would spit a forbidden pebble with force enough to
break a henhouse window. Those which failed to explode owing
to the fuse pulling out were customarily broken at the middle
and touched off for the fizz and flare. Two or more of them, laid
with their broken-open ends facing one another, made a very
passable "catfight."

The other principal class of noisemaker favored by the short-
pants set on The Fourth consisted of caps, torpedoes and other
detonating pieces that needed only a jolt or a whack to go off.
Caps for cap-pistols were in that age big, fat and noisy. An even
bigger, fatter and noisier size of cap was embedded in the tor-
pedo, a balloon-shaped twist of tissue paper filled with gravel, in
the heart of which lay the cap. One of these when hurled upon
the sidewalk would explode with a brave bang, flinging its gravel
in all directions with considerable force, as the scars on many a
now-ancient shin will still attest.

Even more satisfactory than these to use in a crowd were pellets of actual dynamite which enjoyed great popularity for a few
brief years before the law caught up with them.

These were fired from the cast-iron lower end of a special cane
made and sold for the purpose. The cane proper had a handle in
the shape of an eagle's head and a shaft wrapped in red, white
and blue paper, barber-pole style. At the base of the cane was its
working end — a heavy, pear-shaped knob of iron with a slot in
one side of it to receive the dynamite pellet, and a plunger
hanging downward through a hole in the center of the casting.
When the cane was tapped on the sidewalk, the plunger would
be forced upward and would thus detonate the dynamite pellet
you had put in the slot. The pellets were about the size of overgrown aspirin tablets and one of them made such a concussion
as would leave all eardrums ringing within a rod, pole or perch.

Happily, the makers had designed these canes with slots no bigger than would accommodate a single pellet; otherwise there wouldn't have been an ear left in Bradford at the end of a Fourth. As a further slight concession to what was jocularly known as safety, the manufacturers packed their pellets in sawdust-filled cartons.

Older boys and young men also had revolvers shooting blank cartridges, and some enthusiasts in long-pants circles exhumed muzzle-loading muskets and shotguns, of which there were many still around town, and charged them with horse doses of black powder — obtainable by the pound at Behan's on The Fourth or in hunting season. With these, they sought to discover by trial-and-error whether they could blow a hand off themselves. At least one Bradford citizen succeeded during my time there.

By Bradford custom, The Fourth started at midnight. It was held sacrilegious to touch off so much as a squib before then. But when the clocks began to strike twelve, nobody ever heard more than the first two or three strokes. The rest were lost in din, and the remainder of the night was pretty well shattered with explosions and lit up with bonfires.

For this part of The Fourth, my brother and I were forbidden to get up and go out, and during all our years until the final one in Bradford my father enforced this ban. But in 1908 we were sleeping out under an improvised awning on the top of a bay window just outside the Rats' Nest. Being nobody's fools (if you except Nature's) we concealed an ample store of explosives among the bedclothes when we turned in on the third, and took off no more than our caps when crawling between covers. So within a few seconds after we were awakened by the midnight barrage, and before my father could arrive to restrain us, we were down the trumpet-vine trellis and on our way to the Square at a respectable canter.

That was a great night. Willing hands had assembled and piled up in the Square a young mountain of empty tar barrels, boxes and excelsior. This was in full blaze when we arrived, to an obbligato of explosions which flashed in the darkness on all sides. Men with shotguns, youths with pistols and small fry with pockets full of firecrackers were milling around and letting off their blasts in all directions. About 3:00 A.M. there was an alarm of fire from a box within easy running distance, up Standish Street. The whistle roared, the bell boomed and the whole assembly went coursing off like a Roman mob, shouting and firing as it went and seriously impeding the progress of Bradford's Fire Department, which was forced to slow to a trot for fear of running down the runners. The fire proved to be a fairly good one, in somebody's woodshed, and with its subsequent ceremonies of trooping back to the Square, occupied all the time till dawn.

By this hour most of us were getting hungry, so proceedings subsided to a desultory popping as we made our ways through the rose-beige light to our homes. On the way, I remember, my brother and I passed a cherry tree luscious with rich, ripe, black, juicy fruit. From pockets filled with these we sustained our strength for the last few hundred yards. My father was only mildly reproachful at breakfast; there was abundance of oatmeal, sugar and milk; there was steak with fried potatoes . . . the day was off to a good start.

Between breakfast and nine o'clock we managed to get through the greater part of our remaining firecrackers, well aware from experience that the rest of the day would be too crowded with civic doings for much individual enterprise. And by nine we were again on our way downtown to watch and to follow the wonders of the Grand Parade. This was to be even grander than usual (which is saying a lot) because it was Bradford's Old Home Week year, and the parade was scheduled for the added glory of half a dozen visiting tubs for a special prize Playout.

We were only just in time. Already the elm-arched streets downtown were lined with grownups — the women in cool summer dresses of starched linen or ruffled organdy, the men in Sunday best with straw boater hats. It took several shots with our dynamite canes, let off in the rear of people rightly estimated to be nervous, to clear us a passage through to places in front. We got there just as the parade hove in sight.

First came the Bradford Police Force — both of them. Nick and Jim were resplendent in summer gray helmets and best blue frock coats. Their belt-buckles bobbed majestically up and down over their middles as they marched. Next rode the Grand Marshal, Major Capen, upon a monstrous black stallion. He was in full uniform, with gold shoulder straps and brass buttons, and silver sabre hanging at his side. Beneath the visor of his jauntily cocked kepi his eyes were black, and his moustache and imperial bristled white.

Followed the Band. And playing lustily, no soldier's martial tune, as on the graver day, but that exuberant, that brassy, booming air, that crashing, thumping air, "Ta-ra-ra Boomdeay!" Tarara went the brass and Boom the monster drum. You felt your innards jump and saw the leaves adance. Tarara once again and Oompa Boom the bass. Boomdeay, boomdeay, boomdeay! The flashing cymbals rose, the tubas filled their lungs, the drummers poised their sticks. Tarara crowed the horns and BOOM the answer came. Boomdeay, boomdeay, boomdeay . . .

The colors were upon you, almost before you knew it and could snatch your cap off. Massed colors, with a guard of honor from the Grand Army. After them the other military organizations, as of Decoration Day, but this time sprightlier stepping. Tarara Boomdeay!

Next came the six tubs for the day's Playout: five visitors and The Babe. It would be hard to say which was shiniest in mirror-like mahogany or rosewood, in lovingly polished silver, nickel or brass trimmings. Hard, too, to choose between the splendor and neatness of uniforms of their various crews. Each tub was drawn by sixteen men on the white hand-ropes, and flanked by marching files of its remaining crew. Atop each stood its foreman holding the silver speaking trumpet that was the badge of his office. Each and every trumpet was crammed for this great day with red roses.

The tubs were followed by Bradford's own Fire Department: The Steamer with its dapple grays, shining like Phoebus himself and trundling The Reel behind; The Patrol looking as neat as if it had never been to a fire, let alone one in the early hours of that morning; The Hook, with Heber Lambert keeping a watchful rein on the temperamental Bessie and glaring at anybody along the way who appeared likely to let off a firecracker; and last of all The Best ladder truck in its incomparable perfection of white and gold, with its almost-never-used ladders glowing as only affectionately varnished spruce can glow. From Steamer to Best, this section of the parade was nearly unbearable for glamour; perhaps it was as well for youthful breasts that it was followed by a letdown.

This consisted of a long succession of marching organizations: the Templars, the Masons, the Odd Fellows, the Elks, the Grange, the St. Patricks and all the rest. We didn't think much of these; none except the Templars were uniformed (though most were brightly sashed in satin ribbons), and few of them were in step. It was a relief when the Floats appeared.

These were elaborately beflounced drays or other vehicles such as I have already mentioned in the account of my grandmother's defeat by the Demon Rum (and the infant Lily Merrill's defeat by the Demon Water) several years before. They represented societies, organized labor and local industries, and among them took such a fearful wallop at allegory as had not been seen since the MacMonnies statues at the World's Columbian Exposition at Chicago in 1893.

And now approached the final, climactic section of the parade, the Antiques and Horribles.

This, which had been a crowning feature of all respectable New England Fourth of July parades for many years, was a free-for-all, open to any individual who cared to costume himself or herself in dress exhumed from an attic trunk, or in grotesquerie contrived by his own fancy and craftsmanship. Prizes were awarded in each class.

The Antiques section was, as you might expect in a town like Bradford, rich, abundant and genuine. For the town had been going a long time; its attics were capacious and no Old Colony family ever threw away any dress, suit of clothes or hat. Deacon Talbot appeared (as every year) in a rig, complete with powder-horn, from the French and Indian Wars. Half a dozen people still had Revolutionary uniforms around. And there was as usual a whole platoon from 1812 — a war in which few people fought, compared to those who purchased elaborate uniforms with heavy gold fringe epaulettes the size of a scrubbing-brush. George Swan was authentic in a costume of the Beau Brummell period — that is, if Beau Brummell wore a white moustache and gold-rimmed spectacles. Somebody — I forget who — had an early plainman's costume in fringed buckskin.

There were, of course, numerous Indian getups, inherited from grandfathers who had traded a jug of bourbon for a Sioux war bonnet. Beaver hats abounded, with plum-colored coats and tight-fitting snuff-colored pants. So did the crinolines and pantalettes of the same era, and the coquettish bustles of the Elegant Eighties, each set off by a parasol no larger than a soup plate. But of man's costumes from that period, the only ones considered sufficiently gone by to rate a blink among antiques were those that went with high-wheeled bicycles. In these, a speedster was distinguishable from a tourist by his tight-fitting knee-length pants and striped stockings. The tourist wore knickers, a Norfolk jacket and a deerstalker cap, and carried a bugle which he tooted melodiously as he rode. There were four high-wheeled bikes in that parade, but they had a tough time of it, since the rear of the procession went by fits and starts, and any rider was fain to be propped up at moments of halt by a Horace Greeley Free Soiler on one side and an 1812 privateersman on the other.

The Horribles brought up the triumphant rear of our parade. They were fewer in number but far fancier in getup: devils and witches, hayseeds and dudes, highwaymen and hottentots, hobbyhorse knights and an acrobatic two-man personification of Maud, the Mule, a famous comic strip character of her time ("Hee Haw! And her name was Maud," accompanying a terrific kick). There were any God's quantity of clowns. These were funnier than all the rest because they took pokes at their friends along the right of way, and made gestures of invitation to citizens of known eccentricity, implying that if *they* would only join the parade they would win prizes without even trying.

All of us boys, of course, fell in behind the parade. And it is a sweetly solemn thought to reflect that if there were such a procession today, and if we, as we then were in garb and manner, were magically to appear at the end of it, the judges would probably award us, as a group, first prize for Antiques, and — not unlikely — for Horribles as well.

Fond memory insists that The Babe won that morning's Playout at the ball grounds. I have not dared to check this in Bradford's library files. The day, in recollection anyway, was perfect; let it go at that.

That noon we had the traditional New England Fourth of July dinner of cold salmon, potato salad and peas. How this menu had got to be a ritual in those parts for that day, I do not know, but there are anthropologists who insist it was supposed to approximate in color scheme a patriotic red, white and blue.

Leaving our elders to meditate on this and their other sins, my brother and I streaked it for the Square, where the afternoon's Sports were scheduled to begin early. Most of these events were conducted on the Church Green. They included, of course, potato races, three-legged races and sack races, for old and young, together with a large assortment of short dashes for boys and girls by age classes. There were also high and broad jumping for the young men and, along a roped-off course around the Square, a series of sprints and a wildly exciting bicycle race. One of the girls' events was taken by a lithe lass visiting in town, who later parlayed a nice pair of gams into handsome gains in a large city, and the bicycle race was won by an intense young Italian who later shot a compatriot as full of holes as a vegetable grater, thus proving something, but I do not know what. At the close of the afternoon, Nick Banton, the Police Chief, scrambled handfuls of pennies among the small fry, and I got one.

There would be just time in the interval before supper, to set off our remaining firecrackers, including a Six-inch Salute cannon-cracker reserved for this time. This would leave us with one box of dynamite pellets apiece, set aside for our canes during the evening downtown. Going to our stores, however, we discovered the cartons of dynamite missing. Worse, the Six-inch Salute was gone. On experience we suspected our father; he was apt to relieve us, without argument-entailing notice, of sharp knives, air rifles and other weapons he found we were using too freely. Besides, who else would take our fireworks? Surely not our grandmother. And we had not at that time any hired girl or woman.

We rushed inside, full of indignation, to demand our property. But my father not only denied any knowledge of the missing explosives, he scarcely bothered to dismiss them with a word. "I have something to tell you," he said, and took us into his parlor-study. My grandmother was already there.

This, he said gravely, would be our last Fourth in Bradford, and almost our last night. We should be going to Maine for the summer, day after tomorrow. But at the end of this summer we should not be coming back. He had an appointment as head of the biology department in a large school in another state and in a city as big as twenty-five Bradfords. It would be a new kind of life for all of us.

We went in to supper, a sad meal. "I shall feel as badly as you," said my father, "to leave Bradford. So many of our roots are here. My own father pegged shoes and studied for the ministry here. Bradford treated him so kindly, that was why I came back here when your — when you were very little. I have had a happy life here — so many friends. This house I bought, thinking we should always live here among people we know and understand. I — well, I shall be leaving a great deal of me here." He didn't say that it was in Bradford he had lost my mother.

That evening, all the town was out to hear the Band and see the fireworks. For this great occasion a bandstand had been built on the Green, topped with a dome-shaped framework on which colored lights were strung. And out across the Green hung fairy festoons of Japanese lanterns, paler, but no less beautiful, as pink and green and blue pearls to the bandstand's rubies and emeralds and diamonds. Under these, people sat in family groups, or neighborhood groups, or friendly groups, or groups of two alone together among the crowd. The low rail fences around the Green were lined with other sitters like strange black or white birds communing in the dusk. And on the Square beyond, others stood in clusters or walked about quietly. I went over and perched on a ledge of the Library, two hundred yards away.

And from there I had a strange illusion. It was as though the Band under its jeweled dome were like a certain ancient watch I had seen in the Boston Museum of Fine Arts — a watch encased by some mediaeval goldsmith in the semblance of a great beetle whose enameled and jeweled wings would open to show the hour. Now, it seemed, the Band with its gold and silver reflecting the colored lights above, and the dome with its many-colored gems, were that beetle come to enormous life and throbbing its marvelous wings to the time of a gay and yet heartbreaking Viennese waltz.

Even the fireworks that night were sad in their brilliance and splendor. The bombs were like beats of a drum, and the whirr of the rockets like tearing of satin. High through the night soared the arches of brightness, lingered and fell and then burst into beauty, beauty that faded and died.

.   .   .   .   .   .

Late that night we stood on our front porch: my father, my brother and I, looking out over the now-peaceful town of Bradford. Only a few windows were alight, and one by one, as we watched, these were going out.

Presently my grandmother joined us, carrying a lighted joss-stick, as many people did, in those evenings, for the fancied protection of its sandalwood fragrance against mosquitoes. She stood a little apart, saying nothing, communing with her thoughts. Then, as one for whom even son and grandsons were too much company, the little old lady softly stepped down off the porch, walked across the lawn and stood with one hand on the old hitching post in front of the house we were so soon to leave.

What we did not know was that within that post, in a big dry-rotted hollow in its center, my grandmother had jammed the entire contents of the two missing cartons of dynamite pellets — minus the sawdust which she had carefully sifted out. On top of those she had planted our missing six-inch cannoncracker, and tamped the whole business down with dry moss, leaving only the tip of the cannoncracker's fuse protruding. A joss-stick will do (in case you ever run out of punk on The Fourth) to set off any fuse, if you fray the end of the fuse a little to expose its black powder core.

In a moment my grandmother strolled back and joined us. "Well," she began.

At that instant *her* firework let go with a ground-rocking concussion heard all over town, and a blast that flung bits of rotten wood into Charlie Porter's open window a furlong up the street.

My grandmother waited till the fragments began to patter down through the oak leaves. "My!" she said, and softly reentered the house. Humming "Ta-ra-ra Boomdeay."